Leadership for the 21st Century

LEADERSHIP FOR THE 21ST CENTURY

Ann E. Prentice

LIBRARIES UNLIMITED

AN IMPRINT OF ABC-CLIO, LLC
Santa Barbara, California • Denver, Colorado • Oxford, England

Library of Congress Cataloging-in-Publication Data

Prentice, Ann E.
  Leadership for the 21st century / Ann E. Prentice.
    pages cm
  Includes index.
  ISBN 978-1-61069-196-3 (hardcopy : alk. paper) —
ISBN 978-1-61069-493-3 (ebook) 1. Leadership. I. Title.
HM1261.P74 2013
303.3'4—dc23   2013008262

ISBN: 978-1-61069-196-3
EISBN: 978-1-61069-493-3

17 16 15 14 13   1 2 3 4 5

Libraries Unlimited
An Imprint of ABC-CLIO, LLC

ABC-CLIO, LLC
130 Cremona Drive, P.O. Box 1911
Santa Barbara, California 93116-1911

This book is printed on acid-free paper ∞

Manufactured in the United States of America

Contents

Preface

As we move forward into the information-rich, high-tech, global future, it quickly becomes evident that many of the social structures that have sheltered us in the past may no longer suffice. With renewed concern, we need to look at how we interact with others, what new skills and abilities are needed, what aspects of the ways in which we currently interact are essential to future success, and where do we go from here. Who will we trust to lead us? What is our role in leading, in being part of the leadership team, and in making sure that in whatever we do, integrity and core principles direct our actions?

We have seen revolutionary changes in manufacturing as we move from the industrial age to the information age. Communication is now so rapid and pervasive that whatever happens anywhere in the world can be known by others as it happens. Information on nearly every topic is available at the tap of a keystroke. Our educational systems have begun to experience new ways of course delivery whose effects are just beginning to be experienced, and who knows at what rate other aspects of our society will change? Do we have a sense of how to move ahead? Do we have a shared vision?

In thinking about these and related questions, it became evident that leadership and an understanding of what leadership is and can do is the key to moving forward responsibly. With this in mind, I began to develop a graduate course that would serve as a forum for students to discuss these and related issues. The course would bring together research on leadership, the voices of literature—from Shakespeare to Star Trek and beyond—that described leaders and leadership in their own often intense ways, biographies of leaders from all walks of life, and events in our lives as reported in the news media. The course has been a valuable learning experience for those involved and its content is the basis for much of this book.

Many of the questions and comments reported in the book came from discussions in class with a diverse student body: diverse in age, experience, and perspective. My thanks go to them for their thoughtful and insightful comments that demonstrate just how multifaceted the study and practice of leadership is. In addition several chapters and topics, particularly those dealing with team building and social networking, were reviewed by individuals who currently hold leadership positions in science and technology. Special thanks to molecular biologist Holly Prentice, imaging scientist Wayne Prentice, and computing guru Gary Videlock. Thanks also to my editor Blanche Woolls for her support and kind words. And to my husband Don Surratt, both for his knowledge and understanding of the importance of leadership and for being there as deadlines loomed.

Ann Prentice

Introduction

Another book about leadership? What can it add to a long list of books already available? We have books written by and about those who are leaders, those who have been leaders and those who see themselves as leaders. They represent many fields of endeavor, from politics to science to the arts and beyond. A subset of these includes narratives written by politicians and business leaders who appear to consider writing a book about their leadership skills and their ideas about leadership as a requirement of the position they hold or at least as a way to burnish their self-image. Many of the books are thoughtful and have much to tell us about the art and skill of leadership while others are self-congratulatory and have little lasting value. Many of the best accounts of leadership have been written by historians who have the benefit of looking back on the life and career of a person called a leader and being able to evaluate that person's impact on society.

Why is leadership such an important issue in today's world? We live in an environment in which nearly everything is changing at what appears to be an ever increasing rate of speed. The importance of telecommunication and information networks to our economy, our worldview, and our daily lives cannot be understated. What was primarily an industrial economy not so long ago is rapidly moving to becoming an information economy. Many of the jobs that served as the engine for growth of the middle class no longer exist or are no longer performed in the United States. Robots are replacing humans on the assembly lines. Do-it-yourself stations in places including airports, grocery stores, and library checkout counters are replacing clerical staff. Digital books, magazines and newspapers are replacing or radically changing publishing and distribution of information. Each of these examples and many more result in higher productivity and greater speed while at the same time reducing the number of jobs available. New industries and new jobs take time to build and in the meantime there is stress in the workforce and in the marketplace. Demands for a more and more highly educated workforce are changing the ways we teach and the ways we deliver educational services. In the political arena, internet access allows individuals to connect and groups to coalesce independent of existing social and political structures and to do so in hours or days. How do we get our minds around the opportunities and threats of this new information/telecommunication world that is in never ending forward motion?

The changing nature of society and all the issues that this encompasses requires leadership. Who is out there with a vision, a plan? Who has some understanding of the global society that links us, where an economic crisis in Europe impacts the United States stock market the next day or a local uprising in an African country is reported as it occurs? We need leaders to help us deal with the issues of daily living and working and who do so with a long-term vision and the ability and integrity to carry it out. We need to know what to look for in leaders so that we select those who will lead us forward by doing the right thing rather than act in their own self-interest.

Leadership is key to the art and skill of planning, organizing, and managing the many elements of our society with the objective of building a viable path to the future. Those who lead our institutions and organizations have the potential for great power; and, with that power, comes responsibility for doing the right things. As workplace demographics have changed in past decades so that white males no longer dominate, the faces of leadership now can be female, persons of color, and individuals from other cultures. With these demographic changes, there have also been changes in the ways we look at leadership in that it has become a more nuanced concept. Basic principles such as having vision, integrity, and the ability to get things done are enriched by the broader populations and cultures from which leaders emerge. As one looks at the large body of research about leadership conducted since the 1970s, it quickly becomes evident that the majority of studies have been based on white males as leaders and this is so largely because most individuals in leadership positions prior to the 1990s were white males. Since that time, those in leadership roles have become more diverse. Research has reflected that diversity and we are beginning to have a more complete picture of the varied nature of leadership.

The study of leadership began with Machiavelli's *The Prince*[1] in the 16th century, and his comments on leadership continue to be relevant some 500 years later. His view was that leadership is not inherent but can be taught. Those elements of leadership he considered important included the need to maintain a strong self-image others would respect and to enhance this by avoiding association with those who were unprincipled, weak, or otherwise of questionable character. He is best known for his assertion that the primary role of the leader was to maintain order in whatever way appeared most appropriate at the time. In the ensuing centuries, leadership was rarely discussed as an idea or concept. Accounts of the actions of religious, military, political, and other leaders appeared regularly and provide us an understanding of what it took for an individual to lead an army, a cause, or a country in earlier years.

Early studies of leadership tended to focus on the "great man" and how that individual impacted history. Thomas Carlyle, the English historian, wondered if one person would be able to change the course of history and in his writings identified men who made the attempt, some of whom succeeded. We have examples of individuals who took advantage of events in history and gained great power. Hitler saw a power vacuum in Germany in the 1930s and through terror and force, controlled a country and wreaked havoc throughout the western world for decades. Henry VIII was able to exploit the weakness of the Catholic Church and break away from it, thus changing the course of history in England. For historians, leadership has usually been defined as political leadership[2] but in recent years, leadership and the study of leadership has expanded to include many areas of endeavor. As the sciences of anthropology, sociology, and psychology matured in the 19th and 20th centuries, researchers looked at leadership in new ways and from new perspectives. Anthropologists studied other societies and cultures to see how they were organized, and how leadership was practiced. Psychologists looked at human wants and needs and asked if there was a primal need to follow someone who would provide security. Those who studied primates looked to see if similar needs for leadership appeared in simian society. Chester Barnard was among the first to study leadership in the context of the corporation which he described as a social organization.[3] These approaches were strengthened by a growing interest in studying workers in the organization as people rather than as interchangeable parts in a machine as was the fashion among those who championed scientific management in the 19th century.

The scientific study of leadership is a product of the 20th century and can be divided into three periods. The first period (1910–1939) focused on identifying traits of individuals identified as holding leadership positions that made them different from others who were not leaders. The second period (1940–the late 1960s) focused on behavior, as it was thought that the key to leadership was how individuals performed. The third period (1970–present) took a situational approach and looked at how leaders responded to difficult situations to see what commonalities existed.

Most of the studies of leadership conducted in recent decades focus on determining the components of leadership, how they have been applied, and carry the assumption that if one applies them in future, one could be a successful leader. Leaders to be studied were identified by those who worked with them. Those holding positions in the organization that were identified as leadership positions were also studied. Individuals and groups of individuals said to be leaders have been studied in depth. Researchers have conducted content analyses of biographies and autobiographies of individuals recognized as leaders. Leaders in literature are often cited as examples when speaking of leadership traits and their characters used as case studies in discussions of leadership. It was expected that from these various sources and studies, a list of traits defining leadership would emerge. To some extent a list has emerged, and we have examples of how certain traits have helped those in leadership positions and how their absence has resulted in leadership failures. We continue to study leadership in order to try to define and understand this elusive concept.

Another important component of leadership is the perception of the leader by those being led. It has been said that one can understand leadership best from the perspective of the follower rather than from the perspective of the leader. This individual observes the impact of the leader's actions and how they affect others within the organization and to an extent the impact of the leader outside the organization.[4] How do these individuals react to the individual who has the responsibility to lead? What do they respect about the leader? From their point of view, does the leader have their best interests as a priority? Throughout this discussion of leadership, the perspective of those observing the leader and the leader's impact will be included in order to fill out the definition of what makes a leader successful. Much of this information comes from comments by nearly 100 graduate students who represent an age range from the mid-20s to the early-50s and whose work experiences range from clerical positions to management positions in numerous profit and not-for-profit organizations, plus members of the military. It also includes input from scientists who are leaders in industry and in laboratories. Though not the product of a research study, they do represent a cross section of followers as well as some leaders. When one discusses leadership from the view of the leader, the view of those being led, the perspective of the researcher and that of the biographer, there is a strong possibility that a picture of what leadership is, does, and can be will emerge.

DEMOGRAPHICS

While each profession in our rapidly changing world is changing in its own way and at its own pace, there are some issues in common. For example, the baby boomer generation, those born after World War II and prior to 1960, are reaching retirement age which means that an unusually large number of senior people in organizations will be retiring over the next two decades. Who will replace them or will they be replaced? If replaced, what new kinds of skills and abilities will be seen as essential to 21st-century leadership? Given the economic stresses created by the information and telecommunication revolution that in some way affects nearly every job, how will we configure and reconfigure the workforce? Add to this the globalization of the economy and the fact that we are part of a global workforce; what social and cultural definitions of leadership can be put forward that will accommodate such a diverse workforce? What new patterns of work and workforce management will need to be put into place?

The following discussion focuses on the information workforce to see how it is growing and changing and what the expectations may be although many of the findings can apply to the larger workforce. Over the past 50 years, numerous studies have been conducted to determine the growth of the information workforce. It is estimated that "information workers increased from 37% of the work force in 1950 to 59% in 2000."[5] A major reason for this increase was that "technological change within each industry . . . substituted information labor for other types of labor."[6] The decline in goods workers was in large part due to this substitution. While the share of the workforce that consists of knowledge workers grew steadily from 1950–2000 and grew rapidly during the hi-tech explosion of the 1990s, it is assumed to be unlikely that this growth will continue due in part to the outsourcing of knowledge work abroad. Because of lower salaries of information professionals in other countries and the fact that the Internet makes global communication possible, chances are that "the growth rate for knowledge workers in the U.S. will thereby be reduced in the near future."[7]

The definition of knowledge worker expands and contracts depending on whose research one consults. While some definitions include calling anyone who handles information in any way a knowledge worker, other definitions are more limited in scope. Because of varying definitions, one should see these studies as an indication of the breadth of the issue and as a good point from which to narrow the topic. One should be careful when citing statistics from the numerous studies unless the definition of knowledge worker is included.

The Bureau of Labor Statistics noted that in 1998, librarians were seventh among occupations with the highest percentage of workers 45 years or older, and it was estimated that 46.6 percent of librarians would leave the workforce during the decade (1998–2008). Because of difficult economic times during the period, more and more individuals found it necessary to continue working and since 2000 there has been a steady increase of those over 65 remaining in the workforce.[8] This statistic applies to workers throughout the economy. Economic insecurity slows the number of retirements; and this means that there are fewer jobs for those newly graduated persons from academic programs who are looking to replace those currently holding positions for which they have been prepared. However, this does not apply to newly created positions or newly revised positions for which new graduates are often more well prepared because they have new skills and abilities different from those currently in the workforce. In either case, leadership may be in the hands of individuals who began their careers in the industrial era and who may be increasingly uncomfortable leading in the information era. How can we respect the contributions of older leaders and at the same time infuse our organizations with the skills and visions of information society leaders? The need for leaders who have the vision, the integrity, and the skills to move us forward are more important than ever. It is the purpose of this book to move us forward as we seek, prepare, and empower tomorrow's leadership.

NOTES

1. Niccolo Machiavelli, *The Prince* (London: Penguin Books, 1988).

2. Bruce Mazlish, "History, Psychology, and Leadership," in *Leadership: Multidisciplinary Perspectives*, ed. Barbara Kellerman (Englewood Cliffs, NJ: Prentice Hall, 1984), 13.

3. Chester Barnard, *The Future of the Executive* (Cambridge, MA: Harvard University Press, 1938).

4. Nanerl Keohane, *Thinking about Leadership* (Princeton, NJ: Princeton University Press, 2010), 5, 6.

5. Edward N. Wolfe, "The Growth of Information Workers in the U.S. Economy," *Communications of the ACM* 48, no. 10 (October 2005): 37–42.

6. Ibid.

7. Ibid.

8. Edward P. Glasser, "Goodbye Golden Years," *New York Times*, November 20, 2011, Section 4, p.1, 6.

Types of Leaders and Leadership

Leadership is an activity that has been a part of our society since its beginning. It is the process that allows individuals to coalesce into groups and to solve problems together under the authority of an individual selected to lead them. One can cite examples of individuals who have organized and led such groups and have contributed to social progress as well as examples of individuals who have been more interested in self than in society and have done great harm. It is hard to generalize what leadership is, as it comes in many shapes and sizes. James MacGregor Burns, one of the most noted researchers in the study of leadership, said, "Leadership is the most observed and least understood phenomenon on earth."[1] We can observe leadership from the perspective of a particular discipline, from the perspective of different cultures, and from the perspective of different religions, worldviews, or other platforms.

Leadership involves relationships between a leader and a follower, and the two are held together by any number of reasons including ties of mutual need, ties of respect, and the ties of common interest in an idea or project. Whatever the relationship, it is not static but grows and changes as the needs and interests of both leader and follower change. Lindholm commented in his study of the similarities between falling in love and developing the desire to follow a leader that "Leadership is like love in that everyone knows about it but defines it differently, if at all."[2] The leader is defined by many as the individual who serves or leads others for the good of all and not for personal gain.

The most asked question about leadership is "are leaders born or is it a skill one can learn?" In the 1940s and 1950s, a series of studies was conducted asking if those called "leader" had specific physical characteristics or qualities such as intelligence or determination. No clear answer emerged from these studies.[3] Then behaviors were studied to see if one could identify behaviors or styles common to all leaders. In the 1990s, research focused on identifying positive and negative behaviors to see if this answered the question of "what defines a leader?" Weber said that it is the followers who perceive special qualities in an individual and who determine the greatness of a leader.[4] One can read biographies of leaders that focus so completely on the leader that little attention is paid to those who have made the leader's success possible.

Those who study leadership often do so from a particular perspective or bias. One can look at leaders from the context of the world in which they lived. What historical factors influenced their role and actions? Were they leaders or rulers who forced others to act in specific ways? One can also look at leaders of a past era in today's context and thus skew perception by applying today's standards and ideas. Either way, bias creeps into the study of leadership.

Bias can also occur when people attribute more to the leader than is warranted. They idealize the leaders and see them as individuals having more knowledge and wisdom than they actually do, and the leader therefore gets more credit than deserved. This may be due to the need of followers to create wise authority figures they feel proud to follow. Research on leadership, definitions of leadership, and the influence of culture and gender on leadership is to a large extent a product of the second half of the 20th century and continues to attract researchers who look for new insights into this very important component of human activity.

As one reads reports of current research, conducts research, and observes leadership in action, it is evident that certain areas in the discussion of leadership are changing, while at the same time certain core values such as the importance of honesty and integrity remain constant. Among those that are changing is that leadership is increasingly seen as an element of the community rather than as coming from the top of a hierarchical pyramid. The leader can be anywhere in the organization. There can be several leaders, each with special information and/or skills. Leaders are part of a community and while they lead it, most rarely do so from a purely authoritarian position.

Historically, an informal contract existed between employer and employee, between the leader and those led. If employees, the individuals led, were loyal to the employer or leader, their jobs were secure. This loyalty or security contract no longer exists as an absolute, partly because of changes in the ways in which employees may be seen. In some environments, they are resources to be used and discarded depending upon economic conditions while in others, the workforce is an organized or informally organized group that is a power in its own right. Labor unions organize workers, have their own leaders and bargain for worker's rights. In other environments such as the technology industry in the Boston, MA area, members of a highly skilled technology workforce maintain informal connections with one another and are very aware of the opportunities available in the many components of the technology field. This informally organized labor market interacts internally and with management when employment opportunities arise. Individuals or organizations that hire an individual are not the only leadership influences on that individual.

From the employee side of the equation, employees see themselves as individuals in their own right and expect to be treated with respect for what they can contribute to the situation. One can say that those who lead today need to gain the respect of those being led. If this does not occur, employees may go elsewhere. If a contract between leader and led still exists, it has become one in which mutual respect and appreciation have replaced the paternalistic model of loyalty and security. "Leadership [has become] a reciprocal relation between those who choose to lead and those who decide to follow."[5]

Technology has changed the nature of leadership. The leader is no longer the sole owner of information and the means of access to information. Information is now ubiquitous throughout the organization and empowers the entire organization. Ease of communication combined with the availability of information means that the leader and those led use information as a shared resource. Today's leader is more likely to be a server and a supporter rather than an authority figure who dictates actions. The concept of the servant as leader has become increasingly pervasive. The leader helps followers become what they need to become in order to achieve mutually desired objectives. This is neither motivation by whip nor by carrot and stick. It is motivation by expectation of the best efforts of others and by working together to achieve mutual goals. As the workforce in general becomes better educated and today's workforce requirements make a higher level of education essential, workers expect more from their leader. At minimum, they expect to be respected, to be treated fairly, to have access to needed information, and to be able to grow and prosper in the work they do. What remains constant in the leadership-followership equation is that the leader sets the tone of the organization and speaks for the organization.

Numerous studies have been conducted to identify types of leaders and leadership and from this research, leadership components have been organized and reorganized to fit certain categories and to describe types of leaders. In 2006, Mumford conducted a content analysis of the biographies of more than 100 historically notable individuals. This study has its limitations because, of those biographies studied, seven were of women, and seven were of men of color. Individuals from many countries and from many types of activity were included, thus providing a broad cultural—while not a representative—gender and ethnic mix. The intention of the research was to "study leadership not only to understand the nature of leadership as a social phenomenon; we also hope that our understanding of leadership will lead to interventions that will enhance leader performance."[6]

From this study of white males, three basic categories of leadership were identified: Charismatic, Ideological, and Pragmatic. These basic categories served as umbrellas for numerous variations. The Charismatic leader has a vision, looks to the future and builds consensus within the group through that sense of shared vision for a better future that can be achieved by following that vision. The Ideological leader may have a vision, but rather than looking forward, looks to the past and seeks to enforce values and standards that will maintain that leader's vision of a traditional society in which traditional values are enforced. Typically, followers of the Ideological leader have a strong group identity and work closely together as they follow the directives of their leader. Both Charismatic and Ideological leaders have been known to start mass movements that support their vision. Pragmatic leaders, rather than being motivated largely by vision, "exert their influence through an in depth understanding of the social system at hand and the causal variables that shape system operations."[7] Pragmatic leaders are problem solvers and focus on "getting things done." Relationships are based on negotiation, shared outcomes, and mutual respect. Benjamin Franklin is an example of the Pragmatic leader in that his leadership stemmed from the fact that he understood the society in which he lived, was able to identify problems, and to leverage available resources in order to solve those problems.

In describing the similarities and differences among these three types of leadership one can look at the following characteristics:

1) *Performance.* Regardless of the type of leadership, there is something about the leader that motivates others to follow because there are shared goals, because there is an interpersonal relationship, and because the follower trusts the leader.

2) *Problem solving.* The leader displays a grasp of the problems to be solved and has identified a path that will lead to success. The way in which a leader does this is often what separates one leader from another as each leader has identified the problem in a different fashion, has collected data that supports the proposed solution (unbiased one hopes), and intends to implement the solution in a uniquely personal way. The Charismatic leader encourages a range of suggestions for problem solving that may be included in the overall vision. The Ideological leader has no interest in creating a new future but wants to hold on to the past and evaluates existing approaches rather than creating new ones, while the Pragmatic leader just wants to solve the problem and looks for the most potentially successful way of doing so.

3) *Interaction between leader and followers.* In some situations, followers are assigned to leaders and the followers have no choice but to do as they are told while in other situations followers have the opportunity to find leaders with whom they have shared interests. In this latter group, followers can have an impact on the vision and its direction. Charismatic leaders frame issues in terms of people and value trust, participation, and collaboration.[8] Ideological leaders rely on the group to share and reinforce common goals and values while the Pragmatic leader's emphasis is on getting things done.

4) *Communication.* Depending on the leadership style, interactions between leader and follower differ. Ideological and Charismatic leaders rely on emotional appeals and the strength of their vision. If one is part of the team, then one belongs and can be part of a powerful activity. At times the leader may use emotion to bind followers to him/her and may do so in order to enhance personal power and control with little concern for the follower or for the larger society. Other leaders will use emotional appeals to build consensus in support of the leader's vision. Pragmatic leaders rely on objective information rather than emotion and build consensus through expertise and management of the situation.

Regardless of the type of leader, each relies to an extent on personal experiences to shape both vision and approach. The Charismatic leader values persistence and positive thinking as skills to move forward while the Ideological leader values traditional values that reinforce the past; and the Pragmatic leader values observation, analysis, and joint problem-solving. During their careers, leaders may try different styles of leadership depending on the situation or the nature of the group being led. The environment in which the leader works may also have an effect on the leadership style and some blend of these three may emerge at different times and in different places.

ADDITIONAL TYPES OF LEADERS

In addition to the above comprehensive categories of leadership, a variety of additional categories have been identified and studied. Some might be considered as subsets of the above while others are unique in their own right.

Narcissistic Leaders are those who have a vision often supported by good ideas and who believe so strongly in those ideas and their personal leadership ability that they are unwilling to listen to others. Narcissistic leaders tend to be very self-involved and are willing to die for the vision rather than to compromise what they think is right. This type of leader loves the media and loves the persona they want the media to project. They want things to go their way and if they don't, everyone and everything else is wrong. They are risk takers, hate criticism, don't listen, lack empathy, hate to mentor others, and are highly competitive. One comment about this type of leader is that a sidekick is essential in order to keep the leader grounded: "Every Don Quixote needs a Sancho Panza." As we look at the history of cult movements, at certain business enterprises, or at the current political scene, it is easy to identify any number of individuals with narcissistic traits.

Quiet Leaders are very different from Narcissistic leaders. As described by Badaracco, ". . . the most effective leaders are rarely public heroes . . . they don't spearhead ethical crusades. They move patiently, carefully, and incrementally. They do what is right—for their organizations, for the people around them, and for themselves—inconspicuously and without casualties."[9] Badaracco goes on to say that since large problems can only be resolved by numerous small efforts, quiet leadership, although seemingly slow, may be the quickest way to achieve success. Success is therefore the cumulative effort of many people and not the activities of someone who sees him/herself as the hero leader.

Quiet leadership is a way of thinking about people, organizations, and action, and the flow of events. It is what moves and changes the world. Quiet leaders are realists who see the world as it is. They know that individuals do things for many reasons and that many elements are at work in the changing world. They are aware of the limits and subtleties of power. They know that the world is divided between insiders who have power and outsiders who want it. The Quiet leader looks at a situation in realistic terms and knows what can be done and what cannot be done. The Quiet leader looks at the political situation, the personal interactions that must be dealt with, and looks at who wins or loses power personally, emotionally, and politically. The Quiet leader knows that there are no simple solutions.

The Quiet leader is rarely recognized or rewarded. Quiet leaders are less likely to reach the top level of management as they can be upstaged by extroverts who demand more attention and therefore are assumed by some to be better leaders. Quiet leaders are successful because they do their homework, they take many factors into consideration, and they act for the best interests of all. They don't try to save the world all at once. They know that small decisions may get results and that big ones that have not been carefully considered can explode and destroy. Since most issues are complex, they listen to their intuition, to their experience, and rely on as much information as it is possible to gather within a reasonable period and then act. The Quiet leader and the Pragmatic leader have much in common.

The **Alpha Male/Female** may or may not be a leader although many of these individuals see themselves as leaders. Luderman,[10] a psychologist who has spent much of her career working with alpha types, defines them as individuals who make things happen rather than stand back and let things happen. The Alpha NEEDS to be in charge. They can do a great deal to move the organization forward while at the same time most likely lack basic skills in interpersonal interaction. Luderman defines the Alpha by giving advice as to how one should function when in alpha territory.

1) Decide what kind of Alpha you are working for and tailor your input to that individual's way of leading. For example, give a visionary an idea of what you propose to do in terms of how the future will look because of it. Strategists like to see reams of data and cost figures while the executor needs to know everything about how the task will be accomplished. Alphas want brief direct responses.

2) Never ask Alphas to defend their positions. Ask them to explain them. Be interested, ask questions. Stress those areas in which there is agreement. If Alphas think you understand their perspective, you may be able to help them see alternative ways of accomplishing their objectives.

3) Sprinkle superfluous, even erroneous nuggets into your presentations and thank the Alpha for finding the errors. This allows the Alpha to feel in control and to maintain personal superiority.

4) Don't confuse the Alpha's arrogance with total self-confidence. They may try to think that they are smarter than everyone else, but they are never quite sure. They respond well to specific praise but are smart enough to reject flattery.

5) Never complain to Alphas as they see it as a weakness. Ask them to help you deal with a specific situation.

6) If you go over an Alpha's head, be prepared to grovel. An Alpha leader does not see you as an equal; therefore you will make mistakes, and if you make a mistake and then grovel, the Alpha will see you as someone who "saw the light."

7) Don't assume that your battles with Alphas are confined to the workplace. They are everywhere. This type of leadership is all too common and most likely appears when an individual is not a strong leader, is insecure in the position, and tries to use bombast and aggressiveness to cover feelings of insecurity.

LEADERSHIP AND SOCIAL INTELLIGENCE

In the past decade, attention has been paid to the important role empathy and self-knowledge (emotional intelligence) plays in effective leadership. The emerging field of social neuroscience, "the study of what happens in the brain when people interact,"[11] has allowed us to look at leadership from a new perspective. It was found that "certain things leaders do—specifically exhibit empathy and become attuned to others' minds—literally affect their own brain chemistry and that of their followers. . . . Leader follower dynamic is not a case of two (or more) independent brains reacting consciously or unconsciously to each other. Rather the individual minds become, in a sense, fused into a single system."[12]

While there is no clear consensus about what emotional intelligence really means, it is agreed that emotional intelligence is a set of abilities "that shares key characteristics with cognitive and intellectual abilities . . . develops gradually with age . . . and crystallizes in adulthood."[13] Once developed, it is difficult to change. Others define emotional intelligence as "skills that can be acquired with practice and that are focused on successfully negotiating social interactions and on managing one's own behavior."[14] It includes traits and abilities that are related to coping with one's environment in ways that promote social well-being. Because these are learned skills, this has been an opportunity for consultants to develop workshops to assist individuals to manage their behavior and improve their skills.

Other researchers have indicated that informal leadership develops from the combination of "conscientiousness, emotional stability, and centrality to the group."[15] And, this from another researcher: "the moderating role of gender on the relationship of individual differences and team member network centrality" has a strong effect on the emergence of informal leadership.[16] The consensus of those doing research in this area is that leadership has an emotional component much of which is learned through experience, and this component is an essential part of how an individual approaches leadership challenges and how those who are led perceive their leader.

In practice, there are differences in the performance levels of the emotionally mature and those who are less tuned in to their own emotions.[17] Emotionally mature individuals are more aware of the nonverbal cues in the attitudes of others, which is key to being a good listener and to communicating with others. The emotionally mature individual is more open to asking for the input of others, to following intuitive feelings, and to helping foster the development of new ideas with others. The ability to manage and regulate one's own emotions provides a safer environment in which others can contribute their ideas, and this ability results in a more productive organization.

The **Primal Leadership** model builds on neurology and considers the role of emotion in the leadership mix.[18] The importance of mood and tone in information delivery is stressed. When the leader projects a positive mood and tone (resonance), a positive mood is reflected in staff response, while when the leader projects a negative mood and tone (dissonance) this too is reflected in staff response. Staff members not only mirror the leader's moods, they may even synchronize their mood with that of the leader. Leaders who are self-aware and who control their own emotions create a positive atmosphere in the workplace while the clueless leader, the leader who is self-serving, and who tunes out the feelings of others creates a negative workplace.

One cannot overestimate the positive aspects of a workplace in which the leader is aware of the emotions of others, understands and values the contributions of others, and builds a strong team based on mutual respect. Nor can one overestimate the emotional toll that dissonant behavior that may range from manipulation to tyranny takes on a group of people who are responsible for working together to achieve objectives. A dissonant environment damages mental abilities and makes social interaction increasingly difficult.

In some instances, it has been found that the official leader is not necessarily the emotional leader. This may be by design or it may be by necessity. The authoritarian leader who makes the difficult decisions and who is responsible for the safety and welfare of the organization may have an associate whose role is to foster a resonant environment. Think of the high school principal who is aware of the concerns and interests of the faculty and students and responds to them in a resonant fashion. The assistant principal assumes the role of disciplinarian and that individual's role is to ensure that school rules are obeyed by the students. This sharing of the role of leader is not uncommon. In some organizations, the leader's dissonance may result in the emergence of someone elsewhere in the organization who is emotionally mature and who provides a respite from the dissonant leader. This could be the beginnings of a revolt by the staff with disastrous results for the organization.

Right Brain/Left Brain Leadership research has shown that over time, leaders have honed certain processes, values, and actions that [they] are comfortable in using and that succeed.[19] Each leader is different and has a different set of skills and abilities. Some are highly empathetic, some have strong communication skills, some are passionate about their work, and others refuse to give up. Whatever their strengths, leaders need to work outside their usual leadership strengths and patterns and expand their ways of operating so that they can continue to grow in order to be better prepared to meet new problems. "In today's work climate, leaders need to act from a broader, more complete range of business, organizational, and interpersonal behaviors."[20]

Each brain has both a left and a right half. The left brain is ordered, quantitative, logical, realistic and practical, and reasons from the specific to the whole. The right brain controls emotional and intuitive thought and reasons from the whole to the specific. While the two work together, one half is usually dominant. A third set of skills oversees the activities of the right and left brain and coordinates activities. The successful leader continues to learn new ways of doing things, tries new thought patterns, and welcomes new ideas and new ways of approaching them.

COMPONENTS OF LEADERSHIP

A theme throughout leadership research is to identify the components of leadership. Are there specific skills and abilities that one can find in the performance of a leader that could help us identify potential leaders and that might help us determine if an individual is truly a leader? Kouzes and Posner,[21] in one study of more than 400 individuals identified as admired leaders, listed the 10 most frequently used words to describe them: valued, motivated, enthusiastic, challenged, inspired, capable, supportive, powerful, respected, proud. Each of these is a positive term. Their research showed that admired leaders do not place themselves at the center of attention. They place others there. They do not put self first but concentrate on their constituents, their staff, and the public they serve. Staff working with them:

- are proud to be part of the organization
- have a strong sense of team spirit
- see their personally held values as consistent with those of the organization
- feel attached and committed
- have a sense of ownership in the organization.

Successful leaders earn credibility, respect, and loyalty primarily "when leaders demonstrate by their actions that they believe in the inherent self worth of others . . . credibility is earned and strengthened when the leader has a philosophy and acts in ways that are consistent with it."[22]

A Woman's Way of Leading

Mary Kay of Mary Kay Cosmetics is an excellent example of Kouzes and Posner's six disciplines of credibility.[23] These derive from common themes found in the case studies of leaders they studied.

1) Discovering yourself
2) Appreciating constituents
3) Affirming shared values
4) Developing capacity
5) Serving a purpose, and
6) Sustaining hope

A single parent living in Texas shortly after World War II, Kay experienced the difficulties of a woman who needed to support her family in a time and environment in which women were second class citizens and the good jobs were reserved for men.[24] Using all the money she had saved or could borrow ($5,000), a new cosmetics formula she had found, and her skills in direct sales she built a multimillion dollar corporation. She built her international sales force with women, the same women who had had difficulty finding work because they were women or because they had family responsibilities or both. She opened doors to thousands of women who previously had had little or no opportunity to find work unless they had specific skills such as teacher or nurse. These same women who had been told by the prevailing culture that women were inherently incapable of managing became the bedrock of a successful company. She had a vision, built a company and made life better for thousands of women. While we may smile at the idea of a pink Cadillac, which was the award very successful sales personnel received, we can only admire and respect her vision and her ability to make it real.

She believed that emotional leadership is fundamental to leadership success. "Leaders influence the emotional mind set of every individual within an organization."[25] She went on to say that you should follow your vision and be enthusiastic. She stated further that a leader should think like a woman; be empathetic, treat people well, show respect, be honest, fair, and compassionate. Her six virtues of a great leader are:

1) Humility—everyone is to be valued and recognized by contributing to something outside themselves. Seek out the best in others. Don't live in a ME world.

2) Desire to seek the best for others. Support others. Invest in people. Good people in an organization will attract other good people.

3) Have high expectations of excellence from those around you. If you believe they can, they will.

4) Have integrity. Keep your word at all times.

5) Be impatient with the status quo. Stay ahead of the curve. Don't be complacent. Be a risk taker and hire risk takers.

6) Celebrate the human spirit. The most important people in the organization are those who get the job done. These most important people can be anywhere in the organization.

Her six virtues were out of sync with the hard-driving, win-at-any-cost corporate thinking of the second half of the 20th century. She succeeded by following her own leadership styles and values and by refusing to accept less than the best from anyone. As we look at 21st-century leadership, it is easy to see that more and more of her "think like a woman" attributes have found their way into the mainstream.

Geeks and Geezers

Warren Bennis and Robert Thomas[26] were curious as to why some individuals continue to reinvent themselves while others stop growing and settle for whatever they have. They found that there was a strong link between leadership development and development as an individual; and that to be a leader, one needs to practice leadership skills. They also found that distinctive periods in the world in which we live have an impact on how we grow and learn to lead. Consider how World War II, the Korean War, the war in Vietnam, and the wars in Iraq and Afghanistan provided opportunities for many men and women to learn to survive and to lead others. Think of how the industrial world, the wired world, and the information world provided and continue to provide new opportunities and new ways to lead.

They defined geeks as those under 35 who grew up in a wired world dominated by television, and geezers as those 70 years old or older who continue to reinvent themselves. They learned that "older leaders were trained to think of the world in Newtonian mechanical terms; younger ones tend to look at it in terms of constantly changing living organisms and biological systems."[27] While experience and seniority are valued by geezers, geeks are more likely to appreciate new insights. The two groups differ in that geeks have bigger and more ambitious goals at an earlier age, place more emphasis on personal goals, and are less apt to have a hero. They are similar in that both are avid learners and try to transcend limits of all kinds; and both have had a crucible experience, a severe test of patience or belief, that gave them the opportunity to create meaning out of events and relationships that would devastate nonleaders. The authors found that geezers retained the youthful ability to look forward to things yet undiscovered, a characteristic which is called neotony.

WHY SHOULD ANYONE BE LED BY YOU?

This is the title of an article published in the *Harvard Business Review*[28] at the beginning of the 21st century. The authors answer this question by saying that "leadership is a state of becoming, you are always on the journey" and by citing four characteristics that are part of the toolkit of the successful leader:

1) Reveal your weaknesses (but not your fatal flaws). This shows that you are human, that you make mistakes, and that you continue to work toward the vision. When leaders make mistakes, they get up, and continue to move forward. With this as an example, it is acceptable for those being led to make mistakes from time to time and to try again.

2) Rely on your intuition. A good leader has a strong awareness of the environment—social, political, technical—and knows what may work and what may not. Perhaps the term "being aware" is better than intuition.

3) Capitalize on what makes you unique. Are you a good planner? Do you have a sense of who the best staff members to lead a project are? Are you good with people, with numbers? Do you have other talents such as the ability to design space, to lead a social gathering, to cook? An IBMer who always wanted to be a stand-up comic went to a national meeting. He put on a rabbit suit and came on stage as the energizer bunny. No one who saw it has ever forgotten it or the fact that his willingness to do something different brought the group he was addressing together through laughter with and not at him, and his message was remembered long afterward.

4) Be yourself. You cannot try to emulate a leader you respect. You have your own unique combination of skills. Learn how to use them.

SUMMARY

Michael Feiner, in *The Feiner Points of Leadership*,[29] said that effective leadership can be learned and "that leadership is like an iceberg: 90% of it is hidden below the surface. Basing our view of a leader on the public persona deals only with the 10%."[30] As we look around us in our work life, in our interactions in the community, and among our friends and family, we see many kinds of leaders and leadership and observe how effective they are as leaders, and we can learn about our own leadership style and effectiveness from observing the experience of others.

NOTES

1. James M. Burns, *Leadership* (New York: Harper and Row, 1978), 473.

2. Charles C. Lindholm, "Lovers and Leaders," *Social Science Information* 27, 1(March 1, 1998): 3–45.

3. Micha Popper, *Leaders Who Transformed Society: What Drives Them and Why We are Attracted* (Westport, CT: Praeger, 2005), 15.

4. H. Gerth and C. Wright Mills, eds. *From Max Weber: Essays in Sociology* (New York: Oxford University Press, 1958), 358–59.

5. Nanerl Keohane, *Thinking about Leadership* (Princeton, NJ: Princeton University Press, 2010), 25.

6. Michael D. Mumford, *Pathways to Outstanding Leadership, A Comparative Analysis of Charismatic, Ideological, and Pragmatic Leaders* (Mahwah, NJ: Lawrence Erlbaum Assoc., 2006), 81.

7. Ibid.

8. Ibid., 44.

9. Joseph L. Badaracco Jr., *Leading Quietly: An Unorthodox Guide to Doing the Right Thing* (Cambridge, MA: Harvard Business School Press, 2002), 1.

10. Kate Linderman, *Alpha Male Syndrome* (Cambridge, MA: Harvard Business School Press, 2002).

11. David Goleman and Richard Boyatzes, "Social Intelligence and the Biology of Leadership," *Harvard Business Review* 86, 9 (September, 2008): 74.

12. Ibid., 75.

13. Kevin R. Murphy, *A Critique of Emotional Intelligence: What are the Problems and How Can They Be Fixed?* (Mahwah, NJ: Lawrence Erlbaum Assoc., 2006), 39.

14. David Goleman, *Working With Emotional Intelligence* (New York: Basic Books, 1998), 13.

15. Peter J. Jordan, Claire E. Ashton James, and Neal M. Ashkanasy, "Evaluating the Claims: Emotional Intelligence in the Workplace," in Kevin R. Murphy, *A Critique of Emotional Intelligence: What are the Problems and How Can They Be Fixed?* (Mahwah, NJ: Lawrence Erlbaum Assoc., 2006), 203.

16. M.J. Neubert and S. Tagger, "Pathways to Informal Leadership: The Moderating Role of Gender on the Relationship of Individual Differences and Team Member Centrality to Informal Leadership Emergence," *Leadership Quarterly* 15 (2004): 175–94.

17. Sheri Caldwell and Linda Gravett, *Using Your Emotional Intelligence to Develop Others* (New York: Palgrave MacMillan, 2009), 6–8.

18. David Goleman, Richard Boyatzes, and Annie McKee, *Primal Leadership* (Cambridge, MA: Harvard Business School Press, 2002).

19. Mary Lou Decosterd, *Right Brain/Left Brain Leadership; Shifting Style for Maximum Impact* (Westport, CT: Praeger, 2008).

20. Ibid., 7.

21. James M. Kouzes and Barry Z. Posner, *Credibility: How Leaders Gain and Lose It. Why People Demand It* (San Francisco: Jossey-Bass, 1993).

22. Ibid., 51.

23. Ibid., 51.

24. Jim Underwood, *More Than a Pink Cadillac: Mary Kay Inc.'s 9 Leadership Keys to Success* (New York: McGraw Hill, 2003).

25. Ibid., ix.

26. Warren G. Bennis and Robert J. Thomas, *Geeks and Geezers: How Era, Values, and Defining Moments Shape Leaders* (Boston: Harvard Business School Press, 2002).

27. Ibid., 12.

28. "Why Should Anyone Be Led by You," *Harvard Business Review* 78, (September/October, 2000).

29. Michael Feiner, *The Feiner Points of Leadership* (Boston: Warner Business Books, 2004), xiii.

30. Ibid., 10.

Chapter 2

What Does a Leader Do?

The purpose of leadership is to provide a structure for solving problems that require collective action. "Leaders determine or clarify goals for a group of individuals and bring together the energies of that group to accomplish those goals."[1] Leaders have a vision and plans that move activities forward. When a crisis emerges, the leader makes sense of the situation by identifying the cause or source of the crisis, analyzes the range of actions that can be taken, selects the appropriate action, and then builds a plan that will solve the problems that caused the crisis. The leader then implements the plan with input from the team that has been assisting the leader throughout the process, evaluates the level of success, and then moves on to the next task.

LEADERSHIP SKILLS

Knowing the Authentic Self

The first step toward leadership is for individuals to know who they are and to assess personal strengths, weaknesses, personal bias, and other characteristics that define them as their authentic self rather than who they think they should be. Numerous research studies have been conducted to identify those specific skills and attributes that should be part of the authentic self as a way of defining core elements of leadership. In a study by George and Sims,[2] 125 leaders ranging in age from 23 to 93 were asked how they developed their leadership abilities. This diverse group included men, women, persons of color, many nationalities, as well as racial, religious, and socioeconomic groups. Half of them were CEOs and the other half represented leaders in both profit and not-for-profit organizations, some of who were mid-career and others who had just begun their careers.

When asked "How can people become and remain authentic leaders," they provided no universal characteristics, skills or styles but said that their leadership skills emerged from their life stories. Each was constantly testing himself or herself using real life experiences and "reframing their life stories to under-stand who they were at the core." They said such things as

- You do not need to be born with specific characteristics to be a leader.
- You do not need to be invited to lead.
- You don't want to be invited to lead.
- You don't need to be at the top of the organization to lead.
- You will have "the spark of leadership."

"The challenge is to understand ourselves well enough to discover where we can use our leadership gifts to serve others." No course, workshop, or book will in itself show one how to be a leader. The leader's values are derived from be-liefs tested under pressure. When your future hangs in the balance, you learn what is most important, what you are prepared to sacrifice, and what tradeoffs you are willing to make. Leadership principles are values translated into ac-tion. The leader balances practicing values and principles with the desire for reward and recognition. Personal challenges such as illness, discrimination, or the death of a friend help hone the individuals' worldviews and give a sense of what they want to be and to do. "No individual achievement can equal the pleasure of leading a group of people to achieve a worthy goal. When you cross the finish line together, all the pain and suffering you may have experienced quickly vanishes. It is replaced by a deep inner satisfaction that you have em-powered others and thus made the world a better place. That's the challenge and the fulfillment of authentic leadership."[3]

The Leader and the Team

No one leader has all the skills needed to lead a team or an organization. As organizational structure has changed in recent years from the hierarchical to a more participatory structure, it has become more and more evident that the successful leader's task is to develop a team within which the necessary leadership skills are present. The team can be a small select group or it can be a larger number of people representing many aspects of the organization. The size and complexity of the team depends on the purpose of the team, the struc-ture of the organization within which the team exists, and the preferences of those involved. The diffusion of information throughout the organization, rather than its being closely held by a few as was once the case, has democ-ratized the organization by adding more individuals who can contribute to the leadership activities. Decisions are more likely to be made collaboratively in the context of social, political, technological, or other forces. Different stake-holders (vendors, patrons, staff, trustees, etc.) have different expectations of the leader and the leader, with input from team members, may need to present decisions and the rationale behind them to each stakeholder from a slightly different perspective.

Ancona et al.[4] proposed a model of distributed leadership that covers four basic capabilities as a means of compensating for the fact that a single individ-ual rarely excels in each area, thus making it essential to develop a leadership team within which expertise in each area is present. They cite two enabling capabilities and two creative, action-oriented capabilities as being necessary for successful leadership. The first enabling capability is sense making. This involves making sense of the world around you by talking with others on a wide range of relevant subjects, identifying and collecting relevant data, testing posed solutions on a small project, and by being open to new ways of solving problems. How one makes sense depends on the data collected including information, ideas, and perspectives of those with whom the leader discusses the issue. The leader is able to gather information broadly, to evaluate it, and to identify the truly important issues.

The second enabling capability is relating. The leader needs to relate to others by listening to them, understanding their perspective and by not being judgmental. The leader asks for opinions from both those inside and outside the organization and uses this information to clarify his or her individual views. Once the leader has reached a conclusion or settled on a plan of action, it is necessary to explain to the group how this conclusion was reached and to reach agreement on a course of action. While the leader makes the final decision, it is the wise leader who knows that others have discussed and agreed upon the decision. In a networked environment, the leader and members of the team maintain a wide array of relationships to be consulted as one gathers data, makes suggestions, and moves toward a plan of action.

Visioning is the first of two creative, action-oriented capabilities. This dynamic process articulates what the leader and stakeholders want to achieve together. Visioning gives a sense of meaning and direction to the activities of the organization. It charts a course through the possibilities of what could be to arrive at what the leader wants the future to be. The role of the leader is to "sell" the vision—through personal enthusiasm, respected expertise, and building the confidence of stakeholders—that the leader will follow through and if necessary revise course to improve the direction. In the beginning, not everyone will buy into the vision; but if it is compelling and they trust the ability of the leader, others will join in the effort. While the leader may not know exactly how to reach the vision, if it is sufficiently compelling and credible, others will join in and will contribute in a variety of ways to make the vision real.

The second action-oriented capability is inventing. The leader devises new processes to tie the vision to the reality of the organization and to achieve the vision. This usually requires new ways of interacting and organizing. The leader encourages others to think creatively about how tasks can be accomplished. Experimentation such as suggesting new organizational structures or new ways of grouping people is encouraged. The leader keeps asking "Is there another, a better way to do this?" The combined skills and abilities of the team serve as a rich resource in responding to this question.

It is important for leaders to tailor their actions to the situation before them and to make decisions based on the specific situation and not solely on what worked earlier as no two sets of conditions are exactly the same.[5] If one is looking at a stable situation and cause and effect relationships that are easy for everyone to see, then the leader's role is to assess the facts, categorize them, and respond. In a complicated context, there may be several right answers; and, although there may be a clear relationship between cause and effect, it may not be easily seen by those involved. "Here the leaders must sense, analyze, and respond." In a complex context, right answers may not be evident and one must look for instructive patterns. In this situation, the leader probes, senses what the best response is and then acts upon it. In the chaotic context, cause and effect relations shift constantly and there are no manageable patterns, as with 9/11 for example, or the earthquake and tsunami in Japan (2011). "In this domain, a leader must first act to establish order, sense where stability is present, and then work to transform the situation from chaos to complexity."[6]

Disorder is the situation in which none of the above contexts is predominant. Then the leader establishes order by breaking the situation into parts, fits the parts into the above contexts, and then deals with each as appropriate. In each of the situations, the leader brings experience to the problem but does not bring solutions that worked elsewhere assuming that they will necessarily work well again. Leaders know what they want as the end result and work within that vision to solve current problems.

Stephen J. Tractenberg, president emeritus of George Washington University, in an essay in the *Chronicle of Higher Education*, said that "some people have called me a true visionary. But I just had a point of view on one matter and then another and so on and was able to persuade colleagues to turn these ideas into specific goals that we would capture together."[7] To him, vision was not a lofty word but rather a way of bringing people together to move forward. Thomas Stewart, editor of the *Harvard Business Review*, in one of his columns,[8] said that "Leaders help the people around them make sense of the world in which they find themselves . . . A leader has to define 'So What?' before people can decide 'Now What?'"

As was mentioned earlier, no one individual has all of the knowledge, skills, and abilities required of leadership. This is also true of emotional intelligence which is an important component of leadership. Usually leaders are very good at about a third of the 18 emotional intelligence competencies that have been identified.[9] The authors list 4 domains of emotional intelligence and 18 competencies that are key to successful leadership.

The first domain is personal competence which includes emotional self-awareness, accurate self-assessment, and self-confidence. The second domain, self-management, includes self-control, honesty, flexibility, and a drive to excellence, initiative, and optimism. The third domain, social competence, includes empathy, an awareness of the informal organization and its role in the organization, and recognition of customer needs and what it takes to meet them. The final domain, relationship management, includes guiding, motivating, persuading, developing the abilities of others, initiating, managing, and leading in a new direction, resolving conflict, cultivating, and maintaining a web of relationships and encouraging teamwork.

The leader who is self-absorbed and thinks only of personal goals, who lacks a sense of humor, who does not continue to learn, who does not mentor tomorrow's leaders, and who does not regularly seek feedback is moving toward organizational disaster and will drive away good people. Just as it is important to include all four aspects of leadership activity in a team, it is also important to incorporate all aspects of emotional intelligence. The successful leader recognizes personal shortcomings and compensates by including in the team individuals with complementary strengths.

Because the leader has a strong emotional impact on the organization that can be either positive or negative, the leader needs to create resonance, the feeling of positiveness that brings out the best in others. The opposite feeling is one of dissonance in which the person with leadership responsibilities is abusive or manipulative and does not take into consideration the thoughts and feelings of others. The dissonant leader leaves a trail of dissatisfied and frustrated individuals behind and destroys much of the potential of the group.

As each individual has different personal and interpersonal skills, many organizations administer personality tests such as the Myers Briggs test[10] as a means of identifying the skill sets of individuals in order to build teams with a range of emotional skills. It is just as important to have diversity in these skills as it is to have a diversity of cultural, academic, and other perspectives on the team in order to assure the necessary range of problem solving approaches needed to be successful. When there is too much similarity in team member-ship, too few new ideas are put forth and discussions tend to be uninspired.

When looking at leadership in the 21st century context, it is important to be aware that what some call the corporate social contract is no longer the firm contract it once was. The old "loyalty for security" world of work no longer exists as the basis of work life it once was. Today's professionals tend to see their first position not as a lifetime assignment but as a learning experience that will help them hone their skills. They may or may not stay in the same organization but may move from place to place depending on their personal and professional vision. Robert Reich, secretary of labor in the Clinton ad-ministration said that "the most important community for an individual will not necessarily be a company, but a looser community of people with similar skills and social connections."[11] Look, for example, at the information technol-ogy industry in the Route #128, Boston area or in Silicon Valley in California. Companies are born, grow, are bought out by other companies, or are changed in some way as they grow and prosper or die. They employ individuals from the same highly professional workforce whose members move from company to company as appropriate opportunities arise. Members of this workforce are highly networked and support one another. Today's professional is in some ways an independent contractor rather than a cog in the organization. Bring-ing these highly intelligent, focused professionals together to achieve goals re-quires a type of leadership far different from that of the paternalistic autocrat.

LEADERSHIP QUALITIES

The Individual as Leader

What individual characteristics define the successful leader? Are they learned or are they part of the leader's DNA? What are the most important of these and how are they expressed? Can we make a list of these characteristics by identifying leaders and reviewing their activities? Are biographies a useful source of information? What do leaders themselves think are most important? From research, observation, and discussion, the following characteristics are among those most often identified.

Primary among these is that leaders must be ethical and hold a set of values that determine their actions, that define what is right and what is wrong and that tell us what to do and what not to do. The ethical leader sets a high standard of truth, honesty, and fair treatment of others, follows it and expects others to meet the same high standard. In order to gain the respect and confidence of others, telling the truth and telling it consistently is key. If the leader is unwilling or unable to be honest about a situation, about the problems, and pitfalls, how can that person's vision of how to succeed and build a better future be trusted? This can be summed up in one word and that word is credibility.

The leader needs to have the courage to think big and to challenge conventional wisdom by imagining new possibilities. "Moral courage enables people to stand up for a principle rather than stand on the sidelines. . . . Lack of courage stymies positive change at all levels. Consider ineffective politicians who shift positions on the basis of polling data, not conviction."[12] While doing nothing or following the path of least resistance may appear to be the prudent thing to do, it does not necessarily solve problems. It takes courage to support a new initiative or to reject a particular course of action that is not working well. It may appear to be easier or safer to make small changes or to stick with the status quo than to try a new direction that offers opportunity. It takes courage to go against the socially accepted norms if they are not right or fair. "But other paths must be explored, lest we regret the one not taken."[13] Many leaders are remembered for their courage in doing the right thing and secondarily for achieving their goals.

The leader needs to be able to identify a problem, focus on it, and not be sidetracked by lesser crises, opposition from others, or other distractions that draw attention and resources from the important tasks at hand. This does not mean that the leader ignores other things that are going on or ignores comments from team members; but it does mean that the leader does not lose direction because of them. The leader needs to focus on the future rather than get bogged down in daily trivia, and at the same time must focus on what is happening today. This seemingly contradictory statement is an attempt to balance the importance of maintaining forward movement toward important goals while at the same time not ignoring the crises that are directly in front of the leader. We have all seen examples of the individual who has grand ideas for the future but who ignores the fact that a major crisis is unfolding today. The competent leader is both future-oriented and present-focused. How the present crisis is solved can be a step in the direction of moving toward the future.

The leader is always learning and is always open to new ideas. The leader is aware of the latest research, newest ideas, and possible problems. Unlike a recent political candidate who stated in a national forum "I'm a leader, not a reader," the competent leader is indeed a reader, and a listener, and an asker of questions. The leader not only encourages members of the team to become as informed as is possible, it is part of what they are expected to do.

The leader accepts and indeed looks forward to challenges as these are the ways in which the ideas and the vision are tested. While it is possible to learn many of the skills of leadership, the individual also needs to want to lead, to anticipate the challenge of working with a team to solve new problems, to chart new directions, and to make a difference. Being passionate about ideas, challenges, building a vision, and working with others to achieve it is the true mark of the leader.

The most successful leaders are those who have the greatest flexibility in style and perspective.[14] Over time, leaders have honed certain processes, values, and actions that they are comfortable in implementing. This set of skills and competencies varies from leader to leader and to an extent defines that leader's way of setting a vision and working with others to meet the goals embedded in the vision. An important aspect of growth as a leader is to work outside the usual leadership patterns and expand behaviors. "In today's work climate, leaders need to act from a broader, more complete range of business, organizational, and interpersonal behaviors."[15] Research in right brain or left brain interaction shows that the two halves of the brain differ in the approach to problem solving. The left brain is ordered, quantitative, logical, realistic, and practical and reasons from the part to the whole. The right brain controls intuitive and emotional thought and reasons from the whole to the parts. The two work together, but one is usually dominant. Stimulating interaction between the two thought processes encourages new ways of thinking and problem solving. The leader who continues to learn, to question, and to seek new ways of doing things uses much more brain power than the one who sticks with a tried and true path. Researchers have also determined that the brain is hardwired to be social and to have social awareness of others, a basic requirement of good leadership.

Negative Leadership

Some individuals who do not have the best interests of others or of society as their driving force sometimes assume leadership positions. They may be motivated by ideas of personal glory and may have been able to convince others to follow them. This often occurs in periods of economic or social stress such as in Germany after World War I, a time that gave rise to Hitler and Nazism, or the rise of Lenin and Stalin during and after World War I. During periods of unrest under a weak central government, a dictator may emerge who gains control of a group or a country and who builds a regime that benefits no one other than the few in power. Sometimes an individual with a personal perspective on religion can develop a following of individuals who are looking for answers in their lives and follow someone who seems to have those answers. This kind of leader may have a vision and followers but lacks the ethical and moral values that are essential to the leader who looks to build a better future. These individuals use their leadership skills to enhance the self and to build personal power. Throughout history, we have seen examples of evil people who have led or driven others in destructive directions.

Setting the Tone

The leader's attitude and performance sets the tone for the team and for the organization. If the leader acts in an authoritarian manner, those on the team will overtly treat the leader with respect and will do as ordered. If the leader acts in a more collegial manner, a sense of participation will prevail and team members will interact more freely with one another and with the leader. Of increasing importance is the concept of the servant or leader, a situation in which each member of the team, including the leader, works to support the other members. Tasks and activities are performed by the individual most competent to perform the task. Routine tasks are often scheduled in such a way that everyone gets to answer the phone or make the coffee. The quality of the performance is more important than the relative importance of the job. The leader leads by example rather than by preaching or directing and motivates others by example rather than by directive. The leader is still responsible for making the important decisions but does so in a collegial fashion.

The leader respects members of the team and treats everyone in a respectful manner. Everyone is expected to treat everyone else with courtesy and dignity. Close friendships among staff may occur but they should not interfere with workplace activities and personal differences, unless directly related to the tasks at hand, have no place in the workplace. The overly folksy charmer detracts from the professional nature of the workplace while the aggressive, in-your-face leader creates unnecessary stress that interferes with the work at hand. The cold, distant leader who has little or no interaction with others will not foster a collaborative work environment. The ideal leader is even tempered, consistent in expectations, respects others, and fosters an environment in which everyone contributes to accomplishing the tasks at hand to the best of their ability. Humility and a sense of humor are important elements in the workplace as they break down barriers between and among individuals.

Language, both written and spoken, is a powerful way to set the tone of the organization and can be used to unite or divide the team. The tone of voice, the way the leader assigns tasks, the way the leader congratulates or advises a person about a less-than-perfect outcome, can be direct, open and honest or hidden with meanings. When one states the positive and then suggests some changes, it is more positive than when one picks out all the negatives and then says that "except for those flaws" it was a good job. Positive approaches challenge others to do even better. In addition to the use or misuse of language either because the leader lacks the knowledge to use it properly or because the leader wishes to intimidate, there is the fact that different cultures use language differently and what to one culture is a compliment may be an insult to another. It may be necessary to speak to different individuals in different ways to convey the same message in order to be sensitive to different needs.

How one dresses also contributes to setting the tone. The individual who respects self and others dresses in a manner that is appropriate to the workplace. Dress codes are often informal and tend to be reflective of an individual's generation or an individual's culture or both; and they are to be respected. Neatness and cleanliness do count. Personal habits vary but within the workplace there is a standard that should be met. The leader sets the tone here as well. A workplace environment that does not detract from the work to be done contributes to the success of the activities at hand.

We have all worked for individuals who do not bring out the best in others and who treat others in a discourteous manner. These experiences have influenced each of us by having provided a negative model of what not to do. We have been made aware of overt negative activities as well as the more subtle ways of mistreating individuals by ignoring or belittling their efforts or through questionable language. An unprepared or uncaring leader rarely achieves goals and is rarely respected by those who work for the leader. When one is in a leadership position, that individual serves as a role model for others in the group and has an effect on the next generation of leaders.

WHAT DOES THE LEADER DO?

Assuming Leadership

Leaders assume their role in a number of ways. They may have been hired to take over an organization by those who own the organization, and were selected because of their skill in leading other organizations. They may have been promoted from within the organization because their skills were recognized and because it was important to select someone who comes into the position with knowledge of the organization or because internal politics strongly supported that individual. A recent graduate of an academic program may have been selected because that individual has the most up-to-date technical information essential to the operation of the organization. Perhaps an individual has political importance or is supported by a strong political lobby and the organization wishes to build connections. Personal considerations may also come into play. In any case, when leaders accept the role, they come with a set of expectations that certain things will occur because of the new leadership and the new leader is expected to perform and produce. Those who selected the leader to fill that position are the individuals who will assess success or failure. At the same time, the members of the leader's team will also assess the level of success but will do so from a different perspective.

The leader may step into a situation in which the management team or the research team or other team is already in place, and the new leader must learn about the team and develop a means of working with the team to meet expectations. In other instances, the leader may have the responsibility of creating a team and in this case there is the opportunity to select individuals with qualifications uniquely fitted to the task. Within an organization, when an individual is selected to lead a committee, that leader may assume leadership of an existing committee or may lead an ad hoc committee that is brought together to achieve a specific goal. In the latter case, the leader may have a role in selecting members of the team.

An individual may become an accidental leader. A crisis has arisen and someone has to take charge. In that situation, the individual organizes anyone who is available and who has some level of skill, identifies tasks to be done, prioritizes them, and then works with those present to solve the problem. This kind of leadership occurs when there has been an accident or natural disaster—when immediate action is required—and no identified leader is present. The accidental leader keeps things together until help arrives and then turns things over to those most able to deal with the situation or may be asked to be the permanent leader.

A leader may be selected by peers to represent them. In a democratic society, elections are held to determine who will be their representative. In professional societies, members select a leader whose skills they respect and whom they trust to lead the society. Another type of leader is the person with an idea who looks for followers. It may be an individual with a particular religious, political, social, or other perspective who is looking for like-minded people. For example, Martin Luther King was a leader of the civil rights movement who built an organization and led other individuals who believed in equal rights for all in a movement that changed lives. In each of these instances, leadership is assumed and the leader is expected to meet certain identifiable goals and expectations. The advent of social media has greatly increased opportunities for those who wish to bring together like-minded individuals to support a cause or pursue an idea.

Vision

"Being forward looking—envisioning exciting possibilities and enlisting others in a share vision of the future—is the attribute that most distinguishes leaders from nonleaders."[16] The leader assumes that role in order to make a particular vision a reality. It may be presented as a grand idea that will transform the organization or transform society or it may have a more modest objective such as to solve a particular problem. In either instance, the leader is committed to the vision and to making it a reality. The ability to look ahead and envision a new future and to do so in such a way that others wish to participate in the effort is key to making the vision a reality. "The only visions that take hold are shared visions—and you will create them only when you listen very, very closely to others, appreciate their hopes, and attend to their needs. The best leaders are able to bring their people into the future because they engage in the oldest form of research: they observe the human condition."[17] The strongest vision is a shared vision in which all members of the team have the opportunity to include their own ideas and expectations and to participate in making the vision a reality.

In order to translate the vision into reality, it is necessary to state one's priorities and to develop the outlines of a plan of attack that will move the vision forward. At the early stages, this outline is a way of informing others of the leader's priorities rather than being a detailed set of directives. It is an early step in charting a path forward that will be refined with input from the team. The focus of the plan is to look forward to the future, where we want to go and what we want to do, rather than on past successes and failures. It identifies what the leader, and the team, need to know up front and sets targets in terms of short-term, long-term, and very-long-term goals as well as identifies ways of determining progress through feedback mechanisms that are recognized early on. These steps help to translate vision into clear and easy-to-understand words and actions and, in this way, shared meaning is created.[18]

The leader adapts the vision as necessary to meet the changing needs of time and place. This does not mean that the leader loses sight of the vision or dilutes its strength. It does mean that by listening to others, by seeking common ground and by exploring alternative paths, the vision itself is made stronger both through the ideas of others and through the buy-in that results from a shared approach. In a social media world, the leader can expand discussion of the vision beyond a small working group to include the larger organization, and if the vision is sufficiently broad to affect larger segments of society, they too can be involved. When one is open to suggestions and ideas from a wide range of individuals, the opportunity to refine the vision through the expert opinion of others, the resulting vision will become stronger as common threads and common interests can be identified and built upon.

In addition to the refinement of the vision, the willingness to include others in the process shows that the leader is interested in and respects the ideas of others. Such an open process promotes transparency which strengthens the vision as well as provides a way of keeping the vision on course. The leader is thus attuned to the external world and uses the input of others to decide how the vision will change or whether it should change at all. The role of the leader is to make the final decision as to what direction the vision will take. In some instances this may mean that the leader will go against the suggestions others have made. The leader sees the big picture and needs to mediate between differing views in the interest of moving forward in an ethical and efficient manner. The leader also understands the internal and external politics of the situation and the extent to which these forces influence the success or failure of moving ahead in certain ways.

The leader is responsible for articulating the vision and for setting the tone both of the discussion of the vision and for the way in which the vision is made real. Those persons responsible for carrying out the activities that move the vision forward will need to understand the priorities, the goals, and the intended results. Those leaders have an outward focus, are self-aware, know who they are, what they stand for; and they move the vision forward. The leader is the spokesperson to the outside world and champions the vision, its purpose and progress. Within the organization, others manage the activities that drive the vision forward. In some instances, the leader may also be the manager and thus responsible for both external and internal activities.

Team Building

The team is comprised of individuals with a range of skills and abilities and it is the sum of these that provide the strength of the team. The task of team building starts with developing the working tone which is based on trust, respect, and the knowledge by all involved, acknowledging that this is a team, and the input of each team member is valued, indeed is required. Expectations are made clear so that the team knows what is expected and the time frame in which completion of tasks is expected. The wise leader with the team develops a set of norms or rules of the road that guide the team so that each individual's input is respected and discussed as appropriate and decisions are made in a reasoned way. When conflict arises, these rules provide a means of solving most disagreements within the group. The leader encourages discussion and trusts team members to bring ideas and new information to the table for discussion. The leader does not cut off discussion by giving personal opinions but rather asks questions and draws out the input of others. Once the discussion has wound down, the leader then has the opportunity to summarize, and to place the results of the discussion in the context of the vision.

The leader trusts team members and assigns them important tasks that take advantage of the skills they bring to the team. The leader gives them space to do their own thing and does not micromanage. The leader provides opportunities for individual growth by assigning tasks that stretch the individuals' experiences. This willingness to trust team members to function on their own within the group motivates them to do more and think bigger. The leader operates from a position of thoughtfulness, listening, and information-gathering. The leader is open-minded, appreciates diversity of thought, and is interested in hearing of different or unusual takes on a problem. In this way the leader "leverages knowledge to extend an already primed intellect."[19]

The leader practices constructive intolerance, draws a line in the sand, and asserts leadership "through both firm demarcation and rational argument why things must and will change."[20]

Constructive intolerance is a means of instilling accountability, fairness, and integrity.

Collaboration and Communication

Collaboration is based on the ability of the leader to ensure that the team focuses on the tasks that advance the vision and to provide both continuity and momentum. Collaboration requires that the team understand their charge, that they share a common body of knowledge and that they expand this body of knowledge and use it to further the goals that have been set out for them. To do this, the leader needs to know what is going on in the workplace and to guide the direction of work being done without cutting off the creative spark so important to growth and change. This requires a leader who is open to change, is able to deal with conflict, and whose goal is that every member of the team reaches their potential. The leader gives each member of the organization room in which to learn and grow, and the individuals give the organization their best thinking. This is an environment in which the organization is willing to take risks and can turn an idea into reality by enabling the individual and the team both the freedom and the discipline to succeed. It is recognized that each team needs both creators and implementers, those who can dream new ideas and those who can make them reality. The successful organization and the successful leader understand the need for both. Not every idea will succeed but it is important that every idea be heard.[21]

In the collaborative environment everyone has the right, indeed the duty, to influence decisions by bringing their expertise to the table. Trust and mutual respect built over time plus a belief that everyone has a valuable contribution to make is key to building a truly collaborative environment. Everyone understands and follows the rules of engagement which outline the responsibility each individual has to contribute, to respect others, and to provide space for the unusual thinker and for unusual ideas. Every individual has the right to be needed by the group and to enjoy doing what they are doing. They have the right to be involved in decision making and in taking accountability for those decisions, and finally the right to have a role in their future growth and development. To the extent possible, the team should be self-managed with the group responsible for its success. Pride in a job well done should be earned and owned by the team. It is from such a working environment that many of our best ideas are generated.

The leader is not only responsible for the activities of a particular organization or team but is also the link to other organizations and teams through their leaders. Through this communication link, the team has the opportunity to see how its activities fit into the larger picture, if there is overlap, or if parts of the overall vision may have been overlooked. Sharing among leaders allows for even more good ideas and resources to be shared. It also provides the leader an opportunity to see the wider world in which the larger vision will become operational and to look at individual performance in light of the wider arena as well as to build a wider network that connects individuals and teams. Collaboration is internal to the team and external to the interaction among teams and the leader has a role in both areas.

Communication is a key element of collaboration in that the leader must be a competent communicator in order to state the vision and to inform members of the team as to what is necessary for them to do to make the vision real. Team members need to know what is expected of them and to communicate successfully with other team members and with the leader. They need to have the information to do their jobs. Many communication tasks can be learned and can be enhanced by the speed of communications technology such as e-mail and social media. However, while efficient, they lack the personal touch of a phone call or a face-to-face meeting. In order to build the team and grow it as a collaborative working group, the leader needs to build personal connections and does this largely through informal interactions. It is important for the leader to appreciate how others see things including what their values are, what they expect from a leader, and how they judge the quality of leadership.

The leader represents the team in external communication. This is when the leader presents the ideas, work in progress, and the accomplishments of the team to others. The leader is the public face of the team and the successful leader carries the honesty and credibility that is so important to the internal activities of the team to this next level. The extent to which others respect the team's activities is dependent upon not only its activities but also on how well and how honestly these activities are presented.

Accountability

It is important to look at progress toward goals and the vision on a regular basis in order to determine the extent to which those goals are being met. Do the goals continue to be clearly stated and understood or have they been modified to the extent that they no longer serve as guides for action? Have parts of the goals been met while other aspects have not been attended to? Have some objectives been given priority over others and if so, why? Have expectations and deadlines been set? It is important to step outside daily activities to ask these and related questions so that the team can identify problems and evaluate overall progress. It may be that an activity directed toward achieving a goal is not working because resources are not available, because unforeseen problems have arisen, or because upon further investigation that activity just won't work. This is the time to end work in this area, review the overall goal, and plan a potentially more productive course of action. As is true of any venture, success is determined by what one produces (output) rather than the resources one uses to do the job (input) and activities that do not contribute to the overall goals and vision should be revised or removed.

Some may think that working in a collaborative environment means that no one is in charge and that the team has no direction. On the contrary, everyone has a role in seeing that goals are met and each individual is responsible for contributing to meeting them. When evaluating progress, each team member must look at personal actions. How well were assigned and assumed tasks completed? Was there sufficient collaboration with team members? If it became apparent that a problem situation was in the making, did the team member alert others and begin to deal with the problem? These are the questions team members must ask themselves and the team leader must be able to answer to a higher authority for the team as in the end, success or failure is assigned to the leader who either led the team successfully or did not. You always have a gap between what you can control and what is beyond one's abilities to control, but this does not excuse leaders from doing their best to achieve the most that is possible within those limitations imposed.

The team is also responsible to the organization of which it is a part. If it is a not-for-profit group, it is also responsible to the public at large. Transparency of goals and of activities that support those goals is key to maintaining the trust and support of those to whom the team reports. Not only is there the need to do one's best work to meet goals, there is also the need to know that one is a steward of the public trust and one's actions must be honorable and able to withstand questions from the public. The leader represents the team and answers for it in the larger arena and to it internally. Leadership has a moral dimension and the leader who does not adhere to a high standard of honesty, morality, and truth places everyone in jeopardy. One need only to look at the Penn State scandal in 2011 in which an assistant coach was molesting young boys; those in leadership positions tried to ignore the situation rather than dealing with it immediately, showing that immoral leadership is no leadership. There is no leadership without followers and when the leader does not respect and represent the ideals of the organization and the team, followers disappear rapidly.

In addition to regular assessment of progress toward goals, teams also need to review their own internal interaction to assure that each person is doing the assigned job, has the needed resources to complete tasks, and works well with others. It may be that an individual assumed or was assigned a task that turned out not to be a good fit for that person's abilities or the team member assumed too many tasks, or external difficulties such as poor health had intruded. Regular review of how well the team is working will uncover these and related problems if they exist and the problems may be resolved through modification of assignments. It may be found that new skills or knowledge are needed and in this case, a new team member needs to be added or an existing team member retrained. If a team member is not contributing to the team effort, that individual may be counseled or removed. A team member who does not work well in a collaborative environment can do a great deal of damage to the team and the project, and a solution must be found as soon as possible.

Team members may have issues with the leader. Perhaps the leader is not actively involved with the team and does not provide sufficient guidance. The leader may not listen, is more of a dictator than a leader, and is generally difficult to work for. Many leaders are complex and may be sensitive to the needs and concerns of their team some times while ignoring them at other times. Examples of such complex individuals abound; for example, British prime minister Margaret Thatcher or U.S. president Lyndon B. Johnson. Eleanor Roosevelt, well known as a humanitarian, was personally an imperious person and considered by many of those who worked for her to be a difficult person to work for. In some instances, a team member or members resent the leader to the extent that they will rebel. In such cases, the dissident team member may be replaced or if the actions of the leader have angered enough individuals, the leader may be replaced.

Another model is that of the collaborative leader who keeps rivals close in order to use their abilities and at the same time control them. An excellent example of this is Abraham Lincoln's selection of his cabinet members as described by Doris Kearns Goodwin in *A Team of Rivals*.[22] Several of the cabinet members Lincoln selected had run against him in the national election while others were well known for their negative comments about him. Despite this, he brought them together, worked with them, and as a team they provided the expertise desperately needed by a nation at war. He trusted their expertise, believed that they wanted the best for their country, and that they were too proud of their personal reputations to do less than their best. Despite their public dislike of Lincoln and in some cases of each other, they worked together to meet the needs of a nation at war with itself.

SUMMARY

The leader, with the support of the team, works to achieve a vision that will improve an aspect of society or of an organization. This team of individuals represents a wide variety of skills, abilities, and problem solving methods, and they work together, in a collaborative setting, to make the vision a reality. Progress toward goals is assessed on a regular basis in order to ensure that actions support the goals, that acceptable progress is being made, and that any necessary changes are made in order to improve the operation of the team.

NOTES

1. Nanerl Keohene, *Thinking about Leadership* (Princeton, NJ: Princeton University Press, 2010), 25.

2. W. George and Peter Sims, *Authentic Leadership, Discover Your Authentic Leadership* (San Francisco: Jossey-Bass, 2007), article adapted and published in the *Harvard Business Review* 85, no. 2 (February, 2007): 129–38.

3. Ibid., 138.

4. Deborah Ancona, Thomas W. Malone, Wanda J. Orlikowski, and Peter M. Senge, "In Praise of the Incomplete Leader," *Harvard Business Review* 85, no. 2 (February, 2007): 92–100.

5. Daniel J. Snowden and Mary E. Boone, "A Leader's Framework for Decision Making," *Harvard Business Review* 85, no. 11 (November, 2007): 69–76.

6. Ibid., 74.

7. Steven Trachtenberg, "Essay," *The Chronicle of Higher Education* 44 (November 2, 2007).

8. Thomas A. Stewart, "What Kind of Decision Is It?" *Harvard Business Review* 85, no. 11 (November, 2007): 16.

9. David Goleman, Richard Boyatzes, and Annie McKee, *Primal Leadership: Realizing the Power of Emotional Intelligence* (Boston: Harvard Business Review Press, 2002).

10. I. B. Myers, *Introduction to Type*, 6th ed. (Palo Alto, CA: CCP, Inc., 1995).

11. Steve Lohr, "How is the Game Played Now," *New York Times*, December 5, 2005, C8.

12. Rosabeth Moss Kanter, "Courage in the C-Suite," *Harvard Business Review* 89, no. 12 (December, 2011): 38.

13. Ibid.

14. Mary Lou Decosterd, *Right Brain/Left Brain Leadership: Shifting Styles for Maximum Impact* (Westport, CT: Praeger, 2008), 1.

15. Ibid., 7.

16. James Kouzes and Barry Z. Posner, "To Lead, Create a Shared Vision," *Harvard Business Review* 87, no. 1 (January, 2009): 20.

17. Ibid., 21.

18. John Hamm, "The Five Messages Leaders Must Manage," *Harvard Business Review* 84, no. 5 (May, 2006): 114–123.

19. Mary Lou Decosterd, *Right Brain/Left Brain President: Barack Obama's Uncommon Leadership Ability and How We Can Each Develop It* (Santa Barbara, CA: Praeger, 2011), 5.

20. Ibid., 11.

21. David Goleman and Richard Boyatzis, "Social Intelligence and the Biology of Leadership," *Harvard Business Review* 86, no. 9 (September, 2008): 75.

22. Doris Kearns Goodwin, *A Team of Rivals* (New York: Simon and Schuster, 2005).

3

Leadership in Context

The world in which we live is defined in many ways: by the culture in which we live, by history, by the environment, by events of nature, by activities that impact our everyday life, and by our responses to the many conditions and events that surround us. While each of us defines our surroundings differently depending on our own personal filters and on those of the people with whom we associate, certain elements tend to receive a higher value and they are responsible for defining how we see the world around us and how we decide what our role in that world is. In order to be competitive, we need not only to understand the culture in which we live but we must also go outside our own geography and learn how other people live and think. From this we learn how much we don't know, how many other routes to success exist, and how we can identify and use new ways of looking at the world.

Our world is also defined by the speed with which change occurs. In earlier generations, before the advent of instant communication and real-time sharing of information, it took time for change to enter our daily lives. Not so long ago, we had to wait for someone riding a horse to deliver our mail while today, we have instant messaging. We learned about natural disasters or acts of aggression days or weeks after they happened. Now we see them online as they unfold. In earlier times, the disaster had done its damage and recovery was underway before the rest of the world learned of it. Now we see it in real time and are expected to react in real time. We have little or no time to ask ourselves what this means, what its implications are, how we should respond, and what the implications of different responses might be. Emphasis is placed on action rather than reflection. Events of historic importance, such as the Arab Spring in 2012, were influenced by the availability and use of social networking. The collapse of national governments were watched in real time as were the responses of the world powers while everyone with access to social media acted as bystanders who had the opportunity to respond or not as they wished.

Seeing events in real time and feeling pressure to respond in real time has both positive and negative aspects. The positive aspects include the fact that we are able to learn what is happening in our world without having to wait. The negative aspects include the fact that because information is made available immediately, we feel pressured to respond rapidly. We don't have the opportunity to think about our response as carefully as we might which may lead us to respond in what may be an inappropriate manner. Because we are always in some way connected to the world and to our work, when do we have the necessary downtime to reflect on our activities and on events around us? When do we ever have the opportunity to get away from work, from the pressures of interpersonal interactions, and just find a place to be so that we can sort out who we are and how we wish to interact with the world? When are we ever "off the job" in a networked world?

The networked world also means that we can be in touch with friends and family at any time in any place and can be part of their virtual lives. Back in the days when it was necessary to travel a distance to see friends and family, we maintained close relationships only with those who were nearby. Because of the costs of long distance telephone calls, our interaction with others was limited to a relatively small circle. Now the only limits on our social network are those placed by individuals who opt or do not opt to join and participate. Keeping up with distant cousins, friends from high school or college, from earlier work places, or someone we met on vacation is time consuming and takes from our day time that we might otherwise spend interacting face-to-face with those nearest us or alone thinking about our own concerns. The ability to be connected to so many individuals in real time can be seen as a kind of social busy work or extended gossip circle. We are still learning how social networking affects our daily life and how it impacts our environment.

The pressure to respond immediately to what we have learned and not to make mistakes in doing so creates a kind of stressful environment not experienced by our parents and grandparents. In an earlier time, the experience gained by those who came before us was respected and served as a guide to responding to current crises. Older generations were respected for the information they had gained through a lifetime of living and dealing with crises often very similar to those of today. That experience rarely finds a way into how one reacts in a world of instant messaging. While those who came before us may not be conversant with the latest in technology, they have a wealth of understanding of how people interact and the consequences of decisions made carefully or decisions made without proper consideration. As has often been said, time, place, and technology may change but human nature rarely does. This has very important implications for every culture and does so in different ways depending on how deeply one is enmeshed in the world of social networking.

Social networking is but one aspect of the technological revolution that has changed our lives; the way we work, the ways we learn, and how we interact with one another. With rapid communication and the ability to move goods and services on a global level, our economies are intertwined worldwide as is our workforce. This enhances our ability to benefit from a wider range of economic opportunities while at the same time greatly increasing the risk that a crisis in one part of the world will send shock waves across all the economies of the world or that a social crisis in one part of the world will affect the social comfort of everyone. We have only to look at the economic difficulties in the early second decade of the 21st century to see how poor economic choices in one country caused stress in many other countries. Our manufacturing capabilities are also distributed worldwide both in terms of workforce capabilities and the distribution of sites that manufacture parts. The earthquake and tsunami in Japan in 2011 caused a disruption in the manufacture of automobile parts that were intended for Japanese car makers wherever their plants were worldwide, and it took many months before sufficient parts became available to resume planned assembly of cars intended for a worldwide market.

While much of the information that reaches our laptop or other device comes directly from those with whom we work and interact, much also comes from the media that is highly sophisticated in reporting news of all kinds from many sources, and across the range of delivery points from print to digital. Media outlets range from those that deliver the news as accurately as possible to those that deliver the news with a particular political, social, or economic slant. As ways of collecting information and disseminating it have increased so have ways of interfering with privacy of information and this privacy is important to individuals, organizations, and nations. The individual must be ever vigilant not only to protect personal information and that affiliated with the workplace but also to assess incoming information to determine its accuracy and its value.

WORKPLACE CULTURE

External Workplace Culture

Stresses related to the shift in the economy from what was primarily the age of the machine to the age of information have presented themselves in the workplace in many ways. Many of the routine tasks done on the assembly line or in the office, such as packing boxes or filing papers, are no longer done by people. Sophisticated machines now pack and seal those boxes and do so much faster and much more accurately than humans can. One or two individuals can operate the machines thus saving the salaries of numerous workers who once were needed to manage the operation. Filing of hard copy items in an office has been replaced by electronic files that can be updated and searched immediately from a number of locations. In each of these and many other instances, workplace tasks have been replaced by technology and what may have employed several individuals can now be done by one or two individuals who have been given additional training. With the strong emphasis placed on increased productivity, fewer people are expected to produce more and do it faster; and with the development of ever more sophisticated tools, this possibility has become a reality. Multiply this across the economy and one begins to understand why unemployment has grown. One can also see why so many in the workforce are stressed and why those who have lost their jobs have little real expectation of reemployment unless they learn new skills that will make them fit for the new world of work.

A similar situation arose in the mid-19th century, when the economy was moving from agricultural to industrial. As farming became more industrialized with the advent of machines, whether pulled by horses or tractors, fewer individuals were required to grow and process the foods and other products such as cotton and tobacco that the country required. This resulted in a surplus of labor on the farm, and workers had to look elsewhere for work. They went to the textile mills in New England or the Carolinas to find work or to the steel mills in Pennsylvania. Because many of the mills that hired the excess farm labor were looking for healthy individuals who could perform rote labor, there was typically a short learning curve between farm and factory. As the cost of labor in the United States rose and as it became feasible for manufacturing to be done offshore, the jobs that required minimal training left the United States and went to China, to India, or to third world countries where labor is still cheap. We are now learning that although offshore labor is cheaper than domestic labor, quality concerns, the cost of transporting goods from offshore locations, and other costs may erase much of the benefits of cheap labor. As a result, there is a rethinking of what is best manufactured offshore or manufactured domestically.

The transition from industrial to information age jobs is more complex than that from agricultural to industrial because there is a much longer learning curve. Minimal educational credentials would often suffice for factory work but when one deals with robots, computers, and other sophisticated ways of working, a much higher level of education is necessary. Those currently in school or those in the workforce who are able to obtain training for new jobs are in the best situation to move ahead in this environment. Those who are near retirement age or those who are unwilling or unable to learn new skills are most likely doomed to remain unemployed or underemployed. Jobs that require limited technical skills will continue to exist as there is always a need for caregivers and individuals who do routine tasks such as cleaning and maintaining our homes and buildings or working in the fast food industry. These jobs are at the bottom of the pay scale and offer little or no advancement.

The days of getting a job and working one's way up through the ranks in the same company to a position of responsibility with a good salary are over. Many of those jobs no longer exist and more often than not, neither do the factories. Today, it is usually about what you know and how useful you can be today. Recent graduates with specific skill sets replace the loyal worker who lacks the opportunity or desire to develop needed skills and these new hires are often paid at a higher rate. In unionized shops, how does one meet the needs of both sets of individuals and still get the job done? How does the organization support the younger workers who are usually the ones bringing new ideas and new technologies into the workplace while still dealing with union rules and restrictions? Another aspect of this is that in some instances there are too few individuals with specialized skills and although they would like to retire, they are urged to continue working until replacements can be trained and hired.

Another complication for the workforce is that more and more individuals at retirement age are continuing to work beyond the time they had at one time intended to retire. This may be a response to the fact that they truly enjoy what they are doing or more likely to the fact that it is increasingly difficult to survive on retirement income, or some combination of the two. For the employer, this means that there may be too many staff members at the top of the salary scale who although they are doing good work are being paid more than it would cost to hire new employees at a lower rate. This in turn means that there are fewer funds to recruit new hires or to support newer staff. The flexible organization can serve many—often conflicting—needs by looking at senior positions and finding those that can be filled by part-time or contract work and then giving senior staff the choice of working less than full-time by offering early retirement as an option. It is indeed sometimes possible to have the best of both worlds; retain high-performing senior staff on a part-time basis and free up funds to hire new staff. And if funds are freed up, they could also be used to support staff development so that existing staff can become more productive and more prepared for leadership roles.

The public library is an excellent example of the several workforce issues that most organizations, both for-profit and not-for-profit, are experiencing. As an information-based service organization, the library was among the first to benefit from advances in information technology that made it possible to record, store, access, and use information much faster and much more efficiently than before. The card catalogs that at one time consisted of thousands of cards carefully prepared and filed in drawers has given way to online catalogs accessible to the public from any location at any time. Those individuals who prepared the cards, filed them, removed them from the files when an item was no longer in the collection, and who helped the public locate a desired item no longer have a job. A very small staff deals with information items unique to a particular library and enters information directly to the online catalog the majority of whose content has been developed centrally. Systems are now available which allow library users to check out their own information materials and to check them back in when they are returned thus freeing several more staff members from routine work who are then able to interact directly with those seeking information. These and other changes in the way work is conducted have resulted in a leaner staff able to do more things and often in less time. In terms of jobs, this relatively gradual process, rather than resulting in widespread layoff of staff, has been accomplished largely through attrition. What has also occurred is that fewer positions are available for new hires and positions that are available require specific skill sets.

The elimination of routine tasks has provided staff the opportunity to spend more time with those seeking information and anyone who goes to a public library or other library today will find a wider range of information formats easily accessible, more sophisticated search tools, and enhanced services for those using the library. Staff at every level is more highly skilled in dealing with information and the ways in which that information is and can be used by the public. A strong emphasis is placed on continuing professional education so that staff members at all levels are current with the latest innovations and how they can be used to serve the community. Because librarians were among the first to recognize that the massive changes in information technology would have a huge effect on their institutions, they are in many ways ahead of the curve in providing continuing education, implementing new systems, and working with the public to help them understand the systems and how they can work for them.

The need to have an organization that is highly productive, has the smallest possible staff who are highly skilled in the use of information technology and related areas, and continues to meet the needs of the workplace and of society is a common goal. Given that the workforce is in transition with an increasing number of individuals educated for or getting the education necessary to functioning in a high-tech, highly competitive world while at the same time dealing with the unemployment of many individuals who lack essential skills to compete in the information age, we live in a very stressful world and will continue to do so for the foreseeable future.

Internal Workplace Culture

Each organization, institution, or family is defined in part by its internal values and the ways in which they are expressed. A family-owned business is built on the values and expectations of the family. Whether it is autocratic or paternalistic or collaborative depends on the desires of the family in charge. Authority is often tightly held by family members and those who work for the family are well aware of limitations that may be imposed. A college or university, a library, a conservation association such as the Sierra Club, or a socially responsible society such as Planned Parenthood has as its mission strengthening and enhancing the world in which we live. Those who choose to work in these environments bring with them the social values for which their workplace stands and their activities contribute to the mission. A high-tech startup company exists because the creative energy of its founders has produced a product or service that is useful to society. Their environment is one in which the quality of the idea and the product or service it produces is the driving force. Each of the above is an example of the internal context within which we work and live. Combine the external political, social, technological, and economic contexts with the internal environment within which these play out in our everyday lives, and one can see the need and the opportunity for creative leadership.

THE ROLE OF LEADERSHIP

Given this fast moving, ever changing environment in which we live, we have need of leadership that will help frame the future while at the same time helping those who will create the future as well as those whose skills have placed them on the sidelines. Individuals whose work lives have become unsettled and those who have lost the settled path ahead that their parents and older friends have followed often fear for the future and are vulnerable. They don't know who to trust. Can they trust our leaders? Can we trust the social organizations that bring people together? Can we trust our government? Can we trust those who manage our economy? Can we trust the information that comes to us from every direction? Who/what can we trust? Individuals will appear who will try to take advantage of this fear and try to build barriers between groups or find someone to blame for their situation. Individuals who are committed to finding a path to the future will also appear and will help others recognize that "Yes we are in a difficult situation so let's work together to get out of it."

Where will we find today's leaders? Will they be the individuals who were in charge during the pre–information technology days? Will they be the elders of the workplace or the community? Will they be fear mongers who insist that the only way to survive is to belong to a particular group, to believe in a certain way, and to trash anyone who disagrees with their point of view? Will they represent those individuals who fear change and want to go back to the good old days, whatever they were? Will they be the young entrepreneur millionaire whose ideas are changing our social space?

Bennis[1] asked "Where are the leaders when we need them?" The lack of leadership in many areas of our society is a common concern. Wrongdoing in government, in industry and elsewhere is reported daily in the media. In order to function as a society, we need leaders. A small organization may be able to function informally, but a nation of more than 300 million cannot function without individuals who step up at all levels to lead. Some say that when we need leaders, they appear. Others say that it is risky just to hope for leadership and that efforts should be made to prepare individuals to lead. The universities and other educational settings as well as the military have as a major role the preparation of tomorrow's leaders. Bennis goes on to say that "the first step in becoming a leader . . . is to recognize the context for what it is—a breaker not a maker, a trap not a launching pad, an end not a beginning, and declare your independence."[2] Leaders are prepared, organized, and confident that they can make a difference, and then, with a guiding vision, passion, curiosity and daring, make things happen.

David McCullough, a well-known American historian and biographer has said that our history is filled with leaders who exhibit "the fundamental qualities of what might be called timeless leadership."[3] He stressed the importance of history in one's education; knowing about people, about cause and effect, knowing how the demands of leadership change over time and in different cultures, and knowing that luck plays a part in outcomes. He commented on the importance of being able to identify leaders even when the individual doesn't fit a particular mold. "Good leaders also judge people by how they handle failure. . . . Good leaders don't tolerate self pity in themselves or others. The star performer who has never fallen flat on his face or been humiliated publicly, may not have what it takes when the going gets rough."[4]

Leadership as Relationship

Leadership does not occur unless there are those who follow. This is a dynamic relationship in which the needs, interests, abilities, and defects of one influences the actions of the other. It is a give and take relationship that may be based on rational needs or on emotional needs.[5] The charismatic leader can be an idealized figment of the imagination, for example, a father figure who represents safety and security. This is a very personal relationship in which those who feel unwanted can finally find a home. The thoughtful leader who understands that serving as a safe haven is not the healthiest of relationships will work with those followers to help them grow and become more independent. Some leaders serve as symbols of a movement or cause, for example, Lincoln as the symbol of antislavery or Gandhi as a symbol of nonviolent change. Some individuals may attach themselves to a cause and claim that they should be the new leader. They may be supportive of the cause or they may see it as an opportunity to gain a short cut to domination by taking over an existing situation. Transformational leaders "cause the followers to have greater belief in their own ability, enhance their value in their own lives and also lead to more moral and pro-social thinking that goes beyond the cycle of narcissistic needs or self-interest."[6] Martin Luther King is an example of the transformational leader as he would tell others that they have the power to change things.

What Do We Need in a Leader?

The leader understands that leading is more than maintaining the status quo and being a good steward of the current environment. The leader has a vision of what the organization can become and uses this as a guide rather than relying on keeping things as they are. The leader has a sense of purpose, is an individual who knows what the organization should do and what it should not do. The leader asks members of the organization to consider their roles, not only as members of the organization, but also as members of society and in terms of how what they do contributes to the greater good of society. The leader thinks long term and constructs a path, a vision that sets goals for the future, rather than short term, the purpose of which is to solve a specific problem. Above all, the leader needs to know how to master the context. To do this, leaders need to have a strong sense of self, to listen to their inner voice and not ignore what it tells. Leaders learn from the experiences of others and have an understanding of what actions work and those that don't and above all have a strong belief that they can make a difference in the world, and it is this belief that powers the vision. Following a vision is not easy as one has to overcome both the internal and external contexts which define our lives.

In order to be successful, leaders need to be certain that they understand the contexts, that they know what the issues and problems are, and that they are aimed at the most important problems the organizations they lead have to solve. The leader needs to have strong people skills and the ability to work well with others, and the leader needs to be able to adapt personal skills to the environment in which he or she works. There are numerous examples of a leader who is successful in one environment finding it difficult to lead in another. Leaders whose experience has been primarily in business or the military may find it difficult to lead in an academic environment as they may expect to lead without being questioned, without disagreement, and do so promptly. Academics expect that their leaders will consult them, discuss issues, and as a group reach a solution. A business CEO often expects to dictate direction and be followed and when encountering a more collegial environment may find it difficult to make the necessary changes. The practitioner and manager may find it difficult to function in a more theoretical research environment.

Cultural differences in leadership style go beyond the type of organization and may include differences between genders. While it may be useful to discuss a problem in terms of a particular team sport to a group of men, it may not be a helpful analogy in a mixed or an all-female group. It is often recognized that different national groups have their own ways of interaction.

Business representatives and military personnel who are assigned to work with groups in other countries often receive instruction in how the culture with which they will be interacting differs from that from which they come. It is sometimes forgotten that the workforce in the United States is made up of individuals from several cultures and that cultural sensitivity at home is as important as it is abroad.

Leaders may need to adapt the vision to the contexts within which they are working and so long as the vision stays true to the leader's principles, no harm is done. Strategy may change but principles should not. If the leader has joined an organization expecting that it was motivated by a particular vision and has found that that vision differs from personal beliefs, the leader needs to review personal beliefs and make some basic decisions. For example, if an environmentalist joined an energy company that said it was interested in becoming more environmentally friendly and needed someone to lead that effort and then found out that environmental friendliness was a way of covering up activities that were environmentally unfriendly, the environmentalist would either have to live with this or leave the company.

CHALLENGING THE CONTEXT

In selecting a leader, the board of directors, trustees, or other group has done so in large part because that individual's vision, abilities, and leadership style match their view of what the organization needs to succeed. The challenge they have presented the leader is that this person will build or perhaps rebuild an organization so that it is competitive, well-managed, and achieves its mission. They may not be fully aware of the extent to which the existing internal context will need to change in order to meet this expectation.

The first step in challenging the context is for all who are involved to be fully aware of the current situation—both internally and externally—within which one works and leads. Those within the organization need to be informed by the leader that the organization will be looked at from all perspectives and they need to be told why. This overview may be conducted in the context of developing a long-range plan, a reorganization, or as a means of introducing a new leader to the organization. Whatever the immediate purpose, the leader with input from those in the organization has the opportunity to identify strengths and weaknesses, see where problems exist, and to make changes that will make the organization a better place in which to work, and will refocus the organization on its mission by sharpening the vision and identifying a path ahead. This is a "we" task rather than a "me" task and an opportunity for the leader to work to build community. The first step is to explore the current internal situation and to gain an understanding of the company culture. Informal organizations exist in every context and they can be extremely important in defining attitudes toward formal leadership and the goals of the organization. They may be highly supportive of change and new leadership or they may resent change and work quietly to undermine it. Informal organizations tend to be made up of those who are long-term members of the organization and who have seen new leaders and new plans come and go; and if they don't like the new leader, they believe that they have only to wait it out until the new leader leaves and then life can go on as usual. At the other end of the spectrum, other members of the organization look forward to new leadership and the opportunity to move forward in new directions. In either instance, challenging the context needs input from everyone in the organization. It is also very useful to consult with individuals who have worked in similar organizations and other cultures and who can share their expertise with both the leader and those who will be members of the team.

In addition to internal evaluation of an organization, the leader needs to read, study, and listen and gain an understanding of the external world within which we live and what the external challenges, opportunities, and expectations are. For academic institutions, the massive challenge of educating a workforce that can be productive in today's and tomorrow's high-tech industries provides opportunities and challenges and the institution needs to recalibrate its programs and information delivery to meet the need. Every business and industry, as it adapts its activities to take advantage of technological advances, benefits from continuous review of its activities and its competitiveness in the external environment.

Throughout the process of challenging the context in order to assure that the organization has not become calcified by outmoded ways of thinking and doing things and that it is functioning at its optimum level, the leader must communicate constantly with members of the organization so that they are a part of the process and they understand the reasons for changes that are made. A role of the leader is to resist and replace internal systems that are unfair and to make them fair to those within the organization and to those the organization affects. The leader sees the potential of the organization and makes things happen even though it may be difficult. Warren Bennis said "master the context, don't surrender to it."[7]

SUMMARY

In the process of making things better by improving the internal context and by being knowledgeable about the external context and what the organization's role is in the external context, the leader may need to adapt aspects of the vision in order to have a better fit. While strategies may be adjusted, the principles on which the vision is built may not. The leader must stand for something and that something does not change. The strength and power of leaders is dependent upon their having a set of values and principles that do not change as this is what defines the individual and why that individual was placed in a leadership position.

The leader may also need to adapt leadership style depending on the situation. Sometimes a very directive style is needed while at other times a more hands-off style works. Regardless of the need to adapt style to context basic principles and values do not change. The leader must have integrity, and those who follow must know what the leader stands for and that they can trust her or him to do the right thing for the individual and for the organization.

NOTES

1. Warren Bennis, *On Becoming a Leader* (New York: Basic Books, 2003), 1–30.

2. Ibid., 19.

3. "Timeless Leadership, A Conversation with David McCullough," *Harvard Business Review* 86, no. 3 (March, 2008): 45–49.

4. Ibid.

5. Micha Popper, *Leaders Who Transform Society: What Drives Them and Why We Are Attracted* (Westport, CT: Praeger, 2005), 35.

6. Ibid., 55.

7. Ibid., 25.

4

Why and How People Assume Leadership Roles

Where do we find leaders? Some say that leaders are born, others say that they are made, while still others say that leadership is thrust upon an individual. Each one of these paths to leadership has an element of truth and each of us has the opportunity at some time and in some way to be a leader. One can inherit the role of leader as is the case of royal families or one can, very early in life, exhibit special talents that make one a leader. There are situations in which leadership is required by circumstances. For example, an individual is forced into exile and becomes the spokesperson for a cause. The Dalai Lama, a revered Tibetan religious leader, was forced into exile and because of this became a symbol for his countrymen and then found it necessary to add political leadership to his responsibilities. Charles DeGaulle at the start of World War II was exiled from France, went to England, and became the leader of the Free French, a military group who fought for their country from exile. Bennis says that leadership is a product of self-invention by those who have self-knowledge and a strong desire to achieve and that leaders invent themselves by observing, by reading, and by coming to their own conclusions rather than following thoughtlessly or out of duty.[1]

Based on research that has been done to attempt to answer this question, it has become evident that each of us is the sum of our biological heritage, abilities, experiences, and the world we believe in and live in. Studies in the 1940s and 1950s, to determine if those identified as leaders had specific physical characteristics or qualities such as intelligence or determination, found that there were no clear answers.[2] Studies were undertaken to see if leaders shared common behaviors, which then led to studies of combinations of behaviors or styles. In the 1990s attention focused on the attributes and performance of poor or negative leaders. Research to define and understand leadership continues and interest in what combination of factors contributes to the art and skill of leadership increases as the perceived need for leadership in our complex society increases.

THE INFLUENCE OF BIAS ON LEADERSHIP

There are those who say that leadership is a subjective creation of followers in that it is the followers who perceive special qualities and who determine the greatness of the leader and the characteristics that are involved.[3] Biographies, by definition, tend to focus on the individual and often include little or no information on the influence of those who supported the leader and enabled that person's success. The influence of bias—the personal bias of the individual toward certain ways of believing, the bias of the times in which we live, and the bias of those who follow the leader and to an extent define that individual—is often not included in the leader's biography. The individual's bias comes from the world in which they live and from the activities and influences that are considered important at a certain time and place. One's social position and that of one's family and associates influences ways of thinking. If one belongs to a socially prominent group, that individual may feel entitled to being respected and to having the best home, the best education, and a life of ease while if the individual is part of a family that has had to struggle to find sufficient resources to exist and for whom education is a luxury, a very different set of biases results.

Many leaders in history were members of ruling families who led because they had inherited that role. Their families controlled the tribe or the nation's resources and had the power to allocate resources as they wished. Some of these individuals cared about those who lived on their lands and who were expected to serve the ruler while others saw those beneath them as simply resources to be used for personal gain and power. Consider the activities of Catherine the Great of Russia who represented autocratic rule in a land that had been ruled or misruled by an autocratic form of government for centuries. Add to this personal bias based on parenthood and position in a community and level of family affluence, the experience of growing up in a particular environment, and those traits of personality that are inherited and honed by experience, and one has individuals with strong feelings/biases about the world in which they live and what they believe it owes them and they owe it. The individual who has grown up in poverty and has succeeded in spite of that has a very different bias from the individual who has grown up in an affluent environment where basic needs were never at risk. Abraham Lincoln is an excellent example of an individual who understood the difficulty of making one's way in a hostile environment and who truly understood what poverty can do to how an individual thinks and acts. He knew what it meant and what it took for an individual born neither to wealth nor power to succeed in a world which was dominated by those who considered themselves entitled because of the wealth and power of their families.

There is a bias on the part of some individuals for the status quo. These are the individuals who are comfortable in their world and are poorly equipped to deal with change. They often have poor self-image and underestimate their own potential. Learning new things, taking on new tasks is stressful for them as it forces them out of their comfort zone. In some cases, it is possible to force them out of their comfort zone and to take risks. Others will do whatever they can to stay in their comfort zone and will refuse to take part in a changing world rather than following ways of doing things that have proved safe for them in the past, although those ways of doing things may not work today. When they find themselves in leadership positions because they have inherited that role or because they represent a particular group, little forward movement can be anticipated.

There is bias on the part of those who follow the leader. People need leaders, someone who has the ability to create a vision and the authority to make decisions. They place their hopes on the abilities of an individual whose vision appeals to them. To be worthy of their followership, the leader must have qualities that reflect well on their decision to follow. They may attribute to the leader more knowledge and wisdom than that individual actually has. This type of leaders may get more credit for success than they have actually earned and conversely, may be blamed for actions over which they have little or no control. Followers may credit their leader for successes that are more due to the circumstances than specific actions. Followers expect to take pride in their leader and often set high standards for the leader's behavior. When the leader does not live up to these standards, followers may become disappointed and even angry. Some leaders are aware of bias that their followers may develop and they maintain a distance from their followers in order to have a level of independence from followers who would follow their activities too closely. As time goes by, the leader may be seen differently by followers and after the leader dies the image of the leader may change either to idealize that individual as wiser and kinder than in real life or as even more devious than one had thought in real life.[4] Some leaders like Martin Luther King Jr., who had the courage to stay true to his principles and through nonviolent means fought for the dignity and rights of all individuals despite threats against him, continue to grow in the esteem of those who followed them. President Richard M. Nixon, who resigned from the presidency in disgrace and retained the respect of very few of his followers, regained a degree of respect because of his leadership in foreign policy, particularly in his efforts in reconnecting with China and building bridges between China and the United States. As we read the biographies of past leaders, we often see that a leader in his or her own time may have been overappreciated or underappreciated and that as one gains perspective on the leader and his or her actions over time, our attitude toward the leader changes.

Cultural bias toward leadership can be seen in the attitude toward authority. In some cultures the leader maintains a distance and those following treat the leader and the position held with respect. There are often many rules that determine the ways in which the leader is treated and this in itself creates distance. In the United States and in Western Europe, the leader tends to be closer to those who follow than is true in many Asian and Arab societies, and interactions are more direct. Cultural bias also affects the way in which the leader is seen in relation to society. Western society, particularly American society, has great appreciation for the leader who goes it alone and who represents the importance of the individual while other societies, China for example, believe in the importance of the group rather than in the strong individualist. Also, there continues to be cultural bias about the role of women as leaders. Some societies see themselves as totally masculine, a bias which makes it almost impossible for women to assume leadership roles. In other societies, women as leaders have attained leadership roles in business, politics, and other endeavors.

LEADERSHIP ATTRIBUTES

Although studies have found that no particular set of characteristics defines a leader, the individual who assumes a leadership role and is successful tends to have the following attributes.

1) The individual must have the self-confidence to want to lead and be motivated to take the steps necessary to succeed. This does not mean that the individual does not have concerns about the ability to lead, but it does mean that they want the opportunity to get out there with their ideas and vision and start working on them. Some individuals may have been identified by others as potential leaders and been given the opportunity to undertake assignments that test their leadership abilities. They may have been assigned challenging roles early in their work life and given tasks that test their ability to solve problems and to do so in real time. Other individuals may have built their self-confidence through observation, study, and a willingness to try new things and may have done so without the guidance of others and even in spite of the attitudes of others. Being able to learn from experience and to evaluate that experience strengthens the individuals' self-confidence and sense of their leadership potential, and this knowledge is essential to success.

2) Individuals who wish to lead observe the world around them and are curious about how people interact, how government works, and how new technologies are changing the ways in which we do things. They are always observing, reading, asking questions and reaching their own conclusions about how things could or should be done and are unwilling to follow the directions of others because society says it is the expected thing to do. Mroz[5] said that one can find leaders embedded in all aspects of society who are willing to stand up and lead. They are ordinary people doing extraordinary things; trying, risking, crossing boundaries, facing down their fears and taking small steps to effect change. This is true of all cultures, times, and places. He cited the Greensboro Four, young African American men who went to a lunch counter at F. W. Woolworth Co. in segregated Greensboro, NC, asking to be served. They were ordinary people willing to put themselves forward to right a wrong. Despite strong objection to their actions and even the threat of violence, they persevered. It was individuals such as these young men who spearheaded the civil rights movement.

3) Individuals who intend to lead must believe in what they do and must take responsibility for their actions. If they are concerned about social issues, they need to believe that there is a better way of moving forward than that currently being followed. If they are working for a company, they need to believe in the product or service that it provides and be willing to work hard to contribute to the best possible performance of that product or service. They may think of new and efficient ways to streamline performance and to provide greater customer satisfaction.

Leaders are not satisfied with the status quo but are always questioning, learning, testing ways of doing better. Steve Jobs, who in his career at Apple was always looking for a better way to provide information, was a genius at thinking about and devising new industry-changing devices that in turn changed the way we communicate. His interpersonal skills were often lacking and he tended to be impatient with those who did not think as fast or as clearly as he did, but he persisted and won.

4) The successful leader needs to have a vision that is appropriate to today's world, a direction in which to move in order to make a current situation better or perhaps a new and untried vision that has high risk and high reward. Civil rights leaders wanted to move toward a more just society in which each individual was treated fairly. Educators follow the vision of a society that understands its roots, its current issues, and its possibilities. Engineers want to build, doctors want to heal, and artists want to show the beauty of our universe in new and revealing ways. Not only is having a vision necessary, it must be presented in such a way that others become excited about the vision and wish to participate in carrying it out. This requires continuous reading, investigating, asking, and experimenting so that when asked about the vision, the leader is able to describe and discuss that vision within the context of the current culture. The vision is also further clarified and made operational through discussions with those on the team who will be responsible for achieving it. Not only does this process clarify the vision, it allows for buy-in by members of the team for whom the leader is responsible. A vision that is well thought out, meets an important need, and is clarified through discussion and action is more likely to last beyond the leadership activities of one individual or group.

There are leaders with visions that may be seen as "ahead of their time," visions that require scientific inquiry or looking at the world in a new and different way that potential followers are uncomfortable with accepting. At one time, epidemics were seen as what happened when people angered the gods. It took many centuries and scientific discovery to learn that they were caused by rats or other vermin that were carriers of disease. Einstein's theory of evolution was in some ways ahead of its time and it took the scientific community a while to catch up with his vision and only then was he recognized as a leader rather than as some sort of eccentric. There have been those whose vision was built around a political idea that they believed would ensure peace and harmony. While they may have had the strength of their beliefs, it is very difficult to sell such a vision in the world in which we now live. It may be that they see far ahead of the rest of us and their vision is acceptable in small bits and pieces as followers catch up with their ideas. Understanding their role is usually done in retrospect as we look at many years of our history and can perhaps see that they were right.

Not all visions enhance the human experience. Some come from the anger, unhappiness and sheer greed of damaged individuals who want to achieve ends that are detrimental to the world we live in. Think of the vision that motivated Bernie Madoff whose theft in financial markets was the biggest Ponzi scheme ever conducted. Or think of Adolf Hitler whose vision was to lead an Aryan Germany to world conquest. Some individuals who have built religious cults and have found individuals seeking something or someone to believe in have ended their leadership in the disillusionment and death of many. It may take many years for those who followed such leaders or who were harmed by them to recover.

5) The leader recognizes that the vision has numerous components and each of these components needs to be analyzed in order to identify problems that would interfere with achieving the vision. Identifying and solving problems is an ongoing component of the leadership role. One can think of the process of identifying problems and posing ways of dealing with them as a means of bringing order to chaos. As we move from an industrial to an information-based economy, we encounter problems for which there is no precedent and pose potential solutions that have not previously existed. It takes creative, nimble leaders to open the minds of those who are working with them to the possibilities that exist and move them away from depending on experiences that are no longer relevant. We have many examples of leaders who have done just that and they appear in every aspect of society, including politics, technology and social activities. John Adams's vision was tied to the success of the experiment that was the United States as an independent country. Among the problems that were identified and needed to be solved was the need to negotiate trade agreements with other countries, the need to build a merchant navy that would increase the economic viability of this new country, and the immediate need for cash so that the government could defend its shores and build its economic viability. John Adams worked tirelessly with Dutch and French government representatives to solve these and related problems in order to achieve the vision. He built a network of supporters, promoted his cause, and was flexible in his efforts to solve the problems that stood in the way of achieving the vision, and he never gave up. Benjamin Franklin was a man ahead of his time in many ways. He was a businessman, scientist, and diplomat whose reputation as a successful entrepreneur and a gifted negotiator allowed him to represent the newly minted United States to European leaders who otherwise might not have been sympathetic to the American cause.

6) The leader is optimistic about the success of the vision and believes that even though the path to success may be difficult, success will result. Martin Luther King Jr. believed in the equality of all individuals regardless of color and while he knew that breaking down centuries of discrimination would not be easy, he believed that it could be done. He had a strong message, presented it with passion, and lived what he preached. A caveat here is that the leader should be realistic in the level of optimism shown. Some challenges are very difficult to

overcome and some may not be overcome although progress toward the vision may occur. If the challenge to succeed is worth the effort, and if the leader is open and honest about the difficulty, those involved in the effort will have a realistic view of what lies ahead and what the outcome may be. Not all visions are achieved and not all problems are solved but the learning experience involved in trying is in itself important and may well move the organization, the culture, toward a better place.

7) Enjoying the experience of having a vision, sharing it with others, and leading the effort to make the vision real is an essential part of leadership success. Not only does the leader need to believe in the vision, there should be an element of pleasure in identifying and overcoming obstacles, in building consensus, in meeting challenges, and in achieving success. Enjoying the experience and being excited about the challenge of the task ahead is something that needs to be shared by everyone involved. The leader of a research team whose vision has resulted in a scientific breakthrough has every reason to gain pleasure both from the work involved and from the level of success achieved.

8) The final and in some ways most important attribute of the leader, right up there with self-confidence, is to know who you are, know what you stand for, and to not pull yourself out of shape to please others. Successful leaders tailor their vision, not their principles. Individuals who are open and honest about what they believe and how they relate to others will be judged by the extent to which those attributes play out in daily life. Life experiences tend to change an individual's approach to an issue or rearrange priorities and this is to be expected. When an individual supports a proposed action one week and then when that proposed action appears to be unpopular refuses to support it the next week, one wonders what the leader believes in and how strong those beliefs are. Is the leader more interested in being popular than in being consistent? Will the leader follow those who complain the loudest or will the leader look for common ground? There are individuals who are so certain that they are right that they consider there to be no common ground. They can be seen as leaders only by those who share their own particular viewpoint. When two totally different approaches clash and no solution is found because there is no intention of seeking common ground, everyone loses. Being flexible without violating one's core beliefs is a solution that does the least harm and may be the only way to move ahead.

PATHS TO LEADERSHIP

There are numerous ways in which an individual assumes leadership. The individual may have been seen by others as a potential leader and groomed for the role by being given tasks to teach particular skills and test abilities. The individual may have been born into a family such as a royal family or successful business family where leadership is mandated or expected. They may have applied for and achieved a position such as college dean or CEO that includes leadership as an essential component. Promotion to a position within an organization that brings leadership with it or the opportunity to build a new unit within the organization is a chance for leadership. Some individuals assume leadership roles because "it is their turn." They have been part of an organization for some time and have taken their turn serving the organization in various ways. As a reward, they are given the opportunity to become its leader because they have been loyal and have met the organization's requirements.

Many leadership positions are identified by the title of the position. One can be hired or perhaps elected to become a dean, a university president, a business leader, or a local official. That individual will have attained that position because of the expectation by others that the individual has the skills and the potential to grow into the role and to become the leader that the occasion and the job title require. The individual who accepts the position may assume that they have the authority to dictate to those reporting to the position how the organization will work. The reality is that assuming such a position is an opportunity to prove one's leadership. A leadership title carries with it certain benefits and opportunities such as representing the organization, and within the boundaries of the larger organization the opportunity to lead a team, to make a personal vision a reality, and thus to make a difference. It also comes with the responsibility of carrying out the expectations of the position and satisfying the expectations of those who granted the position. The political leader made promises and is expected to carry them out. The college dean has a responsibility to faculty, students, staff, and university administration to work with them to make that college a leader in its field while collaborating with other colleges. Sometimes the person holding the title assumes that the perks that go with the title are entitlements that accrue to the individual rather than to being part of the leadership role, and can either abuse them or perhaps assume that those entitlements will continue beyond the time on the job. One of the best arguments for term limits in politics, education, business, and not-for-profits is that entitlements end when the job ends.

There are those who have become aware of a social need and have proposed a vision that has the possibility of addressing the problem. Wendy Kopp's *Teach for America* plan for a national service corps for teachers came out of her senior thesis at Princeton University. Her vision was that all children should have the opportunity for a high quality education and she built and led an organization that provided a link between new college graduates anxious to teach and public schools that were in need of teachers. Mary Breckinridge who saw the need to provide health care to those living in rural Appalachia developed the Frontier Nursing Service in spite of opposition from established interests. Martin Luther King Jr. devoted his life to civil rights, Cesar Chavez fought for respect and the improvement of wages and living conditions for migrant workers. Our history is filled with examples of individuals who wished to make a difference, had a vision, were willing to work, and made life better for others.

Individuals who are concerned about the world around them and wish to make it a better place may opt to become involved in politics. They may be dissatisfied with the status quo and believe that they can do a better job than those currently holding elected office. Perhaps there is a perceived problem with public education in the community and they run for elected office for the board of education. They may wish to run for state and national office. These individuals have a vision and have to sell their vision to the electorate that will have their vision and competing visions from which to choose who will represent them. Shirley Chisholm, the first African American woman to serve in the U.S. Congress, was a force of nature who represented her New York district, and those she represented knew that she worked for them and they supported her. She challenged the status quo, was frustrated by being told that she had to go through proper channels to be heard, and was never intimidated by anything or anyone.

Other individuals became leaders because early on they understood the implications of the information revolution and saw the opportunities available in this technological revolution. David Brinkely grew up in Wilmington, NC, where in the 1930s, the first and only 100 watt radio station in the region was established. Because of his interest in writing and his general curiosity to do new things, he became a writer for the station and then an announcer. Because of this early introduction to radio, he was hired by other larger radio stations that were looking for individuals with some experience. He was able to build the experience of early entry into radio and add experience with the new media of television to the point that by the 1960s, he was in a position to be a player in forging the model for today's use of the media to present the world's news. Grace Hopper was an early expert in computer programming whose work in the Harvard Computation Lab, which she eventually ran, fueled her desire to make computing understandable and useful to all. Her ability to collaborate with others, and her determination, made her a leader in her field at a time and in a place where women were not particularly welcome.

Military service and the leadership skills learned in that environment[6] are a useful stepping stone into leadership positions in many aspects of civilian life. While in the military, young men and women are given the opportunity to learn how to build a culture of readiness and commitment. They come to understand that the role of the leader is to establish a common purpose, to accomplish the mission, protect the team, and only then to consider personal interests or safety. They learn the importance of teamwork and the need to look out for the safety of those around them rather than competing for opportunity that may result in harm to others.

Individuals may become leaders because of their outstanding talent in sports. Mohammed Ali who first gained recognition as a boxer went on to become known as an advocate for civil rights and as a humanitarian. He used his talent as a boxer to gain the platform he needed to champion what he believed in. Vince Lombardi turned the Green Bay Packers from a losing team into Super Bowl champions by instilling pride, a strong belief in loyalty and order, and a win-at-all-costs mentality into a team that had skill but needed leadership. He had the leadership skills and the team had athletic talent. Perhaps he believed too strongly in loyalty and order but in his time and place, this type of leadership worked. Pat Summitt, Women's Basketball Coach at the University of Tennessee and the winningest basketball coach in history, instilled values as well as skills in generations of young women. Graduates of the program went on to develop women's basketball programs in many universities and largely because of her efforts this sport has grown and flourished, thus providing opportunities for many young women to participate and to become leaders. She is a role model for women who aspire to leadership because of her coaching abilities and her values. Perhaps because athletics is a young person's game, many athletic leaders develop a second career in business or education or other area and take the leadership and teambuilding skills with them to that new career direction.

Individuals who excel in the arts often come to leadership through their abilities. While they often do not seek to be leaders as their interest is directed toward creating new ways of expressing themselves through painting or sculpture or music or other media, they often become leaders as others recognize their abilities and wish to support and/or emulate them. Johnny Cash grew up poor in rural Arkansas. His gift was a musical talent that included songwriting, guitar playing, and singing that spoke to the hearts of millions. Despite his personal struggles with addiction, he became one of the most influential musicians of the 20th century and his impact can be seen across several musical genres. His influence can be seen in the work of other musicians who have followed. Architects such as Frank Lloyd Wight, whose innovations have influenced others, have established schools of thought and design whose products can be seen throughout the country; they are another example of leadership through artistic talent. George Clooney, whose reputation as an actor was well established by the beginning of the 21st century, became an advocate for victims of civil war in Darfur. He was able to shine a spotlight on the misery of thousands of individuals whose lives were at risk because they lived in a place where opposing groups were at war. At any given time, we can see examples of individuals who have made a name for themselves in business, entertainment, sports, or other ventures, and who then use the leadership opportunities their talent has made possible to support worthy causes.

TEAM LEADERSHIP

One can think of many talented individuals whose leadership has changed the way we experience the world around us. Each leader, regardless of how they come to their role as leader has specific strengths and particular ways of leading depending on their personal skills, abilities and worldview. Wise leaders know those areas in which they excel and those areas in which they need to rely on the skills and abilities of others and they bring together individuals whose skills and abilities are mutually supportive. The role of the team is to bring together all the necessary talents into a setting in which they as a team strengthen and implement the vision of how to go forward.

As our organizations become more and more complex, it has been realized that no one person has all the requisite skills to lead an organization and the role of the CEO is moving from being the chief executive to becoming a team builder who brings together individuals whose collective skills are essential to the well-managed organization. Further, these individuals need to know that they are working together and that the organization succeeds or fails based on how well they work together. Leaders of such a team know what their skills and abilities are and select team members who complement their own skill set; they encourage everyone to bring their skills to the table to solve problems. Where yesterday's CEOs were famous for being empire builders with enormous egos, today's CEO is a leader who encourages members of the team and expects the best from their collective input. It is no longer an environment in which the big ego is useful or desirable. Carrying a leadership title is useful to others in that it indicates who is leading the group. In the reality of group leadership, that title identifies the chief encourager and facilitator who will work hard to implement the ideas that emerge from the team's discussions. The leader needs to create an environment in which team members feel safe in presenting ideas as they know that they will be heard with respect and not ridiculed.

"A team is a small number of people with complementary skills who are committed to a common purpose, set of performance goals and approaches for which they hold themselves mutually accountable."[7] The purpose of the team is to focus on issues of importance in our rapidly changing society and to seek a path forward. There are three types of teams: those that recommend things, those that make and do things, and those that run things.[8] Teams that recommend things are responsible for solving a particular problem within a specific timeframe. Team members are carefully selected to ensure that the specific skills and abilities most likely to solve a problem are available to the team. They are also expected to seek the information that the team needs for its activities, wherever it may be found. Teams that recommend new services or teams that make things are part of the ongoing activities of the organization, and teams that run things are responsible for managing a particular activity where group participation under the direction of a leader is the most efficient means of operation. Different levels of leadership are exercised for each of the three types of teams.

The team leader needs to include in the team individuals with a range of skills and experience who can view issues from different perspectives, who are passionate about the work they do, and who see its value. It is also necessary to include individuals who are creative thinkers, who can imagine the future and identify the steps to get there. Individuals who focus on how well the organization functions and who can ask what effect a creative idea will have on existing activities are needed as are individuals who can translate great ideas into terms that others can understand and support if the idea is to gain traction. And teams need to know when an idea or process is no longer relevant and when it is time to move on. The leader may be a cheerleader who motivates team members to do their best work. The leader may be an idea person who looks to the team to study and sort out those of his or her ideas that are worth exploring; or may be the one who sells the ideas of the team to others; or may be the person who says "no, it isn't the right thing to do at this time." Leaders know that they may not be the smartest person in the room on a particular topic and they willingly learn from others. They know that the best answers to "what next" come from the collective wisdom of the group.

In addition to the above skills and abilities, the team leader needs to include individuals who represent a wide range of cultural, educational, and work experiences. The worst possible team is one whose members come from the same educational and work background, who have similar ideas about the organization and who usually are supportive of the ideas of others in their small group more as a matter of courtesy than because those ideas have been discussed thoroughly. The team also needs at least one contrarian who questions well-regarded ideas and who may make outrageous suggestions. Some of our best ideas come from the individual who thinks way outside the box. While one contrarian on a team allows for some outrageous thinking, two or more is a probable recipe for disaster.

Over the past decade, the team approach to management has gained traction in schools of business with faculty team teaching in many areas and with students applying the team approach to dealing with their assignments. In other cultures, the team approach is ingrained in most activities and it is time that we move past the image of the great leader as being the one who goes it alone and sees collaboration as weakness to seeing collective action as the most efficient way to solve our problems.

SUMMARY

Leadership may be a planned career step or it may occur by chance. Regardless of how one becomes a leader, one becomes a successful leader by having self-confidence, by being curious about the world around, by having a vision for the future, by knowing the importance of teamwork, and by being willing to work hard to achieve success.

NOTES

1. Warren Bennis, *On Becoming a Leader* (New York: Basic Books, 2003), 47–64.

2. Micha Popper, *Leaders Who Transform Society, What Drives Them and Why We Are Attracted* (Westport, CT: Praeger, 2005), 15.

3. Max Weber, *From Max. Essays in Sociology* (New York: Oxford University Press, 1955), 358–59.

4. Popper, *Leaders Who Transform Society*, 32.

5. John Erwin Mroz, "Leadership over Fear," in *The Leader of the Future 2* (San Francisco: Jossey-Bass, 2006), 113–20.

6. Michael Useem, "Four Lessons in Adaptive Leadership," *Harvard Business Review* 88, no. 11 (November 2010): 87–90.

7. Ernest Dale, *Planning and Developing the Company Organizational Structure: Research Report* 20 (New York: American Management Association, 1952), 105.

8. Jon R. Katzenbach and Douglas K. Smits, "The Discipline of Teams," in *The Work of Teams*, ed. Jon R. Kaatzenbach (Boston: Harvard Business School Press, 1998), 44.

5

Gender-Based, Cultural, Ethnic, and Other Leadership Approaches

This chapter could be titled "Diversity," but that might lead the reader to refer to the popular and very limited idea that the only differences in the workforce that count are those that relate to women and people of color and are the subjects of legislation or court decisions, when in fact diversity covers many facets of humanity. Each of us is diverse from everyone else. As individuals, each of us represents a particular gender. Our genes, the color of our skin, our age, our talents, our education, where we grew up, our family situation, our work experiences, and our goals in life are unique to us as individuals, and we bring that uniqueness to our daily experiences. When we are placed in a leadership position, the ways in which we respond include some combination of those factors which make us unique.

As one builds an organization, developing a diverse workforce is not just the right thing to do, it is the wise thing to do as it enriches all aspects of the organization and should be seen as an opportunity rather than as a duty to perform. While social justice is extremely important and must be addressed, it is not the only reason to build diversity into our organizations and their leadership.[1] Over the past several decades, discussions have tended to focus on federal requirements that women and people of color be given equal opportunity to learn of jobs, apply for jobs, and be hired. Equal opportunity was and is an essential aspect of workforce management, and compliance with the law in many instances appears to have been necessary to give everyone fair access to the workforce. Many persons in organizations resented what they saw as government interference with their hiring practices and the whole idea of diversity became a flashpoint for anger. Organization staff would conduct diversity training so that their employees would know the legal requirements for hiring and would be able to follow the rules when advertising positions, interviewing, and hiring. Little was said about the value to the organization of diversity. A study of 31 years of diversity training found that if the training was done to avoid lawsuits, it didn't work; but if the training focused on the opportunity to increase productivity, it worked.[2] Understanding the full meaning of diversity and focusing on its benefits is a very important component when building the exceptional organization.

Resistance continues in some organizations and professional fields against hiring and maintaining a diverse workforce; and while one must obey the law, there are other ways in which individuals who do not reflect those in the majority can be made unwelcome. Some individuals in professions including law, medicine, engineering, and other fields traditionally seen as male-dominated have often had difficulty in admitting women and people of color into their midst. Fortune 500 companies have been slow to admit women and people of color to their upper management positions and to their boards. In the case of business and industry, women and people of color, if they were admitted to the upper ranks, would often be given positions such as director of human resources, director of public relations, or director of marketing which are heavy on interpersonal relations but tend not to be areas that lead to CEO positions as do those such as director of finance or director of planning. In the positions they are offered, they would likely not be groomed for more important roles. Women applying for positions in industry that were traditionally held by men, such as work with heavy equipment, would be hired and then often assigned tasks or given working hours that were very difficult to fulfill with the unspoken expectation that they would fail. Social justice continues to be a work in progress and progress is being made slowly as a greater diversity of qualified individuals enters the workplace.

Scott Page when interviewed by a *New York Times*[3] reporter about his book titled *The Difference: How the Power of Diversity Creates Better Groups, Firms, Schools and Societies*[4] responded to the question of why organizations made up of different types of people are more productive than homogenous ones by saying that "it is because diverse groups of people bring to organizations more and different ways of seeing a problem and thus faster and better ways of solving it." He went on to say that "people from varying backgrounds have varying ways of looking at problems, what I call 'tools.' The sum of these tools is far more powerful in organizations with diversity than in ones where everyone has gone to the same schools, been trained in the same mold and thinks in almost identical ways."

When asked to give an example of where diversity has improved an organization or profession, he cited the field of economics.

> Before women got really involved in the 1970s, a lot of the actual labor of women wasn't included in calculations of the gross domestic product. It was as if you had Ma Ingalls sitting around the Little House on the Prairie, eating bonbons, and only Pa Ingall's labor was counted in . . . when you had only men thinking about the economy, they were ignoring the productivity of half the population. By including the perspectives of females, the estimates got more accurate . . .[5]

With a fellow economist, Page

> constructed a formal model that showed mathematically that diversity can trump ability, and when it does . . . what the model showed was that diverse groups of problem solvers outperformed the groups of the best individuals at solving problems. The reason: the diverse groups got stuck less

often than the smart individuals, who tended to think similarly. . . . The other thing we did was to show in mathematical terms how when making predictions, a group's errors depend in equal parts on the ability of its members to predict and their diversity. This second theorem can be expressed as an equation: collective accuracy = average accuracy + diversity.[6]

FRAMES OF REFERENCE

Solving problems in situations offer numerous ways to be approached, and each individual's problem-solving process is directly related to the individual's ways of looking at a problem. Scientists will approach an issue with one set of tools while the social scientist will use another set. People of wealth who have never lived paycheck-to-paycheck and those who have experienced poverty will approach a social or economic issue differently. Individuals raised in one culture will bring a different set of problem-solving tools to the table than those from a different culture. Given the many frames of reference from which each individual approaches the day's activities, it would be very difficult to enumerate and discuss all of them. It would, however, be useful to identify and discuss some of the more important ways in which we are diverse and how they influence how we solve problems and how we lead.

Where We Are Today

For as long as there has been a record of human existence and even before that, human activities were divided based on the need to survive. Men had more physical strength and therefore assumed the responsibility of protecting the tribe or family unit. Women were responsible for bearing the children who would populate the family unit and ensure its continuation. Given that women typically are physically less strong than men and that during the childbearing years they would not be able to focus as fully on protecting the tribe, it was logical that men would be the leaders and make decisions about safety and survival. Research has shown that in an agricultural society, the talents and work of both men and women were essential to survival, and in many communities they were equal partners in providing for and protecting the family. Women tended the crops and the children while men went hunting for food.

Down through the ages, many variations of tribal government appeared and in most cases physical strength was a major component of leadership. In addition, as knowledge about how to hunt and how to make war, and interest in the world around them began to accumulate, men were the ones who preserved and used that knowledge. Women collected information as well; information that related to the growing and harvesting of crops, the birthing and raising of children, and other skills needed for survival. In some instances they shared information while, in others, each held their unique information closely as a means of retaining a degree of power. Both men and women gained knowledge in the healing arts and in the magical arts, and we find both male and female leaders in these areas.

Down through the ages, men developed leadership skills, often with the help of clubs and knives. They protected their own and they went to war against other tribes that may have been a danger to them or held territory they coveted. War was also a way of learning how to lead and how to achieve objectives. Women were not a part of this learning process and of the larger process of male bonding. Rules were developed that dictated how the tribal unit would function and this was done in large part by men. By the time we entered the era in which history was written, the record of human progress was almost exclusively that of men. As has been said, the winners are those who write the history.

Much of human history records a world in which agriculture was the primary activity. Families and tribes worked the land to grow the crops they needed to survive. The laws of the land reflected an agricultural society, festivals were tied to the seasons, armies fought wars to claim or reclaim land, and the family work unit was the farm or estate if one was rich. Men and women worked as a team to manage the farm and they each knew their responsibilities as they had been taught by their parents. While the man was considered the leader of the family unit, the activities of the entire family were required for survival. If the man left the farm for extended periods to go to war, to perform services for a landlord, or to go on a hunting expedition, or to seek new land, the woman managed the farm, cared for the children, and did whatever else was necessary to keep things together. So long as the source of income for the family was in the production of agricultural products, this model prevailed.

Major changes took place with the beginning of the industrial age in the 19th century as—for the first time—the primary source of income was no longer the farm but the factory. Jobs in the factory required that individuals leave the farm, go to a larger community and work for what was often a faceless and nameless employer. In the United States, both men and women went to work in factories. For example, women went to the woolen mills of New England and men went to the steel mills of Pittsburgh. New types of social organizations grew to accommodate the new ways in which individuals acquired wealth or at least earned a wage. Among the more affluent, women found themselves caring for home and children and living on the man's wages. Among poorer families, often including immigrants, men, women and children worked in factories and sweat shops trying to earn enough money to pay the rent and buy food. Education was available to all, indeed in most states it was required, and this was the most important path to a better life.

The gradual change from farm to factory took place over the better part of a century, from the mid-19th century to World War II. During World War II, with the demand for workers to meet the need to build planes, tanks, and other weapons of war to support the men who were fighting the war, internal migration from farm and small town to factory and from the rural South to the North quickened. Women left their traditional roles to work in defense plants. African Americans, many from the South, moved to Detroit and other Northern locations. Often for the first time, individuals in these groups were able to earn a living wage in their jobs. For those who migrated North, a new way of life different from the one they had experienced in the rural South opened up to them. And when the troops came home, although they took back many of the factory jobs, those who had migrated to the city tended to stay in their new communities. Women who had worked in defense plants during the war proved that they could run lathes or other heavy equipment and were not limited by their gender to the lowest rungs of the employment ladder. Rosie the Riveter became a symbol of women who were building the weapons the men needed; and many of those Rosie represented were no longer willing to leave their newfound freedom behind without protest. Women who had joined the military learned that they were competent pilots, were able to manage complex organizations, and were leaders in their own right. After the war was over, it was very difficult for many women to go back to housekeeping and to situations in which they no longer had a paycheck they had earned, situations where their wartime efforts were no longer needed or respected. The press tended to downplay these responses while at the same time glorifying the women who married their sweethearts, had children, made a wonderful home for their husbands, and forgot about their wartime experiences. Women who needed to work because they were single parents or for other reasons often found it very difficult to find any kind of work and many returned to prewar poverty or entered it for the first time.

While a woman's right to vote became part of the U.S. Constitution in 1920 as the Nineteenth Amendment, women continued to be seen as second-class citizens at the workplace, and most of those who worked outside the home were employed in a limited number of professions—teacher, nurse, librarian, or as secretaries and assistants to men who actually ran things. In the 1940s as more and more women and people of color had access to education and to meaningful jobs with paychecks, their unwillingness to return to second-class citizenship increased.

Men and women who were veterans, through the benefits of the G.I. Bill, were able to continue their education, go to college, and enter careers they would otherwise not have been able to enter; and they became economically able to live a life with more opportunity than they had thought possible. Returning military individuals of color, if they had difficulty finding work, had the option of going to college and developing new skills and abilities. Not only did the G.I. Bill provide educational opportunities, it provided a venue in which students of diverse backgrounds would study together and learn more about one another.

Not only had war provided those in the military the opportunity to see more of the world and to meet and work with people different from themselves, it provided experiences that taught them that they had the potential to succeed in life and that they didn't have to live with the status quo. In many ways, the war ended a chapter in our history and those who fought in the war and those who supported them at home had the opportunity to build a new social environment. Not only did they have the opportunity to go back to school and learn new skills, they could also take advantage of new technologies developed during the war. While radio was an accepted part of communication, the 1950s saw the advent of television that rapidly became part of every family's entertainment and access to news. No longer did one just read or hear about what was going on in the world around them, they could now see it in real time. The expectation of every family was that they would have a car and that this would give them the freedom to travel. Having a car also meant that one didn't need to live near where they worked but that they could live outside the city. One of the unintended consequences of having a car was that suburban communities grew up around the cities and with this the need for new infrastructure including schools, libraries, government services, and other activities that provided opportunities for education and for employment.

Advances in medicine made it possible to enjoy a much higher level of health care for all members of the family. Among these was the development of contraceptives that allowed the family to plan for its growth in a way that was medically, socially, and economically advantageous to the entire family. Not only did this ensure the opportunity for the family to grow in the best way for its future, it also freed women from the fear of unintended pregnancy and gave them the opportunity to meet both personal and family expectations in a mutually beneficial way.

The 1960s were the years in which civil rights activism became a national concern and, after years of effort by those who saw the need for a society in which everyone has an equal right to live safely in an environment that is equal rather than separate, the Civil Rights Act was passed by the federal government (1963). It was a major step in recognizing and meeting the need for social justice. This was not easily achieved. Many were imprisoned, and some died for their belief in equality. While the law of the land changed, the process of education and a willingness to live and work together with mutual respect has taken longer and, for some, it has yet to happen.

While one often cites the increasing cost of basic needs as the major reason for women wishing to enter the workforce, a major reason is that for many women, their talents and abilities were not fulfilled inside the home. They had the ability to achieve and had proved to themselves during the war effort that they could indeed compete in the market place; and many women had no intention of returning to a situation in which they had limited opportunity to grow and meet personal expectations. One can read the stories of these women and men, of whom much was expected and who delivered, and then were pushed aside because they were no longer needed after the white men came home.[7] If the times were such that they could not achieve their dreams outside the home for themselves, women and individuals of color could prepare their sons and daughters for a different world which held more equal opportunities. Their children, the baby boomer generation, were and continue to be major change agents in our culture.

Since the 1960s, we have seen a more diverse society largely due to the changes that took place after the war. Prior to that time, white men had little competition in the workplace, in government, and in social interaction. They held power because they had inherited it from their fathers and most intended to keep things that way. Once women and people of color had the opportunity to prove to themselves and to others that they had the intelligence, skills, and abilities to compete in the marketplace and to assume leadership, they began to compete in earnest. Prior to this time, there were women leaders but they tended to fall into two categories: women who had inherited power from men either from being members of a powerful family or because their husbands died and they assumed the husband's duties, or because they were in some respect outsiders who championed a cause.

Outsiders included Florence Nightingale who championed the need for professional nursing care for the ill and injured and for nursing to become a respected profession. Dorothy Day recognized the need to care for those in desperate need for basic services to allow them to survive, and moved from being an idealist who thought about the poor in general terms to a social realist whose work was to help those in need. She and a friend began a movement—The Catholic Worker—that helped those who so desperately needed help. Golda Meir, daughter of a traditional Jewish family, became a Zionist and spent her life working to establish a Jewish State. Susan B. Anthony was a persistent advocate for women's rights. As a man of color who became a leader, Frederick Douglass began life in slavery on the Eastern Shore of Maryland and became an advocate for freedom and equality for his people. Shirley Chisholm was a strong advocate for poor people, and, in her service in both the New York State Legislature and the U.S. Congress, she was a fearsome and tireless champion for those whose needs were so often forgotten.

Those who inherited power included women such as Elizabeth I of England who gained power because there was no male heir to the throne. (Only in 2012 did the British Royal Family, with approval from the government, change the rules of succession to the throne to allow women equal rights so that gender is now irrelevant to the order of succession.) Catherine the Great of Russia married her way to power and once in power showed just how strong a ruler she was when she dealt with the incompetent tsar who was her husband. Katherine Graham, a member of the family that owned *The Washington Post*, assumed leadership of the newspaper only on the death of her husband. Abigail Adams, wife of John Adams, second president of the United States, was a powerful influence on her husband; despite her management of the family farm and raising the children during his long absences, she was respected at the time for her wise counsel and the way in which she advised her husband— without stepping outside her role as wife rather than as a leader in her own right.

Until the 1970s, there were relatively few women and people of color in leadership positions. With the changes—such as access to education—that occurred after World War II, the leadership demographic has changed. Now the pool from which leaders emerge is not just white males but also includes females, people of color and other groups in society that had previously been ignored or underestimated. Rather than white men being a majority from which leadership would come, the addition of these groups has more than doubled the size of the workforce and white men are no longer the majority. White men continue to hold most positions of power but the number of women and people of color in the workforce is increasing slowly as these groups acquire additional education and experience.

The advent of the information age has created new leadership roles that are based more on intellectual skills and abilities than on physical strength. We are a service economy that also builds things but those things are created with mind power rather than solely with muscle power, which means that ability, not who one knows or how much one can lift, are primary criteria for leadership. Manufacturing continues to be an important component of our economy whether it is done in the United States or outsourced, but in that area as well, new technological skills not necessarily based on muscle power are increasing.

Today's world is built on the past and responds to the social, economic, and political needs of today and of the future. Many of the leadership skills men developed in the past continue to have relevance and will be strengthened by the input from other groups of individuals with other approaches to leadership. Not all groups in society are pleased with the need to share leadership and one sees that in the political groups that emerge and demand a return to the past. Nearly all women and individuals of color in the workplace can cite instances of being passed over for a position for which they were well qualified, of being talked down to because of their color or gender, of being called names, of being ignored socially, and of being told in effect "to go back to wherever they belong." It will take time for the traditional leaders in the workplace and in society at large to be comfortable sharing it with others and, for some, this will never happen. In the meantime, it is useful to look at the different approaches to leadership and problem-solving that different groups have and to adapt leadership skills based on what works best in today's society.

What We Can Learn from Male Leaders

"Despite more than 350 definitions of leadership, there is no basic understanding of what differentiates effective leadership from the ineffective or effective organizations from the ineffective."[8] In 1985, Warren Bennis and Burt Nanus conducted a study of leadership that serves as a benchmark for leadership and leadership studies. They discussed the changes in society, economic changes, and the movement from an industrial to an information society, from bureaucracy to networking and to an increasingly high-tech society. "The credibility of the organization has been challenged from all directions and the information age has hatched a new public awareness of leaders and leadership."[9] Because in today's rapidly changing times, new leaders are needed to move to the next steps, Bennis made the assumption that by studying identified leaders from both for-profit and not-for-profit organizations selected to reflect the practice of those who break new ground, a new definition of leadership would emerge. Because at this point in time, there were very few women or minority leaders, nearly all of those interviewed were white males. One can therefore assume that the study reflected the interests and priorities of white males in the late 20th century. Bennis and Nanus selected a total of 90 leaders: 60 CEOs from business and 30 from not-for-profits. This two-year study focused on leaders directing new trends and included interviews using unstructured observations except for three questions asked of all participants:

- What are your strengths and weaknesses?
- Was there any particular experience or event in your life that influenced your management philosophy or style?
- What were the major decision points in your career and how do you feel about your choices now?

From the interviews, four components of leadership were identified.

1) *Attention through vision.* The leader has a vision that has focus and an agenda that leads to an outcome. The leader understands the context

of the vision and sets the direction accordingly. Employees know that the leader has a vision, how the leader intends to achieve the vision, and that the vision has outcomes. The leader's vision may include input from staff, other leaders, opportunities and current trends, and past experience.

2) *Meaning through communication.* It is necessary to articulate the vision and to make it understandable through the development of an agenda. Leaders may use stories or images to describe the vision. If leaders expect others to follow the vision, they need to provide "a common interpretation of reality to guide them so that they know how to act in new situations."[10] "Even the best ideas are only as good as their ability to attract attention in the social environment."[11]

3) *Trust through positioning.* The authors found that trust implies accountability, predictability, and reliability. Leaders need to provide direction if they expect others to follow. The direction outlined should not keep changing but should follow a steady path and show that the leader is persistent and will follow through. The leader needs to position the organization as it relates to the vision in such a way that others will buy in.

4) *Deployment of self through positive self-regard.* Good leaders are very aware of their personal worth, their strengths and their weaknesses. The leader treats others with respect and knows that how individuals see themselves often determines the outcome of a situation.

Bennis and Nanus summarized the study by saying that the leader is a catalyst. They identified five myths of leadership: that leadership is a rare skill; that leaders are born not made; that leaders are charismatic; that leadership occurs only at the top of the organization; and that the leader controls, directs, prods, and manipulates the organization. None of these is true. Leadership can be learned by trial and error, charismatic leaders are rare, there is leadership at every level of the organization, and the leader leads by the quality of the vision and the ability to follow through and not by force.[12]

Men have built a rational means of leading and many have followed the outlines of their methods of leadership. It is generally believed that men see leadership in authoritarian terms and that for those following the leader to question his authority shows a lack of respect for authority. The persons in charge have information others lack, have experience not held by those who follow, have had leadership and authority bestowed upon them by some higher authority and questioning that authority is disrespectful. Key to male management is discipline and a certain toughness that proves that the leader has power and is not afraid to exercise it. Richard Nixon was quoted as saying that "power is not for the nice guy."[13] It is not recognized that power and leadership are different. Men network heavily within their organization and build strong linkages with other members of the organization, and this is a means both of exerting control and of communicating with peers. However, in the information age in which anyone can find out almost anything regardless of where that individual is within the organization, or outside it, it has become difficult for most leaders to maintain control of all relevant information.

It is often said that men see leadership as a game in which there are winners and losers, that leadership is a team sport, and that the objective is to destroy your opponent. This hasn't worked particularly well in the modern organizations as they have developed since the 1990s, and although one regularly reads articles and interviews that champion leadership as a kind of team sport, they are not particularly convincing. As women and other minorities have entered leadership positions, it has become evident that those practicing traditional ways of leadership can learn new ways to lead and that these new ways that modify traditional ways will benefit the individual, the organization, and society.

What We Can Learn from Women Leaders

In the latter part of the 1980s, it became apparent that many organizations were not working well, that companies were in decline, and that many of the old ways of leading were not working. New directions were needed. The military and other organizations were active in determining how best to include women throughout their ranks. Women began to assume positions of authority in this period partly because "as historical outsiders to such positions, women had fresh eyes."[14] Prior to about 1990, most of the literature about women in the workplace focused on their supposed handicaps: they cared too little for the niceties of rank and distinction, they cared too much about relationships and they refused to see organizations as teams in a giant game. When they were admitted to leadership positions, they were told to adapt to the organization they found, to honor the hierarchy, and to model their behavior on that of men in similar positions.[15] A generally held belief by women, that "people don't work well when they don't feel valued, trusted, respected," was seen as softheaded. Women were told to measure up to male standards and to focus on "what's in it for me?"[16] Management and leadership books written for women during this period, and two of the best known were written by women, told women how to play the game the way the men did. They were even told to learn about team sports so that they would understand how to manage.[17] Then, with an increasing influx of women into the workforce, things changed, and the need for restructuring the ways in which organizations were managed became even more evident.

In 1973, Henry Mintzberg's PhD dissertation on how male managers functioned in the workforce painted a picture of the situation in the 1970s and 1980s.[18] Mintzberg followed five white male executives through their day and maintained a minute-by-minute record of everything each one did and from this mass of data he was able to find patterns in their daily work. This new "bottom-up look at management" identified what managers actually did every day rather than what others often thought they did. He identified nine patterns that identified their activities.

1) Executives worked at an unrelenting pace with no breaks. Sixty percent of their time was in scheduled meetings and most of the rest of their day was taken up by brief encounters and rapid problem-solving.

2) Their days were characterized by interruption, discontinuity, and fragmentation. They were always being interrupted by subordinates, were

putting out fires (solving crises), and used secretaries as protection from the stress of unrelenting activity.

3) They spent little time in activities that were not work related. Family and friends received little attention. They rarely participated in interests or activities not related to the work place and they often felt intellectually isolated.

4) They preferred live action encounters such as phone calls or face-to-face meetings to deal with written communication. They delegated as much written communication, mail, as possible to secretaries as they saw it as an unimportant diversion.

5) They maintained a complex network of people outside the organization and 22 to 38 percent of their time was spent outside their office with peers, colleagues, and clients. The purpose of this was to gather information.

6) The pressure of daily needs prevented time for reflection. They had little or no time to become involved in long-range planning.

7) They identified themselves with their job and they enjoyed the prestige of having an important position. Their personal identity was tied closely to the position they held.

8) They had difficulty sharing information as they identified information with power. Hoarding information meant that they knew more than anyone else. It also meant that they could not delegate decision making as they were unwilling to share the information needed for making decisions.[19]

This is "a picture of men who feel pressured by demands and their own importance and satisfaction in their achievement."[20] They liked the achievement rather than the work it took to get there. While men recognized that they had few interests outside the workplace and that their relationship with family and friends suffered, most said that job satisfaction more than made up for it.

Helgesen's study of women as leaders was conducted in the 1980s and she used Mintzberg's methodology to record the daily activities of five women. While Mintzberg's findings about men provide a standard of comparison, her study was not modeled on his work. While he saw his subjects as data sources rather than people, Helgesen "presented the women I studied as people with personalities and histories . . . the diary studies are narratives; the women's days tell a story."[21]

She found the following patterns in the daily life and work of women.

1) Women worked at a steady pace but with short breaks in between meetings and other activities. Forty to sixty percent of their time was spent in attending formal scheduled meetings. The regular breaks were intended to lessen stress.

2) Women did not see unscheduled tasks and encounters as interruptions. They made deliberate efforts to be accessible by having an open door policy and encouraging suggestions. These encounters were considered part of the flow of the day and seen as a way to maintain relationships. They believed in "caring, being involved, helping, being

responsible." Since interactions were not seen as interruptions and were part of the day, secretaries were seen not as protection but rather as conduits.

3) Women made time for activities not directly related to work. Family time was not sacrificed and was seen as an important balance to work life.

4) They did not suffer from intellectual isolation. They read widely in a variety of areas and were well informed on current events. This allowed them to understand the various contexts within which their organization functioned and to be aware of the many interactions.

5) Women leaders maintained a complex network of relations with individuals outside the organization. Like men, they devoted 20 to 40 percent of their day to this.

6) They focused on the ecology of leadership in that they kept long-term goals in focus and, unlike men, didn't get caught up in the daily grind of many tasks to the extent that it caused them to lose sight of the overall direction.

7) Women see their own identities as complex and multifaceted. They are more than their careers. For them, having a family puts work life in perspective. They do not define themselves solely by their title or the job they do.

8) Women scheduled time for information sharing. This was a deliberate process intended to share responsibilities and make collaboration in the work more possible. For women, the hierarchical organization held together by loyalty and control of information is less desirable than an organization within which everyone is valued and respected for their contributions.[22]

Today's economy is different; the structure of the organization is different. Increasing value is placed on creativity and the breadth of the vision. A nimble organization that responds rapidly to change, that can balance demands, and whose members have the opportunity to contribute their skills has replaced the rigid hierarchy filled with rules and requirements for specific behaviors. Women bring different skills that can balance these new demands. Women do not see leadership of the organization as a team sport in which there are winners and losers. They believe in principles of caring; not getting hung up on hierarchy; the need to work as a part of, not separate from, life; and being responsible.[23]

Women are less interested in maintaining a formal organization with its strict hierarchy where decisions are made at the top and filter to the bottom and where communication outside the lines of authority is discouraged. Women are communal. They listen to others, respect the ideas of others, and like to try new things. They prefer a collaborative environment within which members of the organization have the opportunity to be heard and whose ideas are respected.

Women reward competence and the ability to get things done and recognize that more ideas are generated and more progress is made faster in a collaborative environment in which individuals are given the opportunity to shine. This does not mean that women support an undisciplined environment but rather that the discipline is self-discipline of each member of the organization rather than imposition from above. Women leaders believe in shared influence. They establish their leadership credentials by gaining the trust and confidence of others. They innovate, and they mentor others and work toward the success of individuals and of organizational goals. They reward good performance and work with team members to help them do even better. This transformational form of leadership is highly effective in modern organizations.[24] Men on the other hand tend to be transactional leaders in that they have a give and take relationship with members of their team and tend to punish poor performance without helping the individual move in a more productive direction. This approach may actually hinder team performance.

While both men and women spend a large percentage of their day in networking, they do it in different ways. Men tend to focus their networking on internal relationships while women tend to network externally as well.[25] The historical reason for this difference is that for many years there were relatively few women leaders and rarely enough women in one organization from which to build a strong network. As more and more women entered leadership positions and as more and more women started their own businesses, this external network grew and worked well in that it made women's careers more portable as they have contacts in many organizations and know where and when new opportunities arise. It is also a way in which women can build social capital in a wider sphere and gain recognition for their research, their consulting, and their leadership skills. This would not be possible in the individual organizations in which they work, which more often than not are dominated by male networking activities and are not particularly interested in including women.[26] In an era in which individuals rarely spend their working lifetimes in one organization, the ability to "know the industry" and to be known by those outside a specific organization is an important career asset. As time goes by, one can see more internal networking by women and more external networking by men. Both men and women are networking digitally. It is possible to learn a lot about an organization by seeing what is on the websites, what blogs are present, what social networking is in place and what kinds of institutional messages these project.

Contributions by People of Color

Since the passage of the Civil Rights Act (1963), equal participation in educational opportunities, in applying for jobs, and in society at large is a right for all. Men and women of color have a long history of leaders who have had a major impact; but, by and large, this impact has been on the African American community rather than on society at large. Men and women of color were active in the abolitionist movement, including Sojourner Truth and Frederick Douglass; and through the years of segregation and the civil rights movement there have been many strong leaders within the African American community. Here again education has been a key to equal opportunity and despite the efforts of some groups, schools at every level have been made accessible to individuals based on ability and not color. The G.I. Bill that provided education to all veterans provided an opportunity for veterans of color to get additional education and to prepare themselves for jobs and opportunities earlier closed to them. As with women who participated in the war effort, people of color had opportunities to prove that they could compete successfully in military action, in defense plants, and in leadership roles. The Tuskegee Airmen, an all-black fighter squadron, was assembled during World War II. They were given many difficult and dangerous assignments with the expectation by some that they would fail but instead of failing, they became a legend of bravery. Similarly, Japanese Americans who fought in World War II in the Italian campaign were given the most dangerous and difficult assignments. The death tolls in their unit were very high as were the number of medals for bravery. These men had no intention of returning to the same segregated and unequal world. As we become a global economy, more and more people of color are becoming part of a worldwide workforce and this global workforce has provided leadership opportunities for people of color worldwide. People of color are aspiring to and reaching positions of leadership because of their ability to succeed in a multiracial world.

What specific ways of leading do people of color bring to the table? Many of the skills and abilities they bring are the same as those men and women anywhere utilize, but these skills and abilities are practiced with an edge and an understanding developed through centuries of slavery and segregation. People of color know what it means to be prevented from being able to reach their potential. They look at today from a perspective of their history and with the knowledge of how hard fought their victories have been. Masaoka[27] says that this background provides leaders who have both hard and soft skills. Individuals who have struggled to survive are survivors and do not give up easily. Manning Marable, professor of history at Columbia University and author of *Malcolm X: A Life of Reinvention*,[28] said, "The collective experience of pain and hardship, suffering and sacrifice, has given African Americans a unique perspective from which our consciousness has been forged."[29]

Age as a Frame

Some say that young people should not be leaders as they lack experience. Others say that older individuals are past their prime and should be moved out of the way so that others can lead. Strauss and Howe in their study of generations say that "the life cycle experience of ancestral generations tells us, in particular, that the peer personality of each generational type expresses itself very differently from one phase of life to the next."[30] They say that not only is each generation different from the previous generation but that each generation itself goes through phases. They define generation as those individuals born within a 20-year span. Each generation experiences different world events, is exposed to new and different scientific advances, and responds differently than the previous or next generation. They further state that four types of generations exist and they tend to occur in the same rotational order: Idealists who redefine the inner world of values and culture, Reactives who are pragmatists, Civics who rebuild the external world of technology and institutions, and Adaptives who are ameliorators and try to make the world better. Given this scenario, age is less important than the generation to which one belongs.

A more focused study of the relationship between age and leadership was the one conducted by Bennis and Thomas in 2002 in which they studied the differences between Geeks and Geezers.[31] They defined Geeks as individuals 35 years and younger and Geezers as those 70 years or older, and interviewed 43 people with ages ranging from 21 to 93. Nearly all of the Geezers interviewed were men and two-thirds of the Geeks were men.[32] One begins the study with the demonstrated knowledge that the information age has radically changed how we interact with one another, how we gain information, and to an extent how we use information.

Bennis and Thomas found that certain behaviors defined Geeks and certain behaviors defined Geezers, but that both groups shared a large number of behaviors. Geeks tend to have bigger goals earlier in life, are more aware of opportunities, have traveled more, and have a greater sense of their own abilities. They tend not to have heroes whose successes they emulate. They are not particularly impressed by formal structures such as organizations and prefer to follow their own inclinations. Geezers grew up in an era in which they needed to earn money in order to support their family and they believed that if you worked hard, were determined, and paid your dues to society, you would succeed. Organization is important to them as this is the way in which one gains strength.

Regardless of age, members of both groups have had common experiences. They have had family tragedies or difficulties in their lives. They have had life-changing experiences, from being in the military and serving in combat zones to experiencing a failure in business or being fired from their job. These "crucible" experiences served to test their ability to deal with difficult situations and their ability to recover and move on. The authors stress that leadership at any time and any age requires that individuals have such experiences as it teaches them that it is possible, indeed necessary, to overcome the difficulty and move on. From this knowledge that one can move on comes a kind of personal strength otherwise not possible.

Both Geeks and Geezers are avid learners and are always in search of more information. Both seek to transcend the limits of wherever they are and whatever they are doing. They also share a capacity to adapt to existing and developing conditions and engage others in order to benefit from shared experiences and meaning. They have a distinctive voice and have something important to say, and they have integrity. Both groups continue to grow and to change to meet the future and its challenges. They may use different thought patterns and tools to imagine the future but both are moving ahead. Their combined strength of wisdom and approach is truly awesome.

Not all young people are Geeks and not all elders are Geezers. Some in each group fear the future and would prefer to live in a world that changes little if at all. When a Geezer who opposes change is in a position of authority, this causes problems for the organization. Joining an organization and working one's way up in the hierarchy used to be the pattern most individuals followed in the workplace. Today's workplace is less traditional and in order to move ahead, it is often necessary to move to another organization. Young professionals need to take control of their careers, get that first job, learn what can be learned from it and if necessary, move on to move up. As with every other element of diversity, individuals need to look around, look ahead, and find the best personal fit to further their career. This is a very geeky approach, which Geezers who respect the organization would doubtless fault.

Sexual Orientation as a Frame

"Today's workforce is the most knowledgeable, diverse, and empowered in recorded history and old leadership paradigms no longer apply."[33] This statement introduces the first large-scale study of gay males as leaders. When conducting a study of working professionals in many types of organizations, Snyder found a positive correlation between leadership behaviors in organizations managed by gay executives and "significantly higher than average rates of job engagement, satisfaction, and workplace morale reported by their employers."[34] He then refocused his study from one that was initially undertaken "to identify specific leadership behaviors that the next generation of managers would need to embrace in order to achieve and sustain career success over the next decade,"[35] to one that focused on 1000 primarily straight employees in Fortune 500 companies, higher education, government, and small business who worked under the leadership of gay male executives. The gay executives in the study were primarily white, middleclass and college educated, and faced no bias other than sexual orientation. The author noted that all gays in the sample were "out of the closet."

Snyder put forward the term "G Quotient" in which each individual is viewed by the leader "as having the value and authority to play a key role in the success of the organization because of who they are as human beings, it cements a positive, equality based connection between employees and their managers."[36] G Quotient leadership is not restricted to gay males and is not solely a gay management style. It is based on three learned skills that gay men have developed: adaptability, intuitive communication, and creative problem-solving.

Gay men know that they are different and need to adapt their verbal and nonverbal communication to prevent displeasure from others. They have to think consciously about their feelings and reactions. This can result in high levels of personal insight. Gay men build a content filter for thoughts and feelings and pick up on subtle verbal and nonverbal cues. This intuitive communication results in insights to examine feelings and assumptions. Because gay men in some ways are seen as outsiders, they learn to create new paths to solving problems.

From his research, Snyder identified seven principles that define G Quotient leadership:

1) *Inclusion.* This is based on respect for the individual and is defined more by action than words. Each individual is seen as unique and it is important to create an environment where everyone is important and human differences are valuable. Inclusion inspires motivation and fairness.[37]

2) *Creativity* is the "ability to look at ideas in fresh new ways and define innovation as the economic by-product it yields."[38] Develop concepts and original ideas, suggest possibilities, and identify people who can implement the ideas and possibilities. Creative thinking leads organizations to become better and better.

3) *Adaptability* is the "willingness and capacity to adapt to change, particularly in the greater economic, social, and political landscape of the world . . . because change happens so fast, without management's commitment to see, understand, and adapt to its potential effects, the pure momentum of change often leaves the organization behind."[39]

4) *Connectivity* creates meaning through such information-sharing elements as e-mail and web-based interaction, bringing together the many stakeholders in and around the organization. Connectivity is a combination of external networking and internal awareness, an awareness that "the organization must continually draw from outside sources of knowledge to reach full potential."[40]

5) *Communication*'s role is to develop an open system that "actively develops and nurtures interaction in order to create a culture that encourages and supports trust, facilitates organizational candor, and promotes cohesiveness."[41] This encourages direct communication which in turn is facilitated by a flatter organization than exists in the traditional hierarchical structure.

6) Intuition is "a knowledge based process that allows people to discern truths about realities that already exist."[42] It is what Jung defines as the ability to see around corners and what is behind Maslow's definition of "self-actualization."

7) *Collaboration* is based on finding out what matters to people and helping them develop in ways that matter to them so that they will be productive. Boundaries that hinder collaboration, including aspects of organizational structure, bias, and restriction of information, should be eliminated as should too much ego.[43] Accomplishment is more important than who gets the credit.

This approach to leadership is both subjective and objective and focuses on process rather than product. It focuses on the positives and on the present and most importantly, sees each individual as important to the success of the organization.

Culture as a Frame

The culture in which we live has a powerful influence on how we approach our lives and the ways in which we solve problems. Cultures can be defined by ethnicity, language, custom, and geography in that individuals sharing these elements also share a way of living and thinking. For example, in China, Confucian values do not support the idea that leaders should talk without having specific actions in mind. In India, bold leadership is preferred to visionary ideas. In the Latino culture, criticism tends to be indirect so that offense may not be taken while in the American culture, it is often very direct and there is less interest in whether or not offense is taken. American culture is defined by many as one in which everyone is in a hurry and deadlines are always to be met while in other cultures, a more leisurely approach is preferred. In both cases, the job is done on time. For those in a hurry-up world, taking it easier can be frustrating, and vice versa.

Regions of the same country have cultural differences. Different regions of the country often have local customs, which while important in one area are not practiced elsewhere. Differences in urban and rural cultures, for example, include the fact that those living in a rural area have a very different attitude toward distances between places and what constitutes a crowd than do individuals living in a metropolitan area. Immigrants from other countries and other parts of a country bring with them differences in background and experiences that are valuable components in crafting today's social environment and economy. Given the speed of communication and information in our global society, this may be less evident than in the past. As more and more individuals move from one culture to another to seek an education or earn a living, members of other cultures enter one another's workspace and their frames of reference provide new ways of looking at problem solving.

Commenting on the contribution of different cultures to leadership, Derings says that "leadership is now the ability to step outside the culture that created the leader and to start evolutionary change processes that are more adaptive."[44] These transcultural leaders are not members of one culture bringing members of another culture to the organization in order to practice diversity, they are building a vision that combines the best of both cultures into a new set of values and hence a new paradigm.[45] The wealth of experience that resides in the world's cultures and the ways that each culture views leadership is to a large extent a resource that has yet to be fully understood.

Other Frames of Reference

In addition to the several different perspectives that influence leadership, there are also social frames including financial status, social status, political affiliation, religious views, and many more. Veterans returning from military duty "are bringing . . . qualities we really need now: crisp decision making, rigor, optimism, entrepreneurial creativity, a larger sense of purpose, and real patriotism."[46] Their leadership has been tested under extreme conditions and many are ready to assume leadership in civilian life.

One's profession and discipline also influence leadership and the way one looks at problems. The scientist uses the scientific method and carefully collects data and tests hypotheses. The artist whose problem may have a more creative path to a solution follows a different direction. The nurse or doctor who cares for patients has the needs of the patient in the forefront and will "do no harm" to the patient and this priority influences decision making and the path taken.

Each leader, and each follower, is a product of many influences and their leadership styles are dependent on these influences. When all is said and done, it is the individual who complements the team we are looking to hire and we need to look for individuals rather than types or stereotypes.

SUMMARY

Diversity is more than representation. True diversity is highly complex as it includes different perspectives and different worldviews. Diversity provides "a competitive advantage for the businesses that manage it effectively."[47] By bringing together diverse personalities and peoples, we position ourselves in a rapidly changing world by taking advantage of diverse visions and mindsets to work more effectively in a global economy. As more and more individuals from the many groups now competing in the workforce become leaders, they will be role models for others with similar views to follow.

We need to look at people as individuals rather than as representatives of groups. Each individual has a set of skills and abilities as well as several frames of reference from which to lead and to solve problems. It is essential to go beyond the stereotypes that are so often used as shortcuts to define individuals and/or groups. It is also important to know that individuals as they have new experiences usually change and grow. In the end, it all comes back to the fact that each person is an individual and it is the individual and how that individual's skills and abilities mesh with those of the team that matters.

NOTES

1. Thomas R. Roosevelt Jr., "Diversity Management: An Essential Craft for Future Leaders," in *The Leader of the Future 2*, eds. Frances Hesselbein and Marshall Goldsmith (San Francisco: Jossey-Bass, 2006), 55–60.

2. Shankar Vedamtan, "Most Diversity Training Ineffective, Study Finds." *Washington Post*, January 20, 2008, A3.

3. *New York Times* (January 8, 2008), D2.

4. Scott Page, *The Difference: How the Power of Diversity Creates Better Groups, Firms, Schools, and Society* (Princeton, NJ: Princeton University Press, 2007).

5. *New York Times*, D-2.

6. Ibid.

7. Tom Brokaw, *The Greatest Generation* (New York: Random House, 1998).

8. Ann Prentice, *Managing in the Information Age* (Lanham, MD: Scarecrow Press, 2005), 107.

9. Warren Bennis and Burt Nanus, *Leaders: The Strategies for Taking Charge* (New York: Harper and Row, 1985), 2.

10. Ibid., 42.

11. Ibid.

12. Ibid., 222–24.

13. David Gergen, *Eyewitness to Power* (New York: Simon and Schuster, 2000), 80.

14. Sally Helgesen, *The Female Advantage: Women's Way of Leadership* (New York: Doubleday Currency, 1995), xiv.

15. Ibid.

16. Ibid., xxvi.

17. Margaret Henning and Anne Jarden, *The Managerial Woman* (New York: Pocket Books, 1976).

18. Betty Lehan Harrigan, *Games Mother Never Taught You* (New York: Warner Books, 1977). Henry Mintzberg, *The Nature of Managerial Work* (New York: Harper and Row, 1973).

19. Mintzberg, *The Nature of Managerial Work*, 29–30.

20. Helgesen, p. 15.

21. Ibid., 17.

22. Ibid., 19–26.

23. Ibid., 38.

24. Alice H. Eagly and Linda L. Carli, *Through the Labyrinth: The Truth about How Women Become Leaders* (Boston: Harvard Business School Press, 2007), 127.

25. Boris Groysberg, "How 30 Star Women Build Portable Skills," *Harvard Business Review* 86, no. 2 (February 2008): 74–81.

26. Ilene H. Lang, "Co-opt the Old Boys' Club: Make it Work for Women," *Harvard Business Review* 89, no. 11 (November 2011): 44.

27. Man Masaoka, "Ten Things I Learned about Leadership from Women Executive Directors of Color," in *The Leaders of the Future 2*, eds. Frances Hellelbein and Marshall Goldsmith (San Francisco: Jossey-Bass, 2006), 55–60.

28. Manning Marable, *Malcolm X, A Life of Reinvention* (New York: Penguin Books, 2012).

29. Paul Hond, "A Message for the World," *Columbia Magazine* (Summer 2011), 13–19.

30. William Strauss and Neil Howe, *Generations: The History of America's Future, 1584 to 2069* (New York: William Morrow and Co., 1991), 35.

31. Warren G. Bennis and Robert J. Thomas, *Geeks and Geezers: How Era, Values, and Defining Moments Shape Leaders* (Boston: Harvard Business School Press, 2002).

32. Ibid., 44.

33. Kirk Snyder, *The G Quotient: Why Gay Executives are Excelling as Leaders . . . and What Every Manager Needs to Know* (San Francisco: Jossey-Bass, 2006), vi.

34. Ibid., vi.

35. Ibid., v.

36. Ibid., vii.

37. Ibid., 3–19.

38. Ibid., 21–34.

39. Ibid., 35–46.

40. Ibid., 47–57.

41. Ibid., 59–72.

42. Ibid., 73–84.

43. Ibid., 85–100.

44. Isabella Derings, *Trans-Cultural Leadership for Transformation* (New York: Palgrave Macmillan, 2011), 40.

45. Ibid., 119.

46. "The New Greatest Generation," *Time* 178, no. 8 (August 29, 2011): 28.

47. R. Roosevelt Thomas Jr., "Diversity Management: An Essential Craft for Future Leaders," in *The Leaders of the Future* 2, eds. Frances Hesselbein and Marshall Goldsmith (San Francisco: Jossey-Bass, 2006), 47.

Chapter 6

Taking Responsibility

How does one become a leader and how does one know that they have the ability to lead? Assuming a role and actually finding out what you need to do and doing it in real time with real people involved are two different things. When one is given a leadership role, that individual will be in charge of a group that includes individuals with a range of leadership and followership experiences. Some are more experienced than the newly named leader and have seen new leaders come and go and may help the new leader or may wait to see how well the new leader takes responsibility and moves forward. It is possible that someone in the group had wished to be the leader, is resentful of the new leader, and may act in ways that do not support the new leader. In most instances, new leaders have a brief period in which to learn about the organizational culture, get to know the individuals involved, and discuss the ways in which they plan to move forward to attain the goals set forth. If the leader assumes the role in a crisis situation, these steps are foreshortened and the leader steps in, sets the course, assigns roles, and immediately takes charge.

PATHS TO LEADERSHIP

Numerous paths lead to leadership. One can prepare for leadership by attending workshops, taking courses, or being part of a mentoring program. Individuals who are born with the expectation that they will become leaders, such as members of a royal family or those whose families are part of a family business, are often prepared from a very early age to assume leadership roles. Those planning a career in politics often seek out mentors who will guide them through the paths and pitfalls of politics. One can have an idea that one wishes to pursue or join a cause that is very important to one's desire to contribute to society. Other individuals work their way up through the ranks of a profession or business, and then they either apply for or are selected for leadership roles. Often a senior individual in an organization will spot someone they see as having leadership potential and ask that individual to assume a leadership position. In other instances, a crisis may occur and an individual is drafted by members of the group involved to lead. Finally, there are situations in which leadership is desperately needed and no one steps up until finally someone says "I'll do it."

Learning Leadership

Learning to be a leader is a lifelong activity. It is possible to learn a great deal about leadership by reading the biographies of famous leaders and at one time, not so long ago, this was the primary way in which individuals learned about leadership. The body of research on leadership has increased since the latter half of the 20th century and now goes beyond the study of great men and the occasional woman. The emphasis has changed from studying individuals to looking at the environment in which leadership takes place, the motivating factors that compel some individuals to become leaders, and identifying behaviors that contribute to success as a leader.

Many professional societies offer leadership programs for new members of the profession. Typically the society asks members to recommend individuals with whom they work or whose activities they have observed to be part of a formal workshop in which leadership skills are taught. This also provides an opportunity to educate these leaders in training about the values and goals of the specific organization and how they can become responsible leaders in pursuing those goals. Many of these programs include assignment to a project in which the leadership intern can practice the leadership lessons learned in real time and interact with other professionals who can serve as mentors. Another version of this process is often found in the business community where an organization will offer unpaid or paid internships to individuals who have recently graduated from college who wish to learn about the organization. This provides a benefit to both the new graduate and to the sponsoring organization as each can learn about the other and do so in what is specifically a learning context. It may lead to permanent employment, a letter of recommendation, or an understanding by one or both that the new graduate should look elsewhere for opportunities.

Courses in leadership are regularly taught as part of academic programs. These have the benefit of a more leisurely look at the many complex issues that leadership entails. These courses focus on both the research and practice of leadership and give students the opportunity to discuss leadership issues from various perspectives. They often gear leadership examples to a particular profession by citing leaders in that profession—for example, Bill Gates as a business leader who started with an idea and built an empire or Mary Breckenridge who created the Frontier Nursing Service to bring health care to Appalachia. Students read about their careers and observe how they followed a vision, organized individuals and resources to support it, and how they dealt with both failure and success.

An important source of leadership training is that which is provided for men and women who join the military. These individuals are expected to demonstrate leadership qualities and those qualities are emphasized in their training. Once they are on duty, they are given increasing responsibility and are expected to meet expectations and to lead. Men and women in the early years of their work life are thus given the opportunity to assume responsibility and lead. This experience as they transition to civilian life and careers provides them with the knowledge that they have demonstrated their leadership competence under stress and that they are prepared to be leaders in civilian life.

Individuals Who Are Born to Lead

Although it is less common than in the past, there are still examples of individuals who are born to lead. An excellent example is the British Royal Family. Elizabeth II, daughter of a younger son, did not know that she would assume the throne until after her uncle David stepped down from the succession and her father became George VI. Almost immediately, she began to be groomed to succeed him. Her son, Prince Charles, has been groomed all his life to lead and his son, Prince William, follows him. Their lives are led with the knowledge that one day they will be king and that they need to know certain things, and to lead their lives in ways that will bring honor to the title. Families such as Rupert Murdoch's media empire groom younger members of the family to take part in the family business with the expectation that they will at some point lead it. While this often happens, there are many examples of business leadership not going as the patriarch planned. For example, Murdoch's son became embroiled in legal difficulties stemming from how the family-owned newspapers gained information, and his opportunity to lead ebbed. Katherine Graham's husband was a member of the family that owned the *Washington Post* and was its editor. He committed suicide and Katherine, who had not been trained to lead, took over the newspaper and led it to a higher level. Being born to a leadership position may provide an initial advantage but unless the individual has the passion, the ability, and the ethics to succeed, they may falter.

Following a Cause

Many examples of individuals point out those who believed in an idea and who devoted their lives to fulfilling their dream. Martin Luther King Jr., who became a leader of the Civil Rights Movement, started out in Alabama as a minister but was soon caught up in something much larger. While reluctant at first, he was convinced by others and by the events of the day that he should assume a leadership role. For the rest of his life he followed the dream that he so eloquently expressed in his "I Have a Dream" speech at the Lincoln Memorial on August 28, 1963, in front of more than 200,000 civil rights workers, and it was a dream for which he gave his life. That dream was moved forward by others and his leadership continued to be a key element in uniting others to follow the dream. Cesar Chavez fought to have the working conditions of agricultural workers in California improved. He fought to achieve this and in the process became a leader who organized others and gave them a sense that they were worthwhile individuals who could fight for their rights. Mahatma Gandhi's life was devoted to fighting injustice through nonviolence and he was one of the 20th century's greatest leaders against social injustice. Not only did he fight injustice in his own country, he provided a model which was followed by those fighting injustice in other countries. These individuals led because of the strength of their dream, their understanding of the needs and concerns of those they led, and their willingness to devote themselves, often single-mindedly, to a cause. Some who were not particularly adept at organizing a team to support and carry out their ideas would work with another person. Susan B. Anthony, who excelled at demonstrating the need for women's rights but was not a good speech writer, teamed up with Elizabeth Cady Stanton and with their combined skills provided effective leadership for the cause. This is an excellent example of how a great communicator with a worthy cause attracts others who believe in the cause and whose complementary skills strengthen the leadership role. These are the individuals who help build the organization, raise the money, and provide the leader with skills the leader may lack. Leadership strengthened within the team enables the team to achieve the common goal.

The Leader with a Great Talent

When someone has a talent for teaching, for business, for the law, and for other areas of endeavor that require skills and ability, we often take it for granted that that person will be a leader. We may also encounter a leader who holds that position because of great talent. We can name artists including Picasso and Monet, musicians such as Leonard Bernstein, country and western stars including Johnny Cash, and many more. Each of them became known because of their talent and each developed a followership of those who honored that talent and wished to learn from them. In the sports world, Mohamed Ali, the boxer, used his time as a leader in the spotlight to fight injustice. In many instances, these individuals are unintended leaders in that they did not set out to change the world or lead a cause, they were led by their talent to occupy a place on the world stage and then used that place to further their talent or to work for a cause that was important to them. Here too, some had an organization to support them while others did not.

The individual who has a salable idea for a product or service may develop a business and become an entrepreneur. These creative individuals build their own organization around their ideas and lead/control all aspects of development, production, sale, and management. They are often the individuals who do not fit well in a large organization as their ideas and approaches are out of step with the majority and they resist the rules and regulations of a larger organization. If the product or service they have developed is successful, their organization becomes attractive to larger organizations that will often buy them out and they can then begin the task over again with a new idea. These individuals are focused on making their ideas real and building organizational structures to do so. They are special kinds of leaders who often refuse to follow the rules set by others but who lead in their own unique way. Some of our greatest inventors including Alexander Graham Bell are in this category. Scientists who, with their ideas, changed the way we see the world, for example Albert Einstein, were leaders because of their ways of looking at the world but were often reluctant team players.

Working Your Way up the Ladder and Applying for a Leadership Position

This is the traditional way by which many individuals come to leadership positions. You work hard, take advantage of opportunities as they arise, learn what you can about leadership from those around you, make yourself known by volunteering to serve on committees, participate in professional organizations so that you are known outside your organization, and work hard to get good performance reviews. You may develop a special expertise that enhances your job, you may take courses that make you more valuable to the organization, and you make sure that your boss knows what you are doing. Many leaders have looked back to their early years and commented that the mistake they made was to assume that their boss knew what they were doing, that they were preparing themselves for the next level of responsibility. Learning to be a leader is not enough. You need to let others know that you have a career plan, that it includes leadership, and that this is an underlying component of your activities.

The next step may be to apply for or be asked to assume a position within the organization. In this situation you are a known entity and both your new boss and the staff you will be directing know something about you. This is good in that you understand the formal and informal organizational structure and know what the organizational goals are and how your new position fits within the larger structure. What may be difficult is that with your new position, your relationship with the staff at the level above you and below you changes. No longer are you a member of the team who is welcome at lunch. You are now "one of them" who has the power to make decisions that will affect your former coworkers. In addition, if you wish to make changes in the ways in which you interact with others or wish to change work habits or otherwise make changes, it may be difficult as you will be seen as the person you were before your move to a leadership role. Moving to a leadership role in another organization usually occurs after you have applied for the position, been through the interview and hiring process, and have been selected over other candidates to carry out the leadership role. You know that you are wanted because your vision, skills, and abilities match the advertised need. The learning curve is stiff but exciting and you have the opportunity to build new relationships. Should you wish to change your work habits slightly, no one will be able to comment about your early arrival at work or your habit of working late. Growth is expected in both scenarios but faster personal growth is more likely when an individual takes the opportunity to move outside the organization and move on to something new. Leaders, when interviewed, later in their career, have often mentioned that they learned more and learned it faster when they dared to move outside their comfort zone.

STEPS TO LEADERSHIP

The first step toward becoming a leader is becoming a boss for the first time. Linda Hill, who studied the experiences of new managers and leaders for many years and who has both written and consulted widely with for-profit and not-for-profit organizations, says, "Executives are irrevocably shaped by their first management positions . . . [They will remember this as the time] that forged their leadership philosophies and styles that may continue to haunt and hobble them throughout their careers."[1] It is a time in which the new leader has a very sharp learning curve. Not only does the new leader need to focus on the goals, the new leader also needs to provide direction to a group of individuals who are or need to become a well-managed team that will assist in achieving those goals. Leaders who Hill interviewed often commented that their first leadership job wasn't what they expected and that it appeared to have little to do with leadership. One said that the first day of a new job when one is in the leadership role is like day one with a newborn child. You are expected to know what to do; you are responsible for this being and this being isn't listening to you; and you haven't a clue to decide what to do next. You learn very fast as you have no alternative. Further, that newborn is most likely crying loudly, and it is your job to figure out why and to gain control of the situation.

To help "new managers pass their first leadership test, we need to help them understand the essential nature of their role, what it truly means to be in charge."[2] They quickly learn that their new role is more demanding than they had thought and that the power that goes with it has to be learned. The best, actually the only, way to learn to lead is to learn on the job. You stretch yourself beyond your current capacity and learn to work smarter than you thought you could. Mistakes will be made and that is to be expected, but if you learn from your mistakes and continue to grow, things will get better. The leader is responsible for leading the activities of others, not just for the self but for others on the team, and this is a considerable leap to make as it affects the way one plans activities and uses resources.

New leaders may have expectations of the meaning of leadership that are not necessarily accurate. For example, the new leader may focus on the rights and privileges of being boss and the belief that "I am in charge." In fact, the leader's role is to negotiate interdependence, build relationships, and learn how to get things done as a team. While doing this, members of the staff will be looking at how the leader achieves this to see if they know what they are doing and how well they are doing it. The leader is planning their future and most staff members want the leader to succeed because when the leader succeeds, they all succeed. They also want to forge a good working team in which they have roles and responsibilities that are mutually satisfying. These early internal negotiations will set the tone for the way in which team members interact with one another and with the leader.

New leaders often have the impression that they wield authority because of their position and that this power is all that is needed to be successful. In fact, the manager must "establish credibility with subordinates, peers, and superiors."[3] It takes time and effort to earn respect and the trust of those one leads and one does it by demonstrating character and the desire to do the right thing. Demonstrating competence, knowing how to do the right thing is not just knowing how to manage the technical aspects of the activity but also knowing how to work with others to accomplish the task. Knowing everything about a task and showing off your knowledge labels you as a micromanager who doesn't want to give others the opportunity to participate. Listening to others on the team, respecting their knowledge and ability, and delegating activities will build a stronger team and build the regard that team members have for your leadership. Building good individual and group relationships with team members is a strong foundation on which to build a highly functional team. New leaders also need to show that they have credibility outside their area of responsibility and that they are respected for their competence. They are able to use these external connections to enhance the activities within their area of responsibility.

New leaders must be in charge of those for whom they are responsible and those who are direct reports, but the more the power that leaders are willing to share with the team in order to achieve goals, the more the team will accomplish. While the leader is ultimately responsible, listening, sharing, guiding, and appreciating the work of others is the best way to lead. Finally, the new leader is responsible for making things run smoothly. While for some team members this may mean that the leader does not change routines that work and their role is to champion the status quo, this is rarely the right way to go. A major reason for new leadership is that the new leader brings new ideas, new ways of doing things in response to new goals and external factors that make yesterday's tried and true ways of operating no longer desirable. New ideas, new variables, new routines mean that there will be times when things do not run smoothly. The leader guides this creative process and works with the team to build this new approach.

All the above steps are taken simultaneously; and for the new leader, this can be a challenge. New leaders tend not to ask for assistance as they think that this would show that they lack the skills to move forward successfully. They may not know what questions to ask or who to ask. They need to find someone who can help them work through the early steps of leadership. Finding a mentor at the beginning of a career is particularly important as it provides the new leader with guidance from someone who has been in a similar position and can offer suggestions on how to move forward.

Learning to lead is a never-ending task. Each new goal, each new leadership opportunity offers new leadership challenges. While many leaders or managers tend to reach a level of proficiency and then stop growing, it is essential to the success of the individual leader, the team, and the organization that the leader continue to grow. Hill and Lineback[4] set three imperatives for those who do not want to stagnate.

1) *Manage yourself.* "Who you are as a person . . . the beliefs and values that drive your actions and especially how you connect with others all matter to the people you must influence."

2) *Manage your network.* "Effective managers know that they cannot avoid conflict and competition among organizational groups. They build and nurture ongoing relationships."

3) *Manage your team.* "Team members need to know what's required of them collectively and individually and what the team's values, norms, and standards are."

ARE YOU READY TO LEAD?

How do you know that you are ready to lead? Do you have the skills needed to be a leader? Do you have the moral fiber, the self-knowledge, and the determination to succeed as a leader? Do others say that you would be a good leader and that they have confidence in your ability? Is the organization or group you are asked to lead ready for you? Do you have the specific skills and approach that will turn the organization into a team? Do you have all the skills needed to be a leader or are there gaps? Most important, do you want to lead and is this the time?

Few individuals start out in their careers by announcing that they want to be a leader. In the beginning, the emphasis is on gaining skills and applying them. Unless the individual is an entrepreneur, those skills are honed within a larger organization where in addition to honing personal skills, one learns to work with others within the organization. This includes observing how the organization is managed and led. From this experience, it is possible that an individual learns whether taking a leadership role is what they want to do. In the sciences, individuals often have the opportunity to choose whether they wish to devote their career to research or to management and there are two distinct career tracks that emerge and each has its leaders with distinct characteristics. In some other organizations, emerging leaders gain experience in many areas of the organization and are able to develop an overall understanding of the service or product provided. They use this experience to support their move toward a leadership position.

During this early career phase, individuals who show promise as professionals or as individuals who work well with others are often noticed by their supervisors and are given additional challenges which test their leadership abilities. They may be put in charge of a specific project, asked to be a member of a committee that is charged to examine process or policy, or may be asked to prepare a report on a topic of importance to the organization. This allows management to observe their performance and to consider next steps in grooming them for more important roles. Having a mentor at this stage of the individual's career is very important as it is easy to make a misstep or not take advantage of an opportunity that is offered.

Not all organizations are looking for leadership qualities in their employees. It may be a family business where only family members become leaders. It may be a traditional organization where one must follow a predetermined set of steps when it is one's turn to do so. This type of path forward tends to prepare individuals who instead of being leaders are clones of existing management. It is possible that both the formal and informal organization have very specific expectations of what new employees should do and be. One manager interviewed by this author said that the most important role of new employees is to shut up, listen, do what they are told, not ask questions and forget most of what they were taught in school because "it isn't real world stuff." This is the kind of situation that an individual wishing to learn and grow in one's career should avoid at all costs and if in such a situation, get out as soon as possible.

Leading Readiness

Leadership skills are learned as you go and can be learned by observing those in leadership positions to see what methods they use to achieve goals and if those methods work. Leadership styles and their effect on the organization can also be observed and can influence one's personal style. For example, charismatic leaders may speak of the need for major accomplishments and outline a plan of action that places them at the center of attention but then do little to bring staff together to achieve those accomplishments. The quiet leader facilitates the activities of the team so that each individual has a role in achieving the goal and in gaining recognition for the achievement. While the quiet leader may not receive as much personal credit for the activity, the quiet leader and those who follow understand who got the job done. Observing types of leaders and leadership is an important means of learning about one's own leadership style as well as what works best in a particular situation.

An additional leadership skill that is learned by doing is how to deal with conflict. How does a leader deal with conflicting objectives, individuals who do not agree, or individuals who for some reason want to dominate a situation? One learns that a key to resolution is to focus on the situation and not on personal beliefs or attitudes. Learning to listen, to communicate, to treat others with respect, to find common ground, and to act in the best interest of the organization and society is an important test of leadership that is learned over time. The leader who focuses on the task to be accomplished and the best way to do it rather than on personalities of individuals who may not agree or who may wish to dominate will build a stronger team and will have gained in personal stature.

It is often others in the organization, the profession, the community who are the first to say that an individual is ready to lead. They have observed the work of an individual, have provided challenges, have seen how the individual interacts with others, and have noticed if the individual is passionate about what is being accomplished. They also observe if the potential leader can deal with ambiguity and with changing situations and if the individual can learn fast and adapt to new situations. It is often the confidence others have in an individual's leadership potential that motivates the individual to accept a leadership role.

Despite the confidence of others in one's abilities, there is always the concern that maybe one is not ready for the job. What if mistakes are made? What if it is too big a task? Everyone who assumes a new role has concerns about success. Any new role requires a fast learning curve before there is a real understanding of the position and what it entails. For some, this discovery period is the most interesting part of a new position and when the learning curve is less steep, the excitement ebbs. It is usually true that most individuals who are placed in a leadership position feel unready for the position. That feeling is the first step toward learning new things and growing into the position. Mistakes will be made and that is expected. It is also expected that dealing with the mistakes will be an important learning activity and that the individual and the organization will benefit from this.

An additional and in some ways the most important component of being ready for leadership is that you want it. You have ideas you want to test, new ways of organizing and operating and are excited about future possibilities. Those who want to lead, who learn about leadership by study, observation, talking with others who can mentor them and who know that leadership is very hard work but very rewarding have a strong chance of succeeding. Leaders also need to have a strong ego but not a big ego. Leadership is about working with others to achieve a vision that somehow makes the world better. It is not about making oneself important at the expense of others.

TAKING/ACCEPTING RESPONSIBILITY

Taking responsibility implies that the individual is seeking the opportunity to lead and is confident in the ability to lead. It also implies taking responsibility for one's decisions and actions. The person who takes charge recognizes a need and steps up to the challenge. Accepting responsibility may show a more passive stance, or not. The person who accepts responsibility is willing to act, understands what is expected, and acts accordingly. Cultural implications may arise in deciding whether one takes or accepts responsibility. In some situations, women may feel reluctant to act in a way that some would say is too aggressive and therefore would hesitate to take responsibility. In some cultures, it is considered very bad to put oneself forward rather than wait to be asked to accept a new role. The person who accepts responsibility is more likely to be a quiet leader, one who is attuned to the cultural environment, builds teams, facilitates action, and shares credit but not necessarily.

The person who takes responsibility may have a more outspoken leadership style than the one who accepts responsibility but regardless of how this first step was taken, the road ahead is the same. New leaders may not know if others support their actions and may not know if others will participate in the actions the leader takes. Taking responsibility requires a strong ego, a willingness to act, an understanding of what is needed, and the guts to act accordingly. They need to be willing to listen to others and to respect what they hear. Taking responsibility means that the leader is responsible for what happens and when problems arise, the leader needs to take responsibility for them as well.

In some instances the leader who takes responsibility is all talk and lets others do the work while taking credit for accomplishments. Those who are all talk and no action or as some say "all hat and no cattle" do not gain the respect of those who are part of the team or of the larger public they in some way serve. Unless there are strong political or financial reasons to retain the all-talk leader, they rarely last long. In the end, when things go wrong, it is the leader who bears the responsibility for the team's actions.

Leaders who accept responsibility know at the outset that others have confidence in their ability to do the job. They have less need to make a statement that they are taking control of the situation as the situation has been offered. While the beginning steps toward leadership may be different, all leaders are responsible for pursuing the goals and vision of the organization, for achieving results and for taking the heat when things go wrong. Taking or accepting responsibility may well be as much a matter of leadership style as anything else. Some situations call for direct firm action while others may work better if there is a smoother transition in leadership. Either way, leaders must believe in what they are doing and their actions must make the part of the world for which they are responsible a better place.

CLAIMING THE ROLE

What steps are necessary for new leaders to claim their roles and make them their own? In being given the role of leader, one has been given the responsibility of being in charge of a project, an organization, or other entity. Becoming a leader requires additional effort and acceptance of the leadership role by those who are expected to follow. While there is usually acceptance of a new leader, the new leader's actions will be observed closely and the leader will have a sense of the extent to which those being led approve of actions taken. The new leader needs to project a strong sense of self-worth, of knowing what to do and how to do it, and of having goals and a vision others will be willing to follow. This is not the time to show a lack of confidence or feelings of insecurity.

Each of us has a preferred leadership style and it is important to look at a new role in terms of how well that style meshes with the needs and interests of those being led. If the team is made up of part-time students who have had little work experience, an authoritarian approach that is at the same time supportive and gives members of the team opportunities to learn and grow may be the appropriate approach. If the team consists of professionals with a range of skills and a range of ages, an approach that respects and encourages participation is in order. Adapting one's personal style to the background and qualifications of those being led and to the needs of the task at hand is an early step in leading a particular group.

Prior to becoming a leader, there is usually a period of mutual learning in which the individual selected to lead becomes familiar with the organization and members of the organization. At the same time, members of the organization have the opportunity to meet the potential new leader during a search process. If the promotion is internal, both leader and those led have had a period of time to get to know each other and to know the challenges the position offers. If the transition to new leadership was the result of a retirement, a promotion, or the departure of an individual, and the environment left by the former leader was positive, the transition will most probably be fairly free of bad feelings. If the former leader left under less-than-positive circumstances, the new leader needs to identify the issues, how staff members have responded to the problems and the transition, and find ways to heal whatever breaks in trust or performance exist. The level of trust the new leader receives is directly related to the experiences staff have had with the former leader. If staff members are feeling uncomfortable because they know that major problems exist, that tasks have been left undone, that relationships with other units have faltered, they may feel insecure and defensive about what the new leader will learn and how the new leader will respond. It is not the time or place for an insecure leader who is unsure of what to do, who resents questions, who is "always right" regardless of the situation, and who is unwilling to listen. When a leader steps into a well-ordered position, they have time to learn and plan how to move the organization forward. When the position requires action to fix problems immediately and members need to learn how to work as a team, a faster response by the new leader is necessary. A benefit of entering a dysfunctional situation is that the leader has an immediate opportunity to make a real difference and to demonstrate leadership abilities from the outset.

Steps in Claiming Your Role

What does the new leader do to own the leadership role and to gain the respect of those who are part of the team as well as those to whom the leader reports?

Some of these steps can be taken before actually assuming the role and when the position becomes available. Knowing about the organization, its purpose, goals, vision and how well they mesh with personal values is the first step to be taken. If you believe in caring for the planet and its resources, working for an organization that is more interested in plundering the planet will not be a good fit. Knowing how well your personal vision fits that of the organization is also important. If your vision requires resources and expertise not available in the organization and there are no plans to acquire them, this will not be a good fit. Any individual looking to move into a new position needs to learn as much as possible about the organization they might join in order to determine how well the fit will be. Nice and not-so-nice surprises about any new position always occur, but they can be dealt with so long as the overall fit between leader and organization is good.

Steps to making the position your own include the following:

- Identify your resources, including staff and staff expertise, how well the staff is organized to achieve goals, how well the staff works together, the level of communication, what paperwork is available to describe the activities of the team and how much it tells you about where the team is and where it is going. Think of this step as a context analysis, a means of interpreting the situation.

- Determine what type of leader is needed by the organization at this time and how you can become that type of leader.

- Become aware of what you know about the organization and the staff with whom you will work. Also find out what you don't know and figure out ways of finding out.

- Decide whether you will follow the existing course of action toward achieving goals or if you prefer to take a new direction. Whichever action you decide, be open with staff as to why you have made a particular decision, what that decision means to them, and what you expect the result to be.

- Clean up any unfinished business. This may include the need to carry out personnel evaluations and make difficult decisions, the need to reconsider allocation of resources, the need to catch up on undone paperwork and reports, or the need to resolve conflicts that continue to interfere with the work to be done.

- Empower staff. Depending on the history of the organization and the team before your arrival, this may be easy or it may take time. Staff members may need to learn new skills in order to fit into a new direction. They may not have participated in decision making and need to be reassured that their ideas and contributions are important. Some will welcome a more active role while others may prefer to be told what to do. Assure them that there is a mutual responsibility for success and they are expected to contribute.

- Communicate, be approachable, be transparent, and adapt your leadership style to the needs of the team.

- Be willing to take risks and learn from your successes and failures.

- Have a plan, share your plan, and act on it so that the team will see that you are in charge and are moving forward.

You will know you have claimed your role as leader when those you lead respect your decision making, the way in which you interact with them, and that you have a plan that is moving them ahead. You know that you are a leader after you have studied a situation, made decisions, have met challenges, and have moved forward and know that you can really do the job. If there are sometimes gaps in self-confidence, this is understandable. Each leadership decision is an opportunity to learn new things, not all of which are positive. As one leader said, "act like you know until you know."

LEARNING THAT YOU MAY NOT WISH TO LEAD

One learns to lead by doing. In the process it can happen that the desire to lead isn't really there at the time. Perhaps necessary leadership skills are missing or the realization that leadership is harder work than anticipated becomes apparent. Each of us is at one time or other unsure of our skills and our ability to carry out expected tasks. For some, this is a challenge that is met by learning more, trying harder, and in becoming confident. King George VI of England had difficulty with communicating because he stuttered. His solution was to find a speech coach who worked with him to overcome the problem. He wasn't comfortable communicating in public but he learned to manage the problem and he became a symbol of courage and bravery for the British people during the dark days of World War II. Franklin D. Roosevelt contracted polio when he was well into his political career. He had a choice—to suspend his political career or to overcome his inability to walk and to continue his career. He chose the second alternative and led the United States as president during World War II. Katherine Graham, who led the *Washington Post* after her husband's suicide, continued to doubt herself throughout her career despite major decisions such as making public the Pentagon Papers scandal and Watergate, but this did not get in the way of her leadership role. She never publicly expressed her self-doubt until she wrote her autobiography.

In some instances, the time and place are not right. If an organization is well established and there is little opportunity to be creative it may require one kind of leader, while if the organization is new and growing rapidly, it needs another kind of leader. The leader who likes to move into an organization, propose bold ideas, and radically change ways of doing things will not be satisfied with a situation that resists change. When looking at possible leadership positions, it is important to determine if it is the right place and the right time for you to become a leader.

It is possible that while one excels at doing something, there are deficits in other areas that may prevent one from playing a successful leadership role. We have all met leaders who are very good at envisioning a plan of action that will achieve certain goals and are very good at communicating that vision, but they need someone else to actually build the structure, design the steps toward action, and accomplish what the leader proposes. Some individuals prefer to play the second role and let the leader set the direction. FDR was a master communicator and he included among his closest advisors individuals who, while not good communicators, were very talented in dealing with the political realities of the day. He was a big idea man rather than a good organizer and left the daily aspects of leadership to others while he expanded his role as visionary and communicator. As a team, this was very successful.

John Adams, second president of the United States, was involved in numerous important nation-building activities but he was not an inspired leader. He did not excel at communication and since he served between George Washington and Thomas Jefferson, who were famous for their oral and written communication, this was all the more evident. Adams also had an unfortunate habit of blaming others when things went wrong and refusing to accept responsibility for his own actions. He cared deeply about the success of his new country and soldiered on despite his shortcomings.

When you are the leader, you are responsible for those you lead and if something goes wrong, it is your responsibility and conversely, when things go right, you share the credit. Blaming others for problems that occur is not leading. Being able to honestly assess personal leadership skills and determine how best to use them is an essential part of self-knowledge. Some will find that they want to be the idea person out ahead of the crowd and that they enjoy communicating this to others. They may or may not have the skills and abilities to follow through and get things done and need to build a team that includes individuals with the skills and abilities they lack. Other individuals have the will and the ability to lead but wish to do it from "behind the throne." They want someone else to make the speeches and interact with others while they plan what to do and how to accomplish it.

For many leaders, the hesitance to lead is part of the process of testing one's abilities and growing into the leadership role. As risks are taken and experience gained, today's uncertain leader may well become tomorrow's successful leader. It is all a matter understanding one's abilities and finding the best way to use them and to build on them. It is important to be neither overly careful about becoming a leader nor overconfident. Either path is dangerous. Successful leaders are confident that they have the requisite skills, and really want to lead.

THE BENEFITS OF FAILURE

One rarely accepts an opportunity to learn, to do, to lead with the expectation they will fail. This would be depressing indeed. The possibility of failure is inherent in all of our activities and when it is seen as a learning opportunity it can be valuable. Facing challenges, some of which we win and some of which we do not, are the ways in which we stretch our experience and learn to deal with the next challenge in a new and perhaps better way. When we look at a failure, it is important to determine to the extent we can why the failure occurred. Was it because we did not understand the situation in which we were operating? Did we misjudge the interest of those with whom and for whom we worked? Were they less than supportive? Did we misjudge the resources available? What about the interpersonal and political environment? Did we fail because we did not do our homework thoroughly and therefore missed important information? Was our failure due to a movement into unknown territory where, although we had done our homework and had the support of the team, new problems emerged? Was the failure a fluke, something that could not be anticipated? Whatever the reason for the failure, the leader takes responsibility, owns the failure, and moves forward.

Bennis[5] said that one of the most important lessons that failure can teach a good leader is how to understand and overcome the changing contexts of leadership. It is important to master the context and to adapt in order to move toward success. Poor leaders do not own their failure but blame them on prevailing circumstances. This is blaming the context rather than mastering it.

The context within an organization changes and the leader needs to be aware of these changes. In many instances, the leader is in charge of how the aspects of the context change. When a leader goes from one organization to another, studying the context is the first and very important action. Different organizations have different cultures, different formal and informal structures, and different priorities. The leadership style that worked in one organization or in one team may not work in another. Yesterday's experience and yesterday's strategy rarely works in a new environment.

Those who have grown up in environments in which failure was seen as a learning experience rather than something more permanent learn to assess the problem, determine how to fix it, and do better next time. When one looks at the careers of early achievers—those who have found success at a young age and have rarely had to deal with failure—one finds that many of them tend to burn out because they didn't know how to respond. We can look at musical prodigies, movie stars, and others who found fame early and observe their difficulties in dealing with failure when it came, as it always does. Civil war historians suggested that general-in-chief of the Union Army, George McClellan, was unable to make decisions because he feared failure; and this was because he believed what his professors at West Point and members of the press said about his genius and he didn't want to disappoint them.

The first step in learning from failure is to accept that you have failed but don't see this as a permanent situation. Be honest about the situation and don't make it more or less than it actually is. Analyze the situation and see why the failure occurred. What different steps could have been taken? Then decide if and how you will move forward in this area. Has the context changed such that doing the same thing only better is no longer a viable choice? Should we move ahead and, using the knowledge and experience gained, try something else somewhere else? Learn all you can about the failure, move ahead, make changes as necessary, and move on. Those who don't accept failure, analyze the reasons, plan what to do next, and move ahead can be dominated by the experience and not be willing to try again. Not trying again is the greatest failure as it shows we have lost confidence in our abilities and ourselves. As was once said, "failure is one step closer to success." Life is hard. Work is hard. If everything was easy, where is the challenge in living?

If the leader is not challenged by the context and by the vision, why are they leading? Badaracco[6] said that in order for leaders to take responsibility, they need to face a real demand. Leaders must attain self-mastery before being able to lead others and take responsibility for the actions of others. Facing challenges and being tested helps leaders master themselves and see what they are capable of doing.

SUMMARY

Taking responsibility means taking responsibility for the organization you will lead. It is a pledge to work hard, to invest in the vision, the organization and the individuals you will lead. It means that you hold yourself accountable to those you serve and lead for the success or failure of the enterprise. It means that you are passionate about leading and about achieving a vision and that you believe you are ready to lead. You have the skills and abilities to lead and you continue to learn and refine those skills and abilities. As a leader you put the goal and its challenges and the opportunity to be part of something important ahead of your personal success. It also means that you are looking forward to a great adventure.

NOTES

1. Linda Hill, "Becoming a Boss," *Harvard Business Review* 89, no. 1 (January 2007): 44–56.
2. Ibid.
3. Ibid.
4. Linda Hill and Kent Lineback, "Are You a Good Boss or a Great Boss?" *Harvard Business Review* 89, no. 1/2 (January, February 2011): 121–31.
5. Warren Bennis, *On Becoming a Leader* (New York: Basic Books, 2003), 86–91.
6. Joseph Badaracco Jr., *Questions of Character: Illuminating the Heart of Leadership through Literature* (Boston: Harvard Business School Press, 2006), 118.

Integrity

The most important element of leadership is integrity. The American Heritage Dictionary defines integrity as adherence to a strict moral or ethical code and the quality or condition of being whole. When we say that a person has integrity we mean that the individual is honest, does not lie or cheat, and their word and actions can be trusted. Integrity is a demonstration of the individual's core belief system and is practiced every day, with every honest act and action and with every word and deed that supports the principles a person lives by. Integrity is earned over one's lifetime on a daily basis. Integrity can be lost when one purposely makes a false statement or carries out an underhanded action. Once integrity is lost, it may take many actions to rebuild trust and even then it may not be possible.

An ethical leader is one who has a strong sense of self and of the way in which it is appropriate to interact with others. In working with others, the ethical leader puts the good of others ahead of self-interest as "leaders driven by self-interest orient their behavior toward ends that benefit themselves at the expense of followers whose needs and interests are either ignored or trampled on."[1] The ethical leader's vision is focused on ways in which one can benefit the lives of others and society at large. Those who ignore the needs and interests of others and focus on short-term gains that benefit themselves—for example, Kenneth Lay, head of Enron, a large energy company serving the western and southwestern parts of the country, or Martha Stewart, a leader in developing and marketing programs and services focusing on the home, who used quick ways to earn money either directly or indirectly[2]—are representative of a lack of integrity and of unethical leadership.

In response to a 2005 Roper Poll finding that only two per cent of the public "felt that leaders of large firms were very trustworthy . . . a drop from three per cent in 2004," Howard Gardner[3] conducted a study of how people "aspire to do good work—that is, work of high quality that matters to society, enhances the lives of others, and is conducted in an ethical manner." He proposed that the ethical mind is one of the five minds we all need in order to succeed. The minds are as follows:

1) *The disciplined mind.* We apply ourselves in a disciplined way to gain expertise in our chosen field.

2) *The synthesizing mind.* We survey many sources, decide what is important to us and weave these selected sources together in a coherent fashion.

3) *The creative mind.* We look for new ideas and take chances.

4) *The respectful mind.* We try to understand others, to form relationships. We enjoy being exposed to different types of people.

5) *The ethical mind.* We ask ourselves what kind of person, professional do I want to be?

At times the respectful mind and the ethical mind may be at odds. We may respect the leader and report poor conduct, or we may respect the leader and not expose inappropriate behavior. While the latter choice is unethical, it may be selected because of fear of reprisals if one exposes poor conduct.

Gardner asks the question, "Does the need to succeed mean more than ethics?" He cited a Duke University study of graduate students in the United States that reported that 56 percent of students in the United States who were pursuing a MBA admitted to cheating, the highest cheating rate among graduate student groups. "Everybody does it," and "It's the price of success," were representative comments. "A study we [Gardner] published in 2004 found that although young professionals declared an understanding of and a desire to do good work, they felt that they had to succeed by whatever means. When they had made their mark, they told us, they would *then* become exemplary workers."[4] Since markets are amoral and good will does not necessarily prevail, Gardner suggests that it is harder for business people to be ethical as they are often not members of a particular profession. Professionals including doctors, attorneys, engineers, librarians, and others who attend professional schools are socialized to the ethics of a particular profession, and many professions have codes of ethics that are enforced to a greater or lesser degree. Many assume that discussing the role of ethics in the soon-to-be professional's educational program strengthens the individual's desire to live up to the standards that have been set. In least case, professionals have been made aware of the fact that codes of ethics exist and that the profession encourages and expects that its members follow the codes.

Gardner's study does suggest that ethical leaders inspire others and urges that all leaders retain their ethical compass by

- Believing that doing good is for the good of the organization
- Believing in what you are trying to achieve
- Believing in your broad goals of doing good
- Stating your beliefs from the beginning of your role as a leader, sticking to them, and expecting your staff to do the same

He suggests that each leader should rely on knowledgeable and candid individuals to consult in order to get an opinion on "How I'm doing." He also suggests asking, "Would I be embarrassed to have a particular action or decision reported on the front page of the paper or online?" as a good indication of the quality of the action or decision. Listen to a trusted advisor in the organization, listen to someone outside the organization, and listen to a friend who is a peer. These individuals can help the leader keep the moral compass pointed in the right direction. Franklin D. Roosevelt was a more effective president because he listened to his wife, Eleanor, his advisors, and to those with whom he did not necessarily agree before making many of his decisions. Lincoln was more effective because he tested many of his ideas on members of his cabinet, many of whom had very strongly held views that were in opposition to his.[5]

PRINCIPLES AND PRAGMATISM

What happens when one's principles come into conflict with the need to make a difficult decision? Is it right to withhold information if you know that someone may be harmed if you don't provide information or someone else may be blamed? What if you know that the car your friend is selling is not the bargain it is advertised to be but has serious, even dangerous mechanical faults? Do you hope the potential buyer will discover it? Do you hope that the seller will comment? What happens to your friendship if you are responsible for a potentially lost sale? Should you speak or stay silent? What are the costs to your friendship, to yourself, to others? Badaracco defines integrity as "a question of character," and uses examples from literature and history to show how challenges test individuals and how those individuals respond. He cites literary sources to illustrate questions such as "Am I deeply accountable to myself?" "To what other individuals is the leader accountable at the end of the day, the end of the project, the end of a career?"[6]

Badaracco cites Thomas More, Henry VIII's lord chancellor after the death of Cardinal Wolsey. Henry made him lord chancellor because he, More, was widely recognized as an honest man and was widely respected in England and Henry may have intended by this to show that he knew and respected a man of integrity to carry out his decisions and therefore that the decisions had the stamp of integrity. Henry demanded that More take the oath acknowledging him as head of the Church of England. Because More refused, as it violated his beliefs, he was imprisoned in the Tower of London for a year and then, based on false evidence, was beheaded. For several years before his death, he was successful in his profession and in government and was able to protect his family. He was "an honorable man in a position of national leadership trying to navigate deep and dangerous political waters,"[7] who finally had to decide between duty to the crown and his conscience. He chose conscience. He lived his principles and died for them. He did not force others to accept them but in his own behavior and words, challenged others to examine their own behavior. While it might have been possible to compromise, to find a middle way, his principles were in the end more important to him than his family or his life. Historians continue to ask if his decision was one based on thorough consideration of the facts or just plain stubbornness. Literature tells us that "the strands of self-interest and concern for others are lightly intertwined," and the leader is accountable to both self and others.

Shirley Chisholm, the first African American woman to serve in the U.S. Congress, stayed true to her core principles and refused to "go along to get along." Her constituents knew that she worked for them and she refused to be intimidated by those who tried to force her to act against what she saw as the interests of those she represented. Gandhi believed in nonviolent change and despite the frustration of his followers at times, he refused to act in ways that would contradict this strongly held belief. Civil rights leaders in the South followed his principle of nonviolence and were able to prevail against those who intended to deny their rights. Nearly every day, as we read the news or see it on television, there are examples of individuals who do the right thing despite temptations to do otherwise. We also see examples of individuals whose financial dealings and other activities are far from ethical. Many of these individuals lose their positions of power while others manage to squirm their way out of a situation they created because of their lack of integrity and continue to function in a less than ethical manner.

ELEMENTS OF INTEGRITY

To be successful, leaders need to have credibility, trustworthiness, expertise, and an expectation on the part of those being led that the leader is competent and can help them and the organization achieve desired goals. They also need to have a strong sense of self, of what they can and can't do, and not be driven by their ego. Leaders also need to have the respect of those they lead and those to whom they are responsible. In nearly every survey to identify the most important leadership characteristic, honesty was the one most often cited followed by being forward-looking, inspiring and competent.[8]

Honesty

Successful leaders are honest with themselves, admitting areas in which they do not perform well and accepting responsibility for poor judgment when they make the wrong decision. They are honest with others in that they are fair in assessing the abilities of others and in working with them to improve a situation. Honest leaders know better than to believe what is said about them in the media and elsewhere about their performance, as comments from these sources can lead one to develop an outsized or skewed self-image for good or ill. Leaders can create a culture of honesty in which those in the organization feel that their ideas are respected and that they can express them freely. Those from nontraditional backgrounds, those from other cultures, and those with uncommon approaches, ideas, and views feel confident in presenting their ideas and feel confident that they will be heard. The ability to hear and be heard without fear results in a culture of mutual respect, one from which innovative ideas can grow. A part of this openness is that those who express their ideas are held responsible for the quality of the idea and for following up on it if appropriate.

Honest leaders take responsibility for events that occur within their area of authority. Many examples of people in a leadership position show that they, when something went wrong, either blamed someone else or said that they didn't know what was going on. *But they were in charge and therefore responsible.* In 2001 Enron, a multimillion dollar energy company that grew very fast and became very important, crashed, taking with it the savings and investments of many stockholders and resulting in the loss of many jobs. Kenneth Lay, the president of Enron, said that he didn't have any idea that anything was wrong and blamed his financial officer for not keeping him informed. A great deal of blame was passed around with no one willing to accept more than a bit of responsibility. Was the implosion of Enron the result of oversized egos, unwise risks, or poor choices combined with a lack of honesty? As the extent of the debacle became known, there were no apologies to those who lost their savings or their jobs. Perhaps those with huge egos believe that they don't need to apologize as they weren't really at fault. It was someone else.

Trust

Being trustworthy is essential to being a successful leader. It is among the most important criteria looked for in leaders and looked for by leaders when hiring new employees and in building teams. At the outset, leaders need to be clear about the values they live by and that undergird their actions. In early encounters with members of the organization, the leader says, "This is who I am, what I stand for, how I lead," and in this way sets a marker of integrity for future actions. Authentic leaders express the real values they live by, not those they think they should live by or would like to live by. They discuss the vision toward which everyone is expected to work and how they will work together. They are honest about their strengths and those areas in which they will need help and share with members of the team how the team can compensate for areas in which they are not strong. The leader encourages members of the team to bring in new ideas, to discuss them, and to stand up for them without fearing repercussions. Good ideas come from all directions and should be encouraged without fear of reprisal. The leader supports the team effort by urging others to do their best and providing guidance and support when necessary, and avoiding the urge to micromanage. The successful leader builds a winning team and gives the team credit when deserved rather than assuming all of the credit. Leaders accept responsibility for the activities of the team and its members and hold themselves accountable.

For a leader, trust works in two ways, from the leader to those they lead and from those being led to the leader. The leader must trust that any person to whom responsibility is delegated will meet their obligations without being followed around to be sure they are actually performing, and will step in if necessary to provide guidance. Those being led must trust that the leader is competent, has a plan, is delegating appropriately, and will give credit where it is due. Projects in which both the leader and those led trust one another to act with integrity hold high promise for success while those in which there is doubt and distrust rarely succeed. Not only may the project not meet its goal, those involved may be seen in a negative light. Leaders accept responsibility for the actions of those led and hold themselves accountable for achieving or not achieving results. Team members believe what the leader says and trust that the leader's actions will move the team toward the goal in a positive fashion.

Trust is earned slowly with each interaction and each decision. It takes time to be sure that those responsible for achieving goals and working toward the vision actually have the information and the skills to follow through and make things happen. It also takes time to evaluate the decisions made by the leader and to have confidence that the leader will work with the team and support the team as it works toward goals. When a competent leader is in charge, confidence grows and members of the team take pride in what they are doing.

Humility

An overweening ego has no place in the leader's toolkit as the successful leader leads by influence and not by projecting an outsized self-image. Successful leaders often caution leaders with big egos to "check your ego at the door." If leaders think that they have authority solely because of their personal ability and the position they hold, they are mistaken. If a leader thinks that "it's all about me," the work won't get done. It's about what you are trying to accomplish, the goals to be met and the expectations set. Leaders who take unnecessary risks with resources or with the careers of other individuals often do so because they believe that they are smarter than those who caution a wiser path and that they can win in situations that those with a less strong ego dare not risk. They can become so caught up in their vision of how they want to move forward that they lose sight of whether their actions benefit or harm others. In extreme cases of vision-trumps-integrity, pharaohs built pyramids, financial empires were built on less than a firm basis and burst, and careers grew rapidly and then flamed out. The world is littered with the wreckage caused by those whose actions were driven by ego rather than by what their minds, their hearts, and wiser people told them.

Many examples can be shown of people in authority who demonstrate huge egos by becoming bullies in the workplace and demanding that they control every facet of the organization. Howard Aiken who was a designer of the Mark 1, an early computer, demanded absolute control of his lab and in doing so inhibited the climate of innovation so necessary in his field. Bobby Knight, the storied coach of the Indiana University basketball team, so bullied his players and everyone else that he was finally fired. In sports there are many ego enablers among the fans of individual players and teams and many sports figures who believe what the media says about them. If they believe what is said and written about them, they may develop a bloated ego and disaster is not far away.

Shortly after assuming the deanship of the Harvard Business School, Nitin Nohria was asked how he would rethink the School's programs in light of the nation's financial difficulties in the early 21st century. Of the three themes he discussed, leadership, particularly the "development of emotional intelligence and to investigate more deeply the purpose of leadership," was first. He went on to say that

> research demonstrates that character is something one has to work at forming and developing over the course of our lives, just as we focus on developing our judgment . . . what we are trying to do is to allow our students to develop moral humility. We can expose them to the wide variety of pressures that they will face over the course of their careers . . . and show them the wide variety of ways in which good people were led astray because of the pressures that came from their cultures or from bosses, or how they themselves have used incentives in ways to sometimes promote, unwittingly, wrongdoing either by themselves or others.[9]

Being a person with integrity doesn't necessarily mean that you will always make the most morally sound decision. Learning to put one's ethical values into practice is a continuous process of learning and doing.

On Lying and Trust

Is it ever ok to lie? Are there times when lying is the more desirable path than truth? Carl Cannon asked "Why do presidents lie?" and then answered the question by saying that lying is a part of politics. All lies are not equal and the penalty for lying depends on the type of lie. White lies that are told for social convenience are usually not punished. Excuses to rationalize inappropriate behavior are dangerous because the individual is not believed or is often found out to be lying as was the case when President Bill Clinton was accused of having a relationship with a White House intern. The bio-lie, idle boasts such as enhancing one's resume, is usually found out particularly in our Internet world where the real truth is easy to find. Some lies are intended to deceive while other lies may be ones that the liar actually believes is true. Because of the tendency of many of our leaders to lie either for the sake of convenience or due to the desire to mislead, public trust in our leaders has frayed. Cannon concluded the study by saying that "posterity rewards success, not truth . . . for presidents consequences matter more than truth."[10] As one views the many news programs on TV and radio and scans the many blogs dealing with political issues, it becomes evident that a variety of versions of the truth are available depending on one's interests and beliefs. We then wonder, where is the truth in what we see, hear, and, read, and who is standing up for the truth? Truthfulness ultimately comes down to the individual whose integrity depends on it.

SETTING THE TONE OF THE ORGANIZATION

The leader's integrity or lack thereof sets the tone for the organization and the organization is seen as a reflection of the level of integrity of the leader. Leaders are expected to establish policies and procedures that are based on what is honest and what is right, and they expect others to follow those policies and procedures. Ethical followers respect the leader's integrity and follow willingly as they understand that it is important to both the organization and those the organization serves. Leaders who lack integrity tend not to respect others and to act in ways that are self-serving. With this type of leader as a role model, the members of the organization and the organization itself become known as untrustworthy and as entities to be avoided.

Leaders in organizations have visions of what they intend to do and how they intend to do it. For-profit organizations, those that produce and sell a product or service for profit, deal with a specific set of products or services that they make available to the public for money. The law firm advertises that it specializes in a particular aspect of the law, and for a fee, members of the law firm advertise that they will provide high quality service to those who have a particular legal problem. The professionalism with which they provide the service and their attitude toward those who use the service contribute to their reputation. Are they respectful of their clients? Do they perform requested services promptly and for a reasonable fee? Have they built a track record of outstanding service? Have there been situations in which their integrity was questioned and how did they deal with it?

Not-for-profit organizations include schools and universities, libraries, organizations that support our environment, such as the Sierra Club, those that are concerned about our legal rights, such as the ACLU, those that support the arts, such as Public Television, and many, many more. Each of these has a specific purpose and a vision. They wish to make our world safer, kinder, more secure, and more enjoyable. Their statement of purpose may be written in law or it may be developed by those who have specific interests and concerns. For example, the purpose of the Sierra Club is to protect our environment, to preserve the beauty of wild places and spaces for generations to follow and to make those places available for responsible enjoyment. Those with similar interests are invited to join the Club, to contribute financially, and to participate in activities. It represents the interests of members in supporting responsible development and in opposing development that would destroy the environment. As is the case with for-profit organizations, its leadership is responsible for making decisions that fulfill its vision and its promises to its supporters. If a decision is made that violates the vision or promises, the leadership is responsible for explaining itself, and if appropriate explanations are not possible, the organization's integrity is damaged and the leadership is replaced by those who fulfill the expectations of the organization.

The organizational culture is responsible for meshing high performance with high integrity. The leader sets the tone of the organization and serves as a role model of integrity which includes showing respect to the organization and its values and for others both inside and outside the organization. Each individual in the organization from the leader to the newest member of the team is responsible for supporting the shared values of the organization. Not only does this set the tone of the workplace, it contributes to the way in which the organization is seen outside the confines of a building or an organizational structure. The organization maintains its integrity by putting into practice the following:

- Demonstrate consistent and committed leadership. If the leader acts with integrity, one can be sure that it is pervasive throughout the organization. If the leader acts improperly, those actions cannot be tolerated.

- Exceed the formal financial and legal rules. While ethical norms may vary in different cultures, there are some things that must be present everywhere. For example, discrimination is not tolerated.

- Identify ethical issues that may arise in the organization and see how they are handled. Find out what may not be working well and fix it before it becomes a problem.

Finally, hold everyone accountable for maintaining a highly ethical environment in which everyone belonging to the organization and in some way served by the organization is treated with respect.[11]

PERSONAL AND PROFESSIONAL INTEGRITY

Is there a division between a leader's personal life and professional life? Can a leader be honest and forthright in the workplace and at the same time act inappropriately in private? There are those who say that it is not possible to exhibit integrity in a part of one's life while lying or cheating in another. If you cheated on exams in college or stole money from a family member, does this mean that in your professional actions, you will act differently? Will a person compromise his or her principles in some instances and not in others? Is there a cultural component in our definition of integrity? Numerous politicians and business leaders in the United States have been found to have had affairs with individuals who are not their partners. While in the United States this is frowned upon and once made public may damage a person's reputation, in France, for example, such private interactions are not seen as being as particularly damning. In some business cultures, bribes are considered part of doing business while in other cultures, it is illegal. Nepotism is accepted in some cultures and is frowned upon and often illegal in others.

Many individuals believe that even though they have important positions and are often in the public eye, they have a right to personal privacy. What they do in their own time is their business and is personal and private. In our information-rich world that devours facts and factoids with a ravenous appetite, it is very difficult for a newsworthy person to maintain a private life. The advent of Facebook and other social media encourages those with access to computing to go online, tell others about themselves, discuss their thoughts and ideas, and, to do so, on a regular basis, sends a message that *friending* is good and that sharing information is good. To an extent this is true but this sharing should be done with discretion so that those parts of one's private life one wants to keep secure are not advertised to the world. When prospective employers go on Facebook or other social media to learn about an individual, the presence of inappropriate photos or discussions best left for more private places are not to an individual's advantage. Social media is not a place for personal discourse and individuals can themselves compromise their integrity without being aware that they have done so. It is often forgotten that although individuals can erase their e-mail, it never really goes away and can be located by those with a particular interest in an individual's activities.

The media has access to many news outlets online and can locate information on any individual who has had information posted by and about them. It can check any fact and identify conflicting statements. The profiles it can build of an individual can be accurate or can be skewed by including only the information the researcher wishes to include. It is very difficult for anyone to have a truly private life and still be a part of the community.

Everyone has made mistakes, and these mistakes will be uncovered if someone decides to run for public office or finds themselves in the public eye because they have been very successful in a business or profession or have gained public notice by supporting a particular cause. Our culture is usually very forgiving of a single poor choice if the individual has learned from the experience and has moved on to more positive behavior. What is more difficult for the public to forgive are the individuals who loudly proclaim their uncompromising support of a principle they are privately breaking. On a regular basis, the press uncovers private behavior of public individuals that shows poor decision making, and sometimes illegal behavior. While in an earlier, less networked world, it was possible to keep one's private life private, today privacy is a luxury no one can really expect to enjoy and the wise leader acts accordingly.

Most of us are responsible and lead lives that do not lead to headlines in the news and most of us like to feel that to the extent possible our lives should be private. In the public part of our lives, we are connected to a profession, to those with whom we interact professionally, to the organization for which we work, and we need to meet our responsibilities to each of these entities. In our private lives, we have the opportunity to have personal opinions we may not wish to express at work, we interact with our family and friends in a more informal way than we do with colleagues, and we have an opportunity to follow interests in sports, travel, and other areas that are more personal. These aspects of our life are rarely newsworthy. The way in which we conduct our private lives still demonstrates whether we are honest, how well we manage our ego, and how principled a life we live.

Beginning in 2002, Michael Bloomberg, mayor of New York City, insisted that publicly elected officials are responsible for demonstrating their integrity in both their public and private lives. He said, "Politics, no matter what the cynics say, is a noble profession . . . Holders of high office who philander, obfuscate, and act duplicitously cheapen our society. We should insist that officials . . . conduct their personal lives in an appropriate manner."[12] Public office carries with it the responsibility for making choices that affect many other individuals and the results of a poor choice can damage a lot of people. Some may say that this level of pressure on an individual should be taken into consideration and that if they become involved in affairs or are pulled over for driving while impaired, or are otherwise involved in inappropriate behavior, it should be taken lightly given the pressure they are under. Others say that integrity is integrity and good choices are good choices.

How do individuals behave once found in a compromising situation? Do they own up to their transgression and ask forgiveness or do they try to bluff their way through the incident by blaming someone else, by blaming the system? What role does the media play in reporting such incidents? Are there friends in high places who make it easier for the results of poor choices to go away? It still comes down to the fact that integrity is integrity and good choices are good choices.

The question arises of whether a leader should lose that public role because of private actions. President Clinton's impeachment trial had little to do with his performance as president and his performance as chief executive. Should he be held accountable because of private actions that did not affect his public life? Examples abound of leaders who were very able leaders but whose personal lives were less than perfect. In some instances, the line between personal and professional accountability held and they continued to lead, while in other instances, they were removed from their position. The risk of exposure is high and the leader whose personal life is less than exemplary knows this. Some individuals will take advantage of private misdeeds to try to force public actions that harm the individual and the organization the individual represents. While the concept of having a private life is admirable, if one is a public figure the ability to have a private life is limited.

BENDING ONE'S PRINCIPLES

Before discussing the issue of whether there are situations in which it is acceptable to bend one's principles, it is necessary to define exactly what is encompassed by the word "principles," how principles differ from policies, and how they both differ from procedures. According to the Random House Dictionary, principles include the following: "a basic truth or assumption . . . a rule or standard, especially of good behavior . . . the collectivity of moral or ethical standards or judgments."[13] Policies are defined as "a plan or course of action, as of a government, political party or business intended to influence and determine actions and other matters . . . a course of action, guiding principle, or procedure considered expedient, prudent or advantageous."[14] Procedures are defined as "a set of established forms or methods of conducting the affairs of an organized body such as a business, club, or government."[15]

Principles are the basic truths by which we live: being honest with one's self and others, treating others with respect, and being trustworthy. These define who we are and to bend them without a great deal of thought endangers who we are and how we are seen by others. However, if an individual firmly believes that members of another gender or ethnic background are in some way inferior, that belief, that principle is in conflict with the principles of others who as firmly believe that people should be dealt with in terms of their intelligence, abilities, and contribution to society. Some individuals may have among their set of basic truths political or religious beliefs that are in conflict with those of others and may be harmful to others. Those who do not respect their fellow human beings and fail to deal with them with respect have principles that lead to conflict and one has examples of actions by warlords, extremists, and financial operators whose principles do not reflect those of the majority. When the decision is made to select someone to be a leader, careful attention to the principles by which they live is essential.

Policies, which are plans of action intended to influence others, derive from principles and provide direction for an organization. Dorothy Day, an early-20th-century social worker whose life was devoted to helping those in desperate need by providing them with places—hospitality houses—where they could find community upheld her principles of helping those who most needed help. Her policy of never turning anyone away regardless of how needy or disruptive a person might be was a way of implementing her principles. Procedures are ways of carrying out policies that have been set by individuals and groups; and, while they provide structure for action, they can be and are often adapted to the situation as it develops. When we separate actions into these three levels—principles, policies, and procedures—it is relatively easy to identify the category into which a particular situation falls and then move forward. While bending one's principles is very serious as it affects the basic elements of an individual or organization, changing a policy may be an appropriate step if the conditions under which that policy was initially developed changes.

Procedures, agreed-upon plans of action, are developed to provide guidance in certain situations; but they are often guidelines rather than specific orders and are regularly adapted to existing conditions. While one does not arbitrarily change procedures, if good reasons are presented to change them, it is often advisable. An example of changing procedures can be seen in a request by President Kennedy to Phil Graham, then head of the *Washington Post*, that he hold a story on the Cuban Missile Crisis from print until he, President Kennedy, could address the public in a televised news statement. While this was against a policy of not withholding important news from the public, Graham held the news back to give the president the opportunity to inform the public himself.

Jill Ker Conway, during her years as vice president of the University of Toronto, was responsible for dealing with student protests at the university. Prior to becoming a vice president, she was a member of the faculty and in this position gained an understanding of the student body. As vice president, she continued to act with integrity toward the students and developed working relationships with other communities in and around the university. She treated students, the police and others with respect and in this way was able to build working relationships whose purpose was to maintain a level of civility in a difficult time. Rather than trying to clamp down on protest or to highlight difficulties, she quietly interacted with others and used policies and procedures to support the principles that underlie the university and its mission. This is an example of an individual of integrity upholding institutional integrity.

Other examples show individuals who bend principles or adjust policies and procedures for personal gain. Congresswoman Shirley Chisholm (D.NY) in her autobiography cited examples of fellow members of Congress who acted against their conscience for political gain. She was told repeatedly that she would be committing political suicide if she took a particular stand for something she believed in rather than going along with the majority. Her response was that ". . . if you decide to operate on the basis of your conscience, rather than your political advantage, you must be ready for the consequences and not complain when you suffer them."[16] She gained a reputation of being some-one who stood by her principles and her constituents and colleagues knew well what those were and respected her for them. They trusted her as they knew that she operated on principle on their behalf and put their needs above those of self-interest or of political party.

When an individual joins an organization, whether it is an individual re-sponsible for leading the organization or whether it is a new employee, it is important for that individual to know that there is a match between the values of the organization and personal values. Some organizations such as religious organizations are defined by their principles and those joining the organi-zation know at the outset if their principles and those of the organization are compatible. Individuals selecting a college or university to attend become aware of the ethos of the institution as they investigate programs and decide if there is a match. It is often the case that new employees are less attuned to the need to get a sense of the values and principles that influence the actions of an organization they might join.

Some organizations are very paternalistic and their actions appear to be motivated by an almost familial control. Others are new organizations excited about a new product or service and are not really interested in employees. Others see the public to which they provide services as opportunities for mak-ing money rather than as people deserving respect. General Electric is an excellent example of an organization that over the years has prided itself in sustaining both high performance and high integrity.[17] Not only does the CEO set an example, managers who do not adhere to the performance and integrity culture are fired. The company's norms and values are widely shared and the public informed of their actions. When individuals find themselves in organi-zations whose values are in conflict with their personal values, they have the choice of conforming to that set of principles and values, becoming an internal critic or whistleblower, or finding an organization in which they can thrive and still be true to who they are.

SUMMARY

Persons of integrity are honest, ethical, and do what they say they will do. They are loyal to their principles and ideas. They set the tone for the organiza-tion they lead. They refuse to engage in behavior that evades responsibility. Wise leaders know that any deviation from ethical behavior in the networked, information-rich world in which we live is very difficult and to the best of their ability they live lives of personal and professional integrity.

NOTES

1. Brigit Schyens and Tiffany Hansbrough, eds. *Where Leadership Goes Wrong: Destructive Leadership, Mistakes, and Ethical Failures* (Charlotte, NC: Information Age Publishers Inc., 2010), x.

2. Dawn L. Eubanks and Michael D. Mumford, "Destructive Leadership: The Role of the Cognitive Process," in *Where Leadership Goes Wrong: Destructive Leadership,*

Mistakes, and Ethical Failures, eds. Brigit Schyens and Tiffany Hansbrough (Charlotte, NC: Information Age Publishers Inc., 2010), 24.

3. Howard Gardner, "The Ethical Mind: A Conversation with Howard Gardner," *Harvard Business Review* 85, no. 3 (March 2007): 51–56.

4. Ibid.

5. Doris Kearns Goodwin, *Team of Rivals* (New York: Simon and Schuster, 2005).

6. Joseph L. Badaracco Jr., *Questions of Character: Illuminating the Heart of Leadership through Literature* (Boston: Harvard Business School Press, 2006), 139–61.

7. Ibid.

8. James M. Kouzes and Barry Z. Posner, *Credibility: How Leaders Gain and Lose It, Why People Demand It* (San Francisco: Jossey-Bass, 1993), 14.

9. Adam Bryant, "Looking Ahead behind the Ivy: The New Dean of Harvard Business School on Leadership and Character," *The Chronicle of Higher Education* LVII (July 24, 2011): 14–15.

10. Carl Cannon, "Untruth and Consequences," *The Atlantic* 299, no. 1 (January–February 2007): 100–108.

11. Ben J. Heineman, "Avoiding Integrity Landmines," *Harvard Business Review* 85, no. 4 (April 2007): 100–108.

12. Michael Bloomberg, *Bloomberg by Bloomberg* (Hoboken, NJ: John Wiley & Sons, 2001), 231.

13. *The American Heritage Dictionary of the English Language, 4th ed.* (Boston: Houghton Mifflin, 2000), 1395.

14. Ibid., 1358.

15. Ibid., 1398.

16. Shirley Chisholm, *Shirley Chisholm: Unbought and Unbossed* (Boston: Houghton Mifflin Harcourt, 1970).

17. Ben J. Heinemen Jr., "Avoiding Integrity Landmines," 100–108.

Chapter 8

Communication: Listening, Respecting

Communication focuses on the ways in which leaders assess the environment, transmit their vision, and interact with those reporting to them and others affected by their actions. It also focuses on the ways in which leaders use factors in the environment to assess their level of success. It is very easy to become immersed, bogged down, or overwhelmed by the sheer amount of research on communication and the number of books written about the topic. It is also difficult to separate communication from its relation to other aspects of leadership, such as the ways in which gender, age, and ethnic background affect how we communicate or how others communicate with us. Think of this chapter as a lens through which one can look at leadership, a focus that can bring to the fore the different elements of leadership. Snyder said that "as a principle of leadership, communication as an open system actively develops and nurtures interaction in order to create a culture that encourages and supports trust, facilitates organizational candor, and promotes cohesiveness."[1]

TRUE NORTH

Each leader represents a group, a cause, or an organization and leads others through the strength of their vision and their actions. To be successful, leaders must have a strong sense of self, a sense of who they are and what they believe, and must not be afraid to be who they are. Successful leaders follow a set of guiding principles, a true north, and these principles influence the kind of leader they are. They are enthusiastic, even passionate about their work and the causes they support, and exude positive energy as they move forward. Leaders have emotional intelligence. They know that leading effectively is less about mastering skill sets and situations and more about "developing a genuine interest in and talent for fostering positive feelings in the people whose cooperation and support you need."[2] Leaders also have social intelligence, "a set of interpersonal competencies built on specific neural circuits that inspire others to be effective."[3] Many very intelligent people are not always successful leaders and this may be because they are impatient with social conversation. Steve Jobs revolutionized our lives with his development of numerous path-breaking communication and computing tools; yet, while he was a genius, he lacked empathy and social skills and was often tone deaf as a leader. He did not meet the leadership standard to control his emotions and to be calm, thoughtful, and positive. His leadership was accepted despite his lack of interpersonal skills because his strengths in other areas were so strong. Barbara McClintock, a Nobel Prize winner in the sciences, was an excellent communicator via the written word and when she was discussing her work, but she was less successful with informal social conversation. As with Steve Jobs, her leadership was accepted because of the strength of her intellect and her accomplishments.

Leaders understand their work environment and are able to focus on what is important to advance common goals. They provide continuity and momentum. They are aware of the history of the organization, how it has developed, and how its history informs both present and future. In order to provide an environment in which individuals are confident and free to explore, leaders need to know what is going on in the workplace and deal with conflicts that may arise so that each individual has room to grow. They know that the legal contract as the basis of their working relationship only goes so far. They have tapped into the body of tacit information that, while unwritten, influences actions and relationships. Leaders owe people space to grow and to learn together as they collectively and individually work toward common goals.

Leaders are trustworthy. They have integrity and can be relied upon to stand behind their principles, to treat everyone fairly, to expect high-level performance, to both appreciate and respect others, and to lead by example. They know that there is a difference between principled leadership and managerial skill. They respect the organization and its goals, individuals within the organization, and themselves. They know what they are good at doing and those areas that are not their strength, and they are willing to discuss their strengths and weaknesses with others in order to build a team that matches their abilities and lack thereof with others in the team. Finally, leaders assess situations and learn what can be changed and what it is difficult or impossible to change. They have sufficient humility to deal with failure and know how to learn from it, and they have sufficient humor not to take themselves or their environment so seriously that they lose the passion for doing their best. The Welches, Jack who was the CEO of General Electric for 21 years and Suzy who was editor of *The Harvard Business Review*, said that all great leaders have one thing in common. They are authentic. "To quote the great philosopher, Popeye, you often hear authentic people give you some version of 'I yam what I yam, and that's all that I yam.' You know what we mean . . . they acknowledge without phoniness where they've come from and who they've become, both the good and the not so good, through life's accidents and their own hard work and ambition."[4] They do not bend their principles to avoid offending others and they are consistent in what they stand for. They are not afraid to say that they have made a mistake, are open about it, and then open about what they learned and how they recovered. Having principles, working hard, enjoying success, working back from failure, and doing so in pursuit of a vision are all part of being authentic and being a leader others can trust.

Life experiences have been a major factor in how they lead and how they communicate with others. Those achieving leadership positions who grew up in a stable environment and had families who provided for their needs and encouraged them to succeed come to leadership with a different set of expectations than those whose life experiences were different. Winston Churchill's story is an example of how an individual overcame early difficulties in order to succeed in life. It also shows the effect that early experiences have on ways of leading later in life. His parents, although they represented British aristocracy and American wealth, were remote and unresponsive leaving Winston emotionally insecure. He was dyslexic and therefore found school very difficult. To compensate for these difficulties, he became very ambitious and somewhat impulsive throughout his career. He always had to be braver and more accomplished than his peers. At an early age, he made a name for himself in the military and as a correspondent. After a number of years out of favor politically in England, he led his country through the agony of World War II and held them together with the force of his vision, his courage, and his abilities. Not everyone loved him but he was widely respected and he got the job done.

Fanny Lou Hamer, an early civil rights leader whose parents and siblings were field hands, knew firsthand what it meant to be poor, black, and a target of those wishing to attack her. She spent her life fighting for the rights of others and later in life, as the civil rights movement gained traction, she was able to look back on her early years and see that the poverty, abuse, and neglect had made her the strong leader that she was. Each individual who becomes a leader has a story and that story influences the leader's values and approach to leadership. Some learn how to be a successful leader while others whose experiences may have been difficult come to a leadership role without the requisite passion and understanding and perhaps with an attitude that "the world owes them."

Learning to be a leader is a priority of the military and young men and women who join the armed services are given opportunities to learn to be responsible for others and to test their leadership abilities at an early age. "They have a standard of leadership that is different from someone right out of college . . . they understand that it's not about them. They have a huge running start. They're smart. And they've already met a certain bar."[5]

ASKING, LISTENING, AND UNDERSTANDING

Asking

The first step in communication is for leaders to get the attention of their staff. The many competing sources of information and many demands often make it difficult to get someone's attention. Getting the attention of numerous individuals at once is even more difficult. The leader needs to help those in the organization focus on the vision and activities needed to achieve it. This can be done in the following manner:

- Focus on a few things when communicating, particularly those of greatest importance. For example, if a crisis looms or if major changes are being contemplated, focus on that.

- Resist scaring staff with threats or other negative information. This may be an attention getter, but such extreme measures should be used only when there is a real emergency and then only when absolutely necessary.

- Don't let distractions cause you to get off message. When you have the group's attention, stay on message and express it clearly.

- Keep others engaged in what you are doing.

- Personalize your interactions with others. Focus on specific individual contributions and needs and let others know you are aware of what they are doing.

The leader communicates (listens with a purpose) both formally and informally. Formal communication provides a way

- To present statements of vision and related formal directives in written form

- To discuss issues in a formal setting with others in the organization and external to the organization

- To teach. Teaching is not always seen as a means of formal communication, but when the leader wants to inform others at length about vision, direction, or changes in direction, it may take the form of a seminar, a formal presentation, or the invitation of an expert to discuss issues.

In these contexts the leader does the following: assesses the environment, assesses how the leader's vision connects with the environment and, if changes are needed, teaches others what they need to know in order to move toward accomplishing the vision, and is able to learn from others what they know and can contribute. In this context, leaders have the opportunity to assess how others view their success as leaders and how clearly the vision has been projected. It provides an opportunity to clarify statements or actions so that everyone understands the situation and the direction.

What do leaders do when there is disagreement? The leader may ask for understanding and "When leaders ask for understanding, they cede power to others instead of asserting their own authority, they encourage others to trust in others, and they indicate their strength and confidence by acting with modesty and humility."[6] This is often the beginning of discussions that lead to finding common ground. In looking for common ground, ask those involved in the discussion how they see the situation differently because of gender, age, ethnic, political, or other perspectives. If they are part of the same organization, there should be a degree of common experience and support of the vision on which the organization is based and this common ground is then enriched by diverse perspectives. It is rare that within an organization there are major disagreements on basic issues and values. More often the disagreement is on tactics. The leader can use disagreements as an opportunity to help others think about an issue differently and act differently. If agreement is difficult to reach, the leader never blames someone or something else for the problem. It is the leader's role to lead, not to complain or find excuses. The leader also knows when it is time to stop talking about an issue and to make a decision, and it is the leader's role to make the decision and move forward after having heard the concerns of others who are involved.

Listening and Understanding

Listening requires patience and respect for the speaker as well as acknowledgment of the message. Leaders need to listen to each person who has something to say, not just those who are in agreement with the leader's perspective. Individuals with different perspectives, for example, ethnic, gender, economic, or political, are often those who can contribute valuable and different insights. Individuals need to know that they have been heard. This shows that the leader values and respects the input of the speaker. If the leader wants to get honest feedback, the leader needs to listen actively and to respond to what has been heard. When the leader only wants affirmation for current activities and decisions and discounts anything that is in conflict with that, the most important means of knowing what is really going on will quickly shut down. President Lyndon B. Johnson was an expert at soliciting the opinions of others. However, as time went on he tended not to include those with views contrary to his own in the group of individuals to whom he listened. This began to limit the range of views, ideas, and opinions to which he listened and damaged his decision making. As president, he no longer followed his earlier emphasis on listening to all sides of an issue and this impacted his ability to lead.

Different members of the community often have different ways of presenting their views. Men and women often have differing conversational styles and some women may sound tentative in their contribution by prefacing their remarks with a phrase such as "I was wondering if . . . " rather than saying "Here's what I think . . . ." Depending on the sensitivity of the leader, the more tentative approach may be dismissed as the statement of an unsure individual rather than a turn of phrase.[7] Men often tend to talk over or past one another and not listen to the contributions of others, which is a form of bullying and a way of announcing that the other person's contribution is not worth the group's attention. Grace Hopper, an early leader in the development of computing, was the rare female leader in an overwhelmingly male world. She learned to communicate her ideas and the reasons for her actions using the language of senior managers and in this way was able to be heard. Because of her ability to listen and to understand the language of different disciplines and groups, she was able to lead quietly and persuasively.

Individuals from other cultures may not come directly to the point as quickly as is common in the United States as to them, the direct approach may seem disrespectful. Leaders need to listen not just to what is said but also to how it is said and who says it and to sort out what truly contributes to the discussion. When a leader welcomes those from another culture by saying a few words in their language, this indicates respect and a desire to connect. It was often noted by individuals from other cultures that President Obama would speak a few words of welcome in the language of his hosts when he visited their country or when he was hosting them at the White House. This created an environment in which important conversations could begin.

When one watches news and opinion programs on TV, it is common to hear each guest and the moderator talking at once. To the viewer, this means that they are not interested in what the other person is saying and are only interested in expressing their own opinion more loudly than other participants. At the end of the program, few ideas have been stated clearly as each individual has been trying to drown out the others. In addition to wasting everyone's time, it is highly disrespectful to interrupt, talk over, or talk past others. While this type of bullying may be acceptable in the entertainment world, it doesn't work in the real world. In an organization, a team, the leader needs to take control, ask each individual to speak while others listen, give each individual an opportunity to talk, and then together they can sort out the positive aspects of the discussion and propose next steps. It is the responsibility of the leader to sift out those aspects of the discussion that are valuable contributions to the discussion and to use those contributions to inform future action.

MOVING FORWARD

Setting Expectations

The most important task of the leader is to have a vision and to articulate, communicate, and enforce it. The leader is clear and direct in describing the vision and in setting expectations. The leader does not suggest what the vision might be nor does the leader hint around or hedge the truth. The vision and what is to be done is stated clearly and often. There is a long-term view of the vision and short-term tasks to be accomplished to move forward. The leader makes it clear that everyone is important and brings value to the table and everyone is expected to perform at a high level and to contribute to meeting expectations. Failures will occur and so long as they are learning experiences that move the team a step or two toward success, they are not to be feared.

In order to assure that the vision has been clearly communicated, it is helpful to ask the following questions. What is the context? Why is the vision important? Whose life are we improving by carrying out the vision? Why are we the ones who are going to do the work? What do we hope to achieve and is it doable? How will we measure progress? When will we finish? Each individual on the team will be part of expectation-setting meetings, each will bring different personal answers to these questions, and each will bring different skills and abilities. It is important at the outset to develop a common understanding of purpose and of the direction in which the group is going.

Cesar Chavez, a farm worker in California, was concerned about the poor treatment and low wages of his fellow farm workers and wanted to organize them into a union that would represent them and fight for fair treatment.

Most of the farm workers had had bad experiences when they tried to organize before to improve their working conditions; and they were fearful that if they were too vocal, they would lose their jobs. Few farm workers could afford to pay union dues that would be needed for initial startup costs. Chavez met one-on-one with the farm workers telling them that this was no easy task, but if they were successful, they would be able to improve their lives. Chavez treated each individual with respect and showed them how important their participation would be. His unflagging efforts received national attention and, with the help of many farm workers, those efforts resulted in the creation of the National Farm Worker's Association. While this is a very straightforward example of a need, a vision, work toward a vision, a measure of progress and success, it includes those elements necessary to achieving the mission and the communication necessary for success.

Setting Direction

Even though the leader sets the direction and has clearly stated what the organization is expected to achieve, each individual processes the information in a slightly different way depending upon individual perspectives and experiences and may well arrive at different assumptions about the vision and how they are to contribute. It is essential that the leader make certain that everyone has the same understanding of the vision and is on the same page when it comes to how they are expected to contribute. Otherwise they will be working at cross purposes and not achieve at the desired level.

While the overarching responsibility of the leader and the organization is to develop and pursue the vision that guides organizational activities and the vision is a constant, the ways in which the vision is pursued is always a work in progress as environmental factors change, as different individuals become involved, and as needs and interests change. Regular discussion about strategies to move forward is an important component of being sure that the organization is vital and responsive to society's needs and interests and that the members of the organization are continuing to work together and have not veered off course. Open and honest discussion of issues is essential. In a healthy organization, everyone has the opportunity to be heard. Each individual has special perspectives and skills that contribute to the discussion and to direction-setting and everyone should be given the opportunity to lead in some way so long as activities are focused on the vision and working toward it.

It is the role of the leader to hear all contributions and then take ownership of the discussion and make a decision. Martin Luther King said that a genuine leader is not a searcher for consensus but a molder of consensus. King said that while a majority of African Americans might prefer violence as a strategy, he would reject it in favor of nonviolence and provide an explanation of his actions. If the majority recommends a course of action that the leader's principles reject, the leader should then show them the way to go. Ultimately, the leader is responsible for the actions of the group and with this responsibility goes the need to make the right decisions even if they may be unpopular.

Uncommunicative Leaders

Not all leaders are successful at communicating their vision and in setting direction. This may be because they are uncertain in their role as leader. They may have been hired for a position they are not prepared to fill or their existing position may have been changed to include new responsibilities that are not within the leader's expertise. A new leader may need time to learn what is expected both from staff and from those to whom the leader reports. While the individual stepping into a new leadership position needs time to learn about the new organization, new responsibilities, and how they fit into the new organization, in most cases the learning curve is very short and the leader needs to be in charge from day one. One needs to be a very fast learner and not make too many missteps. This is where communicating who you are, what your values are, what you are good at and not good at, and what you expect from the organization demonstrate your leadership skills.

Sometimes leaders give a promising employee new and different tasks as a way of grooming that individual for a leadership role but don't tell the individual that this is the case. The individual who is personally secure and likes a challenge will thrive while the less experienced individual may feel inadequate to the challenge and not know what to do. If this new challenge is very general and the individual has to develop a new activity but is given little or no direction even when asked, the individual may not make all the best choices when communicating with those with whom they work. As the individual becomes more assured with new tasks and builds a new team or works with the existing team in new ways, communication skills and confidence will grow. Leaders who are testing potential leaders need to provide sufficient guidance and support to potential leaders so that they can make the most of their opportunity.

Some individuals who have been placed in leadership roles lack the skills and abilities to serve in that role. They may be political appointees or a family member or other individual whose connections and patrons outweigh ability and experience. They give orders or delegate responsibilities that may be incomplete, inconsistent, or unintelligible and then complain when members of the team do not produce the expected result. When directions are unclear, it is impossible for staff members to know what is expected. They would be able to get the job done, if they knew what the job was. This type of leader rarely answers questions, is never satisfied with results, and blames others for lack of success. Such leaders may overcompensate for their lack of understanding of the job by micromanaging those aspects of the job they do understand.

The poor leader may lack the skills and abilities to lead and is uncertain in the role. The poor leader may not want to lead and is doing as little as possible hoping to be removed. The poor leader may have a passive-aggressive personality and gives impossible or conflicting instructions, refuses to answer questions, and is always dissatisfied with the results. Such leaders tend never to write things down as it would provide a record of expectations and then they say they forgot what they wanted. One intern who was assigned to this type of nonleader complained of being nothing but a gofer and of learning little or nothing about the organization and its activities. This complaint resulted in a poor recommendation to the sponsor who was told that the intern had a "bad attitude." Poor leaders tend to be insecure, inarticulate, and unsure of expectations. As they report to their superiors, they may present a different face and blame their staff for work not done or done poorly. Good leaders understand their role, support the organization and its members in achieving goals, and provide constructive and positive feedback to those for whom they are responsible.

ASSESSING PROGRESS

As one climbs up the ladder, there are fewer and fewer sources of honest feedback available to the leader, and the leader needs to be in a continuous self-assessment mode.[8] In your leadership role, it is important to ask yourself: How often do I communicate my vision and priorities so that those following me know what I am up to? As a leader, do I give regular feedback, am I good under pressure, and does my leadership style reflect who I am or have I become too tentative or too politically correct? Spending too little time and effort examining how well one communicates the vision creates problems throughout the organization the leader is committed to serve.

President Lyndon B. Johnson relied on the opinions and interpretations of his advisors as a way of assessing how well he was doing but because of his difficulty in accepting criticism, relatively few of those who advised him dared tell him the truth. He wanted affirmation, not honest statements. So long as he was making progress on his agenda, he would accept mild criticism but when problems arose, he wanted affirmation, not honesty. He knew his failings but didn't want others to suggest he change direction. Because of his bombast and unwillingness to accept advice, many advisors either remained silent or resigned. President John Adams relied heavily on the wisdom of his wife, Abigail, who was able to soften his often loud and brusque manner that could get in the way of his ability to communicate his ideas and wishes. He had a habit of expressing his opinions and could become quite heated in debates. Throughout their lives, they functioned as a very successful team, he holding center stage and she providing the human touch. She was a source of strength for him during his often rocky political career, and they were among the first husband-and-wife political teams in American history.

Leaders are under constant scrutiny by someone: staff, those who benefit from the activities of the organization, the media, friends, and colleagues. Leaders need to find means by which they can assess their progress toward stated goals. In some situations there is an annual performance review by a board or individual to whom the leader is responsible. In others there is no real place or position to whom the leader reports. In either case, leaders must have individuals whom they can trust to tell the truth about the current perception of the vision, their accomplishments, and their leadership style. This type of assessment is informal and continuous. The most difficult type of assessment is personal; am I too harsh, have I lost direction due to personal difficulties, am I beginning to believe my press releases? Having good and trusted friends who will respond to the difficult questions prevents the leader from becoming isolated and from veering too far off track.

When it comes to being sure that the vision is on target, that external variables are identified, and that a new way of organizing staff responsibilities to accomplish tasks more efficiently is in place if necessary, professional seminars, leadership retreats, and other meetings of leaders who can share experience and expertise are useful. Comparing one's performance to that of leaders in similar or more responsible circumstances is a good means of self-assessment. "Leaders gain the strength that matters [quiet confidence and assurance] by meeting hard challenges and learning about themselves and leadership from the challenges."[9]

In addition to self-assessment, the leader is responsible for assessing how well the organization is moving forward and if changes in strategy, in assignments, in resource allocation need to be made. Group discussions that evaluate progress are useful in that individuals can bring problem areas to the fore and as a team find ways to solve them. Discussions with individuals may be necessary when a team member needs additional support in carrying out assignments or when that individual is not meeting expectations. The leader has certain expectations of staff members that need to be met if progress is to be made. It is important that leaders have available staff members who are involved, are willing to speak out and are comfortable in doing so. They do not require constant supervision but are self-directed in pursuit of organizational goals. They stay current with tasks at hand, anticipate potential problems, and fix problems when they arise. In return, the staff expects clarity of direction, frequent and specific feedback, and accessibility, honesty and candor from the leader.[10]

Transparency

Transparency, defined as sending light so that images can be seen as if there was no intervening material, can also be defined as the condition of being open and honest, guileless, and having nothing to hide. Transparency is tied to trust. If an organization has nothing to hide, it should want to discuss its vision, its goals, objectives, and operations with the public it serves. While at one time organizations and their leaders held power in part because they had information no one else had, information today is much more widely available and relatively little information can be kept confidential. Those limitations or aspects of the organization that by law or because of necessary confidentiality of records cannot be shared with the public are known by both the news media and informed members of the public; however, both have expectations that all other information is available to them.

In today's world, responsible organizations seek public approval by sharing some of their information, particularly that which supports decision making. Because there have been numerous examples of lack of transparency within government, within the business world, and within our political structure, the public has lost confidence in much of what they are told. In discussing the importance of candor, O'Toole and Bennis said that "we won't be able to rebuild trust in institutions until leaders learn how to communicate honestly . . . and create organizations where that's the norm . . . Honesty is the first step but true transparency like a healthy balance sheet, requires ongoing effort, sustained attention, and constant vigilance."[11]

It is also important that, within the organization, the leader creates a culture of transparency in which everyone knows what the organization is about and what their role is. Transparency starts with everyone having an accurate and up-to-date description of their position, its responsibilities, and how it is evaluated. Transparency carries on throughout the organization with a statement of vision and purpose and of who will benefit from the organization's activities. When something goes wrong, leaders are expected to take responsibility, to explain what went wrong and why, and to fix it. The leader meets frequently with staff to discuss ongoing progress, identify problems, and propose solutions. There should be no surprises.

Communications are clear and as complete as is possible. If a topic cannot be explained briefly, simply, and clearly there is the suspicion that the leader is incompetent or is trying to hide something. While relatively few situations are so simple that they can be explained simply, an effort to do so may clarify the situation for those inside and outside the organization. If one clearly states the organization's objectives, who is funding it, how it operates, and how it is evaluated, the public will have a better understanding of the organization's purpose and value. Transparency has become an important watchword in the media, and leaders are responsible for shaping the message both internally and externally. In a world of instant communication, leaders need to respond responsibly, accurately, and immediately to issues that may affect the organization, its members and its mission and do so as fully as possible. Numerous examples of organizations show that they immediately reported a problem. For example, an automobile company recalled a particular vehicle because a problem had been discovered in the design. The company apologized to those affected, indicated how the problem would be fixed, and fixed it at no cost to the owner. We also have examples of an organization that tried to hide a problem by stalling for time and perhaps providing incomplete or inaccurate information. BP tried to minimize the extent of the oil spill in the Gulf of Mexico in 2010 and then, when it could no longer hide the problem, it grudgingly provided as little information as possible. Once containing the spill became a national issue, the media kept the public informed as efforts were made to contain the damage. The media continued to report on the problem as BP worked to restore the environment and reimburse those whose livelihoods were destroyed by the destruction caused by the oil spill. Trying to hide information in a networked world is rarely successful, and those who try to hide it through obfuscation pay dearly in public support and public trust.

NETWORKING

Networking occurs within the organization, among organizations, and with society at large. It has been called the nervous system that informs activities at every level. Networking begins with individuals who interact with a small group with whom they have a common interest and grows to include larger and larger groups. Networking is built through relationships, one-to-one interactions. For many, networking begins during the early years of their career and builds as they have different opportunities and experiences and as they look for expertise in new areas. Networking at its most basic and most important level is personal. Leaders network by walking around to chat with those in the organization to see what they are doing and if they need something. It is a very important means of identifying needs and problems before they get too large for an easy fix. Leading by walking around is not only a wise way to learn what is really going on but the personal attention given to staff members at every level is greatly appreciated as it says that the leader is interested in them and how they contribute to the overall success of the organization.

Leaders network with their counterparts in similar organizations to learn what they are doing, to find areas of common interest, to cooperate when appropriate, and to get to know what the competition is. Leaders reach out to the media in order to build an image of the organization and its activities and to become known by members of the media in case a crisis occurs and there is need to contact the media to discuss it. Networking with the media also provides an opportunity to make available news items that describe the organization and its vision and would be of interest to the public, and enhance the organization's image in the community.

In the age of the Internet, networking has exploded and it is possible to communicate anywhere, anytime, with anyone we wish. No longer are we limited to communicating face-to-face, by letter, by telephone; now we can belong to online networks that bring individuals together in many ways. Intranets within an organization allow for much closer communication among team members and within the organization. Professional networks provide both the leader and the members of the team immediate access to individuals and information that can assist in problem solving and in making connections. Networking is a means of expanding the organization's vision. It is a powerful tool for the leader who uses it and in today's networked world, nearly everyone uses it.

Despite the ubiquity of online networks and social media, many leaders continue to appreciate the fact that the best interaction is face-to-face and by phone as these interactions are personal and for some things, personal contact still trumps other interactions. For example, when there is disagreement on an issue it is often more difficult to retract a written statement than a verbal statement. It is much easier to discuss an area of disagreement than to go back and forth with written messages.

SUMMARY

Communication is the way in which leaders keep the organization healthy and on track as it works to fulfill its vision, its goals and objectives. "The key [to a successful organization] is to create an environment where people can thrive without unnecessary dysfunction, confusion, and politics. This requires a cohesive team . . . clarity, communication, and reinforcement through human systems."[12] When Doris Kearns Goodwin, author of *Team of Rivals*, a collective biography of Lincoln and his Cabinet, was interviewed about Lincoln's leadership skills, she highlighted the following:

- Include your able rivals on your team as they will provide different perspectives and are confident of their skills and are not afraid to take issue with the leader.

- Not only is it important for leaders to surround themselves with people who are unafraid to challenge the leader's ideas, it is also important to include those with temperaments different from the leader. Lincoln, who was often too kind to punish subordinates, benefitted from Stanton's more hard-nosed approach.

- Leaders must both share credit for success and responsibility for failures.

- Leaders must connect with the larger public as did Franklin D. Roosevelt with the radio broadcasts of his Fireside Chats and Barack Obama with his weekly television program.[13]

In looking at Lincoln as a leader, Goodwin said that he had "an extraordinary amount of emotional intelligence. He was able to acknowledge his errors and learn from his mistakes to a remarkable degree. He was careful to put past hurts behind him and never allow wounds to fester."[14] He was able to communicate with many individuals and groups; treated everyone with grace and humility; never lost his sense of where he was going or what was important although the environment changed almost daily; and took responsibility for his decisions. He continues to be a role model.

NOTES

1. Kirk Snyder, *The G Quotient: Why Gay Executives Are Excelling as Leaders and What Every Manager Needs to Know* (San Francisco: Jossey-Bass, 2006), xxx.

2. David Goleman and Richard Boyatzes, "Social Intelligence and the Biology of Leadership," *Harvard Business Review* 86, no. 9 (September 2008): 75.

3. Ibid.

4. Jack and Suzy Welch, "What Do Great Leaders Have in Common? They're Authentic," *Fortune* 165, no. 5 (April 9, 2012): 58.

5. Adam Lashinsky, "How Amazon Learned to Live Veterans," *Fortune* 165, no. 7 (May 21, 2012): 219.

6. Joseph Badaracco Jr., *Questions of Character: Illuminating the Heart of Leadership through Literature* (Boston: Harvard Business School Press, 2006), 154.

7. Deborah Tannen, "The Power of Talk: Who Gets Heard and Why," *Harvard Business Review* 73, no.5 (September/October 1995): 138–48.

8. Robert Kaplan, "What to Ask the Person in the Mirror?" *Harvard Business Review* 85, no. 1 (January 2007): 86–95.

9. Badaracco, p. 195.

10. James O'Toole and Warren Bennis, "What's Needed Is a Culture of Candor," *Harvard Business Review* 87, no. 6 (June 2009): 54.

11. Ibid.

12. Patrick Leonconi, "Leadership Attitude Adjustment," in Issie Lapowski "Strategy, Tactics, Tactics, Trends, Politics," *INC* 34, no. 3 (April 2012): 104.

13. Doris Kearns Goodwin, "Leadership Lessons from Abraham Lincoln," *Harvard Business Review* 87, no. 4 (April 2009), 43–47.

14. Ibid.

Chapter 9

Leadership and Social Networking

In the past decade, the speed with which communication and information technology innovation has become part of our work life and personal life has changed many of the ways in which we interact with one another. It has been estimated that one in eight individuals on the planet is connected to Facebook and that by 2016, three billion people, which is half the world's population, will be online.[1] Numerous special purpose networks exist that connect professionals who have common interests, that help individuals manage their careers, and that help one find a romantic partner, provide opportunities for participation in games online or to build social groups centering around a hobby or interest. Being connected through the Internet and social media fills many hours in the day of countless individuals who might have socialized face-to-face in earlier days. Social networking continues to grow and to absorb many hours of time for millions of people both for work and pleasure. Social media also has demonstrated value in the workplace as a means of bringing people together within an organization, with other organizations, and with those served by the organizations with the objective of adding voices to the discussion of the purpose of the organization, the products and services it provides or should provide, and the level of satisfaction of those who use the products and services. In the political arena, discourse has expanded from the powerful few to those in the street who are making it increasingly difficult to be ignored. Social networking democratizes the playing field so that anyone with online access can participate in many interactions. The downside to this is that not all of the interactions are thoughtful and fact-based.

USES OF SOCIAL NETWORKING

The major uses of social media include networking, internally and externally, provision of communal services, and advocacy. Social networking is in a state of change and how it may be described at one time is out-of-date nearly as soon as it is in print. However, it is possible to identify some trends and directions that can help us understand this virtual world, the directions in which it is moving, and implications for our work life. Since 2001, social media has changed and its uses have expanded to include the following trends:

- More social media content
- More access to Facebook or other personal content
- More important connections in the business and academic worlds
- More confusion as search and monitoring tools disappear and are replaced by new ones

It has been found that social networking tools are particularly useful in certain types of research relative to the needs of leading an organization, particularly because they can keep this research current by providing a continuous stream of new information. They can be used for the following:

- *Public relations and communication.* Immediate reaction to announcements, activities and the like, making it possible to monitor the impact of your efforts on a real-time basis.
- *Technical updates.* Applying technical tools to specific problems providing a value-added component. Having access to the entire body of information relating to the tools allows technologists to be limited only by their imagination and ability to locate the enabling information.
- *Competitive intelligence.* Determining how you are doing in relation to others in terms of the successful use of your products and services.
- *Reputation management.* Anticipating a crisis, identifying it, and fixing it before a situation deteriorates.
- *Product and service brand management.* Learning quickly what people like or dislike about your organization and its products and services.
- *Marketing.* Using social media, marketing is often called "word of mouth on steroids."[2]

Leaders may incorporate one or more of these social media uses into their activities in order to increase productivity and to have an enhanced awareness of how their products and services are liked or disliked by those they serve or wish to serve.

Networking

Networking is the key to individual and organizational success both internally and externally. It "helps . . . gain influence . . . broaden expertise . . . learn new skills, and find purpose and balance. [It has been determined that] executives who consistently rank in the top 20% of their companies in both performance and wellbeing have diverse but select networks . . . made up of high quality people who come from several spheres and from up and down in the corporate hierarchy." These top performers participate in "six critical kinds of connections, which enhance their careers and lives in a variety of ways."[3] To network successfully, one needs to have a small set of core contacts, those you really rely on and who successfully connect the many aspects of your work in a balanced way and serve as models for positive behavior. Some of these networks were built long before what we now call social networking appeared and each now has a virtual component that has expanded the possibilities well beyond the earlier face-to-face connections. These six networks are as follows:

- People who can offer new information and expertise
- People in formal and informal power positions who can mentor, guide, help to coordinate
- People who can challenge decisions in order to improve them
- People who give personal support
- People who provide a sense of purpose
- People who promote a work and life balance[4]

Internal Networking

Leaders are gradually becoming aware of the possibilities of social media as a means of enhancing collaboration within their organization and of supporting an innovative environment. They have come to understand that while technology provides the vehicle for more and richer collaboration, it is the individuals themselves who make things work. Some leaders have been quick to see the benefits of social media while others are reluctant to expand their communication networks too rapidly. Bradley and McDowell[5] identified six basic categories into which leader's attitudes toward social media fall:

- *Folly.* Leaders with this attitude see social media solely as a source of entertainment with no business value and they tend to ignore it. The leader can be convinced of its value only if it can be shown that it can provide a specific strategy that is of benefit to the organization.
- *Fearful.* These leaders see social media as "a threat to productivity, intellectual capital, privacy, managerial authority, regularity compliance. . . ."[6] They may discourage or prohibit its use which stifles or eliminates any benefits social media may have for the organization.
- *Flippant.* These leaders don't take social media seriously and if they use it, they see it as a technology-centered activity where the organization "provides access to social media and hopes that . . . value will spontaneously emerge." They don't see the possibility that social media can be a way to "catalyze and mobilize communities of people to act in a way that delivers value to the community and the organization."[7]
- *Formulating.* These leaders recognize its potential value so long as its use is organized and focused on specific strategies that add value to the organization.
- *Forging.* Here the entire organization is developing competence in the use of social media "to assemble, nurture, and gain business value from communities . . . they should also promote additional grassroots

social media efforts as critical in becoming a highly collaborative social organization."[8]

- *Fusing.* This type of leader "treats community collaboration as an integral part of the organization's work, ingrained in how people think and behave . . . this is a description of a social organization," and the basis of organizational strength.[9]

Bradley and McDowell's analysis indicated that most leaders of organizations had not progressed beyond the formulating stage and therefore had not achieved much success in using social media as a leadership strategy. The level of acceptance is to a large degree dependent on the age of those involved in that those who have grown up in a world that accepts social media as the next good thing welcome the possibilities while those whose careers predated the online era are less accepting of the potential social media offers. Wilson et al. went a step further in assessing progress in the workplace by analyzing the strategies and practices of more than 1,000 companies worldwide and conducted interviews with "70 executives who were leading social media initiatives."[10] They identified four distinct strategies being used to bring social media into the workplace.

Productive practitioners identify a specific area and develop a program that would enhance the organization's activities such as the development of a website to bring customers and providers together to brainstorm. This is an activity with stated objectives and measurable goals. Creative experimenters go a step further and embrace uncertainty by "using small scale tests to improve discrete functions and practices." They take advantage of social media by listening to customers and employees who communicate on platforms such as Twitter and Facebook. They also mine internal social networks to gain a better understanding of organizational strengths and issues. One experiment was to identify expertise within the organization that could be tapped rather than hiring outside experts to do what could already be done internally. Social media champions build large initiatives designed for predictable results that will have a major impact on the organization; and the final strategy, social media transformers, facilitate the use of internal and external collaboration to identify emerging trends and thus move the organization forward. The four strategies allow the leader to start small and gradually move to a more sophisticated use of social media.

Social Networking among Organizations

Social media provides an opportunity for continuing dialog among those who have common interests regardless of where they live and work. A role of the leader is to be a global connector by being tied to different social worlds and by connecting the organization to those worlds. This includes the need to cede a level of control in order to enable and empower those in the organization to seek out the wealth of views that enhance and challenge the organization. Beginning at the top of the organization, the leader collaborates with other organizations and builds bridges between and among people in order to share ideas. The leader also has the responsibility to devise teams represent-ing many ideas and approaches and organizations and to manage these teams so that there is a steady stream of new ideas to challenge the organization. "Left to their own devices, people will choose to collaborate with others they know well—which can be deadly for innovation,"[11] so it is important to lead in an environment in which change is the constant.

When collaboration is focused on working together to develop new ways of doing things, when it is devoid of political games and turf battles, when there is diversity in the membership, and when new team members are added on a regular basis, one has the recipe for innovation and communication at its very best. With the assistance of social networking, a collaborative approach to leading is replacing the old command-and-control way of leading and it brings together individuals and groups with diverse abilities and experiences to work on common problems. It fits well within the ways in which the Internet gen-eration has grown to want to function as it provides the opportunity for work-ing together and contributing to common objectives. The successful leader guides but does not dictate. Networking across organizational lines enlarges the pool of individuals who can offer new information and expertise and who can challenge decisions in order to improve them. It also provides individuals a wider opportunity to find mentors with whom they can develop a successful relationship.

Social networking is also a very inexpensive and productive means of learn-ing about those the organization serves. It is a means of getting feedback about the success of the product or service provided which can be used to improve the product or service and to develop new products or services where there is a gap. It is also a way of accessing demographic information on those being served and using this information to develop new products and services that potential users would enjoy. Social networking is also a way for professional societies to get closer to their membership, learn what their interests are, how they are changing, and how to respond to evolving needs and interests.

Control of Social Networks

Those who use social networks in the workplace as a means of enhancing communication, sharing ideas and concerns, and keeping up-to-date on the progress of group initiatives and organizational information need to have ac-ceptable guidelines for participation and follow them. The guidelines include the necessity of separating work life and social life activities so that there is no overlap, being careful not to divulge internal organizational information that is private, not to divulge personal private information, and not to use infor-mation for personal advantage. Legal implications arise when certain types of confidential information find their way into the networks. Everything an indi-vidual enters into a discussion can be used as evidence. Disclosing company secrets, speaking improperly about or to a colleague, sending inappropriate documents all become part of the archival record and it almost never goes away. Once information is recorded in some way, there is no getting it back. It is important that social networking be used in an environment of trust; trust that participants can speak candidly and respectfully and not be penalized for unpopular comments, trust that personality conflicts will not drown out an individual's comments, and trust that there is a level of confidentiality in that sensitive conversations within the organization will not be broadcast more widely. However, one should have the expectation that all content is potentially public.

A side effect of online discussion is employee turnover. Online contributors whose comments are exceptionally thoughtful can become the targets of recruiters. From the employee's perspective it is in their best interest to put their ideas forward in this way in order to enhance their own career prospects. Given that many organizations have reorganized, downsized, and otherwise changed the workforce, this is a way in which individuals can have some control over their future. Judicious use of social networks by leaders and an awareness of its pitfalls provide information about the organization and the external world that will enhance the organization's goals and objectives.

Several colleges and universities have developed policies for the use of social networking and others are in the process of doing so. Ball State University's policy includes the statement that privacy does not exist in the world of social media. It is also recognized that "social media sites 'blur the lines between personal voice and institutional voice.'" When an individual uses a university or a business website, that individual speaks for the university or the business regardless of the intention of the speaker. Great care needs to be taken to avoid situations in which a personal comment inadvertently is assumed to be an institutional statement.

Networking within the organization is also an excellent way to bring the top tier of the organization closer to the workforce by developing "a Facebook inspired app for companies that allows users to keep track of their colleagues and customers and share information and ideas."[12] Such an internal network does not mean that the leader is creating a democracy or a consensus because the organizational culture is one of meritocracy, not democracy. What the internal network does is to provide an opportunity for discussion and for the expression of different viewpoints. While the leader welcomes different ideas and different perspectives, the leader still has the responsibility to make the decisions.

External Networks

While social networking within the organization or among organizations is determined by leaders in the organizations involved, social networking in the world outside traditional organizations is very fluid and anyone can put forth an idea or plan and find others who agree. Anyone with access to the Internet can state an idea, encourage action, and monitor that action in real time. Social networking outside traditional organizations has become a new tool for those protesting unjust societies. Tom Friedman, an expert on the Middle East, author, and *New York Times* correspondent, said that "the main driver in the Arab Spring was the combination of globalization and the information technology revolution. Social networking is democratizing weak states and individuals are becoming super powered as they now have a voice and a platform." He went on to say that "the days of leading countries or companies via a one way conversation are over."[13] Dov Seidman, author of the book *How: Why HOW We Do Anything Means Everything*, said that "command and control is being replaced by connect and collaborate." We now need to have a two-way conversation and "as power shifts to individuals . . . leadership itself must shift to that . . . the role of the leader now is to get the best of what is coming up from below and then meld it with a vision from above."[14]

In many countries, movements have arisen which enable people to declare their "freedom from" and they need to take the next step to determine how to use this freedom to move forward in a positive way. With the help of social networking, centuries of control over those without power are coming to an end as anyone with computer access can be heard, can join a movement or lead one, and can act. An example of this was the attack on the Taj Mahal Palace hotel in Mumbai, India, in November 2008. The leaders of this attack used high-tech tools, from Google Earth 3-D maps of the target to Blackberries, satellite phones, and GSM handsets to carry out their plans.

2011 was the year of the Arab Spring in which several governments in the Arab world—Tunisia, Egypt, Libya—found themselves in unexpected situations. Flad Teichberg, cofounder of Global Revolution, said, "All of a sudden, a bunch of young people [in Egypt] using social media were able to mobilize not just 500 or 5,000 people but 50,000 people . . . They inspired us with their courage and techniques."[15] Social networking has become a new tool for those protesting unjust societies. Not only is it possible to announce gatherings and protests widely, it is also possible to maintain contact with those who are protesting in real time. Mobile teams can provide a live stream of information on a designated website and thus control the narrative not just for local consumption but for the world. Police brutality demonstrated by their use of pepper spray, firing on unarmed citizens, and other actions ordered by those in power are no longer rumored; if they actually occurred they were seen as they happened. The leader(s) of the protest could be nearby or far away in a place where those whose activities they were protesting could not locate them. Despite efforts by the Egyptian government to shut down communication by shutting off the Internet and mobile phones, a great deal of information about the uprising leaked out of the country to the extent that it was impossible for the United States and other countries to ignore the extent of what was occurring. What social networking did was to provide so much information that instead of a gradual shift of support from the Mubarak regime to the protesters, the process was much faster. The downside of so much information so fast is that those receiving the information lack time to process the information and to understand its true meaning. This leads to confusion in the decision-making process, and the possibility of unwise responses to information available at the time may not be the full story. The opportunity for international misunderstanding is greatly expanded.

After the downfall of Libya's dictator, the U.S. State Department began "creating a twenty first century structure for a world where social media and instant communication have empowered people relative to their rulers."[16] While traditionalists in the State Department were reluctant to see social media as a powerful tool, it has become an important way to use soft power and to reach many organizations and individuals in a country, not just the elite. Social media "takes diplomacy out of capitals, out of government offices, into the media, into the streets of countries . . . because given social media, given the pervasion of new communication technologies everywhere, no leader is any longer able to ignore his people."[17]

The next very public use of social networking to lead a movement was the "Occupy Wall Street" activity that was, to an extent, patterned after the experience of Egypt earlier in the year in terms of what worked and what didn't work. Chafkin who had conducted an oral history of the movement and interviewed several occupiers found that "the amazing thing about the Occupy Wall Street movement is not that it started, but that it worked."[18] Initially it was a vague idea with no formal leadership structure and almost no budget. Despite this, it inspired similar protests worldwide. Srdja Popovic, founder of the Centre for Applied Non Violent Action and Strategies (CANVAS), worked with people from 46 countries. Graduates of Popovic's program included organizers of the successful movements in Georgia, Lebanon, Egypt, and the Maldives and they said that for "the Occupy Wall Street movement to succeed, had to make sure it got three things exactly right: a clear vision of tomorrow, a clear plan for pursuing that vision, and a clear understanding that whatever happens in New York or Boston or Denver is connected to a larger global movement that stretches from the alleyways of Cairo to the beaches of the Maldives."[19] The next steps for those who have led uprisings via social media are much more difficult. Responsible leaders do not only protest against injustice, they also use their skills to work to replace the injustice with a better world.

From the experience in Cairo, lessons learned included the need for on-the-ground organizing as well as online organization, a need to communicate, and the need to control the message. We live in a savvy world and many of the "Occupiers" were part of the most tech-savvy generation to date. It was not at all difficult for them to develop and put into service the online tools to further their objectives. Now that we live in a 24/7 news cycle, protest happenings anywhere in the world are available in print and pictures immediately. An unfortunate aspect of this immediacy is that there is little or no time to check the facts behind the documentation or to place events in a larger context.

The website www.change.org is a social action platform that empowers anyone, anywhere to start, join, and win campaigns for social change. Millions of people each month sign petitions in support of thousands of issues that concern them. Some are local, others national and international. Here again, anyone can lead the charge for change and be supported by others of like mind throughout the world. In political races, numerous websites exist that support candidates and causes. In each of these instances, information is available on who supports a cause and what those causes are.

When social media is used outside the confines of a particular profession or organization and is used to promote a cause, right or wrong, it has been demonstrated time and time again that it is very powerful. The Dalai Lama had been invited to South Africa to help celebrate with Nobel Peace Prize Laureate Archbishop Desmond Tutu this great honor. The Dalai Lama was then disinvited because the People's Republic of China, which had strong economic ties to South Africa, objected to the visit. However, he joined the celebration online and was able to participate from a distance. While politics could keep the two leaders apart, social networking brought them together. The power of social media, when turned on the sad and troubling case of a teenaged young black man in Sanford, Florida, who was shot and killed by a neighborhood watch person, shed light on an issue of national importance and opened a needed dialogue. At its best, social media can be an agent of change, and at least, is a means of shedding light on issues that need discussion. T. D. Jakes, leader of a megachurch in the United States, said in an interview published shortly after the 2012 shooting that "social media is changing the way we amass public outcry."[20] Women, who live in societies in which they are not allowed to be in public places unless veiled and whose ability to interact with others outside the confines of their home is limited, are finding social media to be their opportunity to experience the wider world and to have their voices heard.

The Wisdom of Crowds

Which is better at solving problems and reaching wise decisions, larger groups of people or smaller groups that are well informed about a topic? "The concept that the research efforts of a group of people with varying opinions, when aggregated, can result in better information than a specific expert could come up with 'crowdsourcing' has been around for some time."[21] Wikipedia, the online encyclopedia whose articles are written and edited by individuals who contribute their knowledge and then reviewed and edited by other individuals, was founded on the premise that information resides in crowds and that tapping it provides universal benefit. Beginning with Suriwiecki's *The Wisdom of Crowds*[22] published in 2004, research has been conducted that supports the hypothesis that a variety of approaches to a problem can be identified by a diverse group and can often result in useful information. Scott Page who conducts research on diversity indicated that "for a crowd to be wise, its members must be individually smart or collectively diverse. Ideally they would be both."[23] Leaders have used crowdsourcing to conduct market research and to identify trends in politics.

To show the power of crowdsourcing, Cepeda cited the decision of the executive leaders of Handel and Komen to disassociate themselves from Planned Parenthood in 2012 in order to continue to support their mission of curing and eradicating breast cancer in a different way.[24] "The crowd—which is to say those who were enraged by this turn of events and rose up in a fury of social media—pressured Komen into reversing its decision. Before you knew it, Handel was out, the foundation had been rocked to its core, and though Planned Parenthood's funding has been restored, it's unclear how the foundation can move forward with prochoice and antiabortion supporters disappointed."[25] Cepeda cited other issues that have been decided by crowds; the Gap clothing chain reverted to "its decades old logo after those who despised the new look took to Facebook, Twitter, and blogs to complain."[26]

The Stop Online Piracy Act was derailed by protests aired on social media. While Cepeda says that there is nothing wrong with giving the customers what they want, or with leaders of an organization being responsive to stakeholders, there is a problem "when the crowd has such an outsized effect that even the possibility of its social media wrath drives leaders' decisions."[27] Cepeda went on to ask if ". . . we are in danger of becoming slaves to the 'crowds' reaction . . . and routinely acting in anticipation of them—making them [leaders] nothing more than figureheads reliant on correctly forecasting change, organizational petitions, public opinion polls, and tweets-per-minute to make tough decisions."[28]

Many views on a topic from a large number of people can be helpful and provide new perspectives which the leader can consider in making decisions. Since it is difficult to know the composition of a crowd—are they biased, do they have an agenda, do they have sufficient information to make informed decisions—their input can have limited value. Still, they are a potential source of good, new, powerful ideas and worthy of a listen. However, members of crowds can become bullies where the loudest noise rules and those who suggest other approaches are drowned out. In any case, the wise leader considers the comments made by crowds and factors this information into the decision-making process while at the same time taking responsibility for the decision. This is what leaders do.

Control of Social Media

While it is possible to set rules for how social media is used within an organization and among organizations, this is not the case when one considers social media at large. Government plays a role in defining the Internet and its use. The extent of that role and when it impinges on personal freedom is of concern to anyone who uses the Internet. Currently, there is relatively little control over social networks and the efforts by the government to place some control have been met with a storm of objections by those owning and using the networks because they project this control to a possible future that is heavily government-controlled. In January 2012, Congress was scheduled to vote on bills aimed at stopping online piracy, SOPA (Stop Online Piracy) in the House of Representatives and PIPA (Project IP Act). The reaction from bloggers, Twitter users, and social media giants was so strong that Congress opted to postpone action on the legislation. Social media leaders feared that the legislation would give media companies too much power and lead to Internet censorship. As part of this protest, Wikipedia took its site down for a day (January 18, 2012) and thousands of other sites joined the protest. The *New Media Index*, a weekly report on the news agenda of social media and part of the Pew Research Center's Project for Excellence in Journalism provided continuous reporting of the ways in which "blogs and other social media sites have allowed news consumers and others outside the mainstream press to have more of a role in agenda setting, dissemination, and interpretation."[29] An overwhelming agreement came from many companies and organizations that the proposed legislation would be detrimental to freedom on the web. This was an indication of the power of the web to stand up to the possibility of government control and win.

An additional report from *The New Media Index*[30] focused on Facebook and looked at changes in its privacy settings as well as its privacy policy. Part of the interest was because "many analysts have suggested, the personal data of the site's 800 million users is a large part of what is being leveraged during the IPO." While social media continues to improve and add to the ways in which it can be used, users continue to be at risk because of their lack of thoughtfulness about what they place on the site, their lack of control over who has access to it, and how those with access may use someone's personal information.

Monitoring of social networks is a continuing concern. Charlie Savage of the *New York Times*[31] reported on a concern that the U.S. Department of Homeland Security was monitoring Twitter and Facebook not just for information on terrorist activities but also "for reaction to major government proposals with homeland security implications." A recently published departmental manual included numerous keywords with the potential of gathering information well beyond the responsibilities of the Department. A Freedom of Information Act lawsuit stated that First Amendment issues are at stake and suggested that the government was "overdoing its looking around."[32] Concern over the power of social media is not limited to the United States. "The Chinese Communist Party has long felt threatened by overseas websites and social media outlets . . . and has blocked both Twitter and Facebook as well as tens of thousands of other websites that the government deems a threat to hold on to power."[33] The balance between regulation of the Internet in order to enhance its efficiency and control of the Internet which would have the potential of limiting free speech is one that will concern leaders and users of social media for a long time and its outcome is of critical importance.

ADVOCACY

An advocate is defined as one who argues or recommends publicly on behalf of an individual or an idea. It can be as simple as asking someone to support a neighborhood trash pickup project or as complex as asking others to join in overthrowing the government. Advocacy groups can marshal support for issues and do so faster over a larger area and more graphically than any medium to date. Nearly every professional organization has an advocacy component that educates the public about what that association stands for and what it does. The professional association also advocates for its positions with government agencies, businesses, not-for-profit agencies, as well as groups and individuals. Candidates for political office are advocates for their interests and those of their constituents and usually have a staff whose role is to spread the message. Since the 2008 presidential election, social media has become an integral part of politicking and many campaigns since then have hired digital directors to lead the virtual effort.

The American Library Association (ALA) is an excellent example of a professional society that uses the Internet to publicize who it is and advocate for what it does. In 2001, ALA began a multiyear campaign to promote the value of libraries and librarians.[34] The @ Your Library website was launched in 2009 "aimed at increasing and improving the use of libraries by reaching out directly to all kinds of people of all ages and building on direct outreach efforts the campaign had already taken."[35] It delivers content and serves as a source of tips and hints, recommends books, movies and music and provides connection to libraries where these materials can be located using WorldCat. In 2010, Library Advocacy Day replaced National Library Legislative Day, a day on which librarians and other advocates for library and information services would visit their Congressional representatives in their offices on Capitol Hill. Now representative advocates from all 50 states and the District of Columbia can contact their representatives from home and are able to organize a virtual meeting date online to discuss issues of concern. This type of advocacy makes it possible for anyone anywhere to participate in the discussions and contribute their ideas.

SUMMARY

Social media has enlarged the role and reach of the leader to an extent not previously imagined. In order to take full advantage of the information and information technology–rich world, the leader must accept the role of global connector by being tied to different social worlds and connecting the world outside the organization to the world inside. The leader is an active networker who builds bridges between people and people and people and ideas, someone who engages talent from everywhere, collaborates by beginning at the top and continuing on every level of the organization, and builds a collaborative environment in which open discussion is encouraged.

The successful leader needs to be aware of both the benefits of having more information and greater access and the difficulties presented by a loss of control over access to information, its tone, and its accuracy. The leader must assure that the narrative of leadership is consistent with that of the society in which we live. Successful leadership will drive the discussion with great ideas that advance a compelling narrative rather than reacting to existing narratives.

NOTES

1. Idea Watch: Vision Statement, "It Keeps Growing and Growing . . . ," *Harvard Business Review* 90, no. 10 (October 2012): 32.

2. Rob Cross and Robert Thomas, "A Smarter Way to Network," *Harvard Business Review* 89, no. 7 (July/August 2011): 149–53.

3. Ibid.

4. "Where Does Social Media Monitoring Stand," *The Information Advisor* 23, no. 6 (June 2011), 1–3.

5. Anthony J. Bradley and Mark P. McDowell, "The Six Attitudes Leaders Take Toward Social Media?" *Harvard Business Review BLOG Network.* http://blogs.hbr.org/cs/2011/10/the_six_attitudes_leaders_take.html.

6. Ibid.

7. Ibid.

8. Ibid.

9. Ibid.

10. James H. Wilson, P.J. Guinan, Salvatore Parise, and Bruce D. Weinberg, "What's Your Social Media Strategy?" *Harvard Business Review* 89, no. 7/8 (July/August 2011), 23–25.

11. Hermina Ibarra and Morton T. Hansen, "Are You a Collaborative Leader?" *Harvard Business Review* 89, no. 7/8 (August/September 2008), 72.

12. Daniel Chudnov, "Social Software: You Are an Access Point," *Computers in Libraries* 27, no. 8 (September 2007): 41–43.

13. Thomas Friedman, "op ed" *New York Times*, December 12, 2011.

14. Dov Seidman, *How: Why HOW We Do Anything Means Everything* (Hoboken, NJ: John Wiley and Sons, 2011).

15. Max Chafkin, "Revolution Number 99," *Vanity Fair* 202, no. 618 (February 2012): 74–82.

16. Massino Calabresei, "Head of State," *Time* 178, no. 18 (November 2 2011), 28.

17. Ibid., 33.

18. Chafkin, 75.

19. Liel Liebovitz, "The Revolutionist: The Secret Architect of the Arab Spring Casts an Eye on Occupy Wall Street," *The Atlantic* 309, no. 2 (March 2012): 21–22.

20. "Interview with T. D. Jakes," *Washington Post*, March 31, 2012.

21. Sanhita Sinha Roy, "Libraries Tap into the Crowdsource," *American Libraries* 42, no. 11/12 (November/December 2011): 22.

22. James Surowiecki, *The Wisdom of Crowds* (New York: Doubleday, 2004).

23. Scott E. Page, *The Difference: How the Power of Diversity Creates Better Groups, Firms, Schools, and Societies* (Princeton, NJ: Princeton University Press, 2007), 234.

24. ejc@estherjcepeda.com

25. Ibid.

26. Ibid.

27. Ibid.

28. Ibid.

29. http://www.journalism.org/print/228189

30. http://www.journalism.org/print/28272

31. Charlie Savage, "Hearing Held on Program Monitoring Social Media," *New York Times*, February 23, 2012, A17.

32. Ibid.

33. Andrew Jacobs, "American Recounts Beating by Chinese Agents Suspicious of Social Media, *New York Times*, February 14, 2012, A11.

34. Leonard Kniffel, "Pipeline to the People," *American Libraries* 40, no. 10 (October 2009): 63–65.

35. Ibid., 63.

Chapter 10

When Leadership Falters

Leadership can be a difficult undertaking and is not always successful. The world in which we live is always changing, which requires that the leader be able to anticipate and implement new strategies when needed. Sometimes change overwhelms individuals and organizations as in the case of a natural disaster such as a hurricane or tornado. Other changes occur when the vision changes, which can happen when the organization one works for has been absorbed by another organization and the new owner imposes a vision which may be different from the one formerly pursued. Because of any number of possible events, leaders may be placed in situations in which new leadership approaches are needed and they have to learn how to lead in this new environment with little or no preparation time. Perhaps the individual placed in such a situation does not have the skills or experience to take command immediately and is slow to come up to speed. This may cause leaders to lose confidence in their own abilities, which can be difficult for everyone involved.

In addition to changes in external factors that can cause leaders to falter, leaders may develop and exhibit behaviors that do not enhance their ability to lead. Leaders may believe what the media, colleagues, and competitors say about them. If the leader is praised for a job well done, that is a good thing and the leader should be appreciative. If however, that praise goes beyond what is appropriate to the situation, the leader may become overconfident, forget to be as self-critical as is necessary, and make poor decisions. On the other hand, if the leader is unduly criticized for actions taken and believes the criticism without considering the source or its validity, the leader may lose confidence and the ability to lead.

Some leaders become arrogant and forget that leadership is a humble task in which the leader is responsible for achieving a vision with the collaboration of others and that success is a collective activity and not due to the efforts of a single individual. Arrogant leaders tend to believe that they can treat others with disrespect, and this can result in a dysfunctional workplace. Others placed in a leadership position may be insecure in their ability to lead and therefore go on the attack by bullying and complaining about those they are expected to lead, micromanaging every activity, and treating others with little or no respect. This results in the destruction of any sense of teamwork and community so necessary to success.

Leaders who compromise their integrity by overlooking actions that are ill-advised and could be illegal destroy their integrity and the reputation of the organization they represent. Ethical lapses ranging from the small lie to the hiding of gross misbehavior when found out (most do emerge from the shadows given the ability of investigators in a networked world to track even the most complex activity) destroy the ability to lead. While lack of leadership performance due to inexperience or even poor decision making can be understood and a second chance often given, evidence of the lack of integrity and ethical values is rarely if ever forgiven or forgotten.

Leaders, even the most competent and confident ones, can reach a point in their careers when they no longer wish to be responsible for a vision, for inspiring others to do great things, and for devoting their lives to making our world a better place. Wise leaders, when they reach this point, usually find a gracious way to move aside and let others take responsibility. Some stay involved in activities related to their leadership activities while others take the time to pursue interests which they formerly had no time to enjoy. Wise leaders leave the leadership position on their own terms while they are at the top of their game and before someone suggests it is time to leave.

WHEN THE VISION CHANGES

Leadership is in a sense situation-based, in that there is a fit between action, style, and situation or context.[1] As organizations change, leadership styles may need to change as well. Individuals who have a vision for a new organization or of how to lead an existing organization create an organization or environment to fit the vision. The leader then translates the vision into reality by clarifying the focus, setting the direction, and communicating this to those who are part of the organization. Once the organization is operational, the leader constantly seeks to improve the way in which it functions and expands communication with others who could be impacted by the organization. As the organization matures, the vision may change either through the actions of the leader or because of external circumstances. The leader who has the creativity to design an organization and translate the vision into reality may not be particularly interested in maintaining and nurturing the organization once it is up and running. We often see idea people who once their idea is made operational by the addition of people and organization charts, lose interest and want to move on. Individuals who are excellent leaders at one stage in an organization's development may not be the persons to lead it through its maturity. Knowing one's strengths and knowing when to move on is an important attribute of a leader.

The leader who is part of a larger organization may have been hired to energize a particular unit or to implement a new program. That leader may also follow the same trajectory and as soon as the creative building process is over may wish to move on. Sometimes, others in the organization may change its vision, and they may no longer wish to pursue an earlier program or product and the unit responsible for its development or implementation is shut down. In this situation, the individual's leadership is not at issue but rather what is going on in the larger context. If an organization for which the leader is responsible is shutting down, the leader may well be the individual responsible for dealing with this difficult task. To some this may indicate a loss of leadership as they see their role disappearing. To the contrary, it is an opportunity for one to practice one of the most difficult of leadership activities, that of ending the hopes and economic security of others and doing so in a responsible way. This is the time when leaders are called upon to use all of their skills and abilities to assist those who are forced to make transitions in their work life.

Looking Ahead

Leaders have the responsibility to anticipate changes in their organization and changes in the larger community so that they can be prepared for different leadership challenges. The leader who does not look ahead and anticipate that the social and economic climate will change, sometimes rapidly and sometimes slowly, and that the context within which the organization functions will change, will have failed as a leader. In a survey of tens of thousands of working people who were asked what they looked for and admired in a leader, their number one response was honesty. Their number two response was that the leader be forward-looking. While 27 percent of respondents wanted this of a colleague, 72 percent wanted it of a leader. Those who become leaders need to add envisioning to their top priorities. "Leaders on the frontline must anticipate merely what comes after current projects wrap up. People at the next level of leadership should be looking several years into the future."[2] Further, respondents want to be part of the envisioning process so that they understand how the leader got to that vision. "The only visions that take hold are shared visions—and you will create them only when you listen very, very closely to others, appreciate their hopes, and attend to their needs."[3] Leaders who fail to share the vision with those they lead so that everyone is aware of the direction of the organization, what the future may look like, what opportunities and what difficulties may emerge are failing in an important component of their responsibility to lead.

NOT KNOWING HOW TO DO THEIR JOB

One of the most common issues that leaders face is that they either overestimate or underestimate their abilities. Leaders who are overconfident about their abilities tend to be convinced that their way of doing things is the right way, indeed the only way. They refuse to understand the culture of the community or organization which they have become a part of and refuse to treat those for whom they are responsible as their equal. This form of bullying may be because they indeed believe that they are right in their decision making or it may be because they are insecure in their decision making and think that if they are sufficiently loud and dictatorial no one will challenge them. Leaders who underestimate their ability can appear to be hesitant and unwilling to make decisions, and can lose the respect of those they are responsible for leading; but respect is not gained by how loud they trumpet their decisions. It is expected that an individual entering a leadership position will take a reasonable amount of time to assess the culture, assess the specific leadership challenges, come to understand the skills and abilities of those to be led, and then move forward with specific plans and actions. Neither overestimating nor underestimating one's leadership abilities is an important component of success.

Blaming Others

Leaders who lack an accurate sense of their skills and abilities as leaders often resort to blaming others for their failures. They complain about the abilities of those they are expected to lead. They complain about the lack of resources, about the problems they are expected to solve. If there is a poor decision, it is someone else's fault and not theirs. Some will say that they are not appreciated for the creativity of their approach to leadership, which is shorthand for saying that they haven't studied the situation and don't know the parameters within which they are expected to work. For others, saying that they are creative is an excuse for being sloppy. Either way, they will blame others for nonperformance.

Poor leaders have not developed the self-discipline to know what the important tasks are and to organize their time so that they prioritize the important things. They spend too much time dealing with issues of importance to them rather than assessing the situation and dealing with what is truly important to the organization. Nothing is getting done because it is nearly impossible for one person to amass all relevant information in a timely fashion. They refuse to let anyone else make decisions and therefore deadlines are not met. They then blame others for lack of progress.

It's Not "All about Me"

The poor leader believes that "it's all about me" when in fact it is "all about us" and it is the strength of the team or the organization that leads to success. The leader has been given that title and then must earn the title of leader by actions that enable and empower others. The leader is the spokesperson for the team and the designated leader but this does not mean that the leader is in any way better than others. If anything, the leader has the greater responsibility to ensure that every member of the team contributes to the vision and that every member is treated equally and fairly. The leader does not play favorites as it skews the energy of the team and creates dysfunction in its operation. Every team member deserves and expects fair and equal treatment.

Having the title of leader may cause an individual to act in a way that is self-serving rather than serving the organization. This may become evident if it is found that the leader manipulates information and withholds all or part of it or presents it in a way that can be misinterpreted. Leaders may claim credit for ideas and actions of team members or blow out of proportion a small error on the part of a team member in order to demonstrate that one is a strong leader who keeps the team in line. Sometimes a self-important leader appears to have a large support group. These are often the individuals who benefit from the leader's actions and who would find themselves in a tenuous position if the leader were to fall.

Incompetence in a leader can be divided between those who brag about how important they are but really don't know what to do and those who truly don't know. The braggart who refuses to use new or existing methods that would improve operations is probably revealing an unwillingness to learn new things and a fear of failure in trying new things. When individuals in a leadership position say "nobody told me," they see that statement as an excuse while it is actually an indication of incompetence. Leaders need to know and when they don't, they find out rather than blame others for their failure.

There are individuals who truly are "in over their head" in a situation for which they have little experience and aren't sure where to turn. This is less a matter of incompetence than of needing to learn very fast and make decisions in difficult situations. The leadership team is important here as they can add their expertise and decision-making skills to the problem and, if needed, can request added expertise. Such a situation can be a learning experience for all. Or, as in the case of the aftermath of Hurricane Katrina, leadership may refuse to admit that they are in an overwhelming situation and try to address critical issues with bravado and other techniques that do not work.

Leadership or Loudership?

Psychologists have long known that part of being a successful leader is to act the part. "Speak up, speak well and offer lots of ideas, and people begin to do what you say. Yet what if someone acts like a boss but thinks like a boob?"[4] A research study conducted at the University of California, Berkeley, found that "the people who spoke up the most [were thought] to be higher in such qualities as 'general intelligence.' The ones who didn't speak much scored higher in traits like 'conventional' and 'uncreative.'" Two sets of teams were given math problems to solve and when the task was finished, those who spoke up most often were rated as leaders and perhaps even as math whizzes. Any talking seemed to convince observers that those who spoke were leaders. When the answers were checked, it was found that the loud mouths were not the ones with the right answers, just the most answers, and that when checked against their SAT scores, the loud mouths were often those who had the least demonstrated mathematical ability.

Mario Batali, a well-known chef, was interviewed by the *New York Times* for its weekly contribution to the business section on leadership.[5] He said that his opinion of yelling was that it is "the result of the dismay you feel when you realize you have not done your own job," and it is easier to yell at someone else than to admit one's own shortcomings. The individual who resorts to verbal abuse and loud noise is not a leader. No correlation is found between the level of yelling and the ability to lead. Just the opposite—behaviors that damage the self-confidence of others and get in the way of progress prevent teamwork and a satisfactory working environment.

DESTRUCTIVE LEADERSHIP

Destructive leadership goes beyond not knowing how to lead to exploiting a leadership position for purposes of self-interest. "Leaders driven by self-interest orient their behavior toward ends that benefit themselves at the expense of followers whose needs and interests are either ignored or trampled on."[6] Some organizational cultures support this type of leadership either overtly or passively. In these cultures, destructive leaders dominate followers in such a way that it slows career growth, controls the effectiveness of teams, and emotionally stresses employees. Destructive leaders take credit for any successes and punish others for any failures. They insist that they have complete control of the situation and their tenure often resembles a reign of terror.

Destructive leaders tend to emerge when social systems are in crisis and there appears to be a lack of leadership. For example, Hitler emerged in Germany during a period of economic and social crisis. A charismatic leader and an ideologue, he promised a better future for those who would follow his leadership. He was enthusiastic, had strong beliefs, and used these beliefs and values to demean the ideas of others. He marginalized those who did not believe in what he said and demeaned them as "the other." Because he saw his ideas as superior, and he and those who followed him looked down on those who did not share his ideas seeing them as inferior beings, he had no difficulty in destroying them. Like all destructive leaders, he practiced selective information processing. Reality was distorted; information that did not agree with his point of view was distrusted and was punished.

In order for destructive leaders to prevail, there needs to be an environment in which they can function. Four universal factors must be present in the environment for this to occur:

1) The organization has no checks and balances and destructive behavior is institutionalized.

2) The environment is unstable and threats are perceived if control by the leader is not present, and

3) Cultural values must support this type of environment.

"Toxic leaders + susceptible followers + conducive environments = a toxic triangle."[7]

The media serves as a major means of preventing destructive leadership. The media's exposure of the Enron scandal in the 1990s, its criticism of the ways in which victims of Katrina (the hurricane that devastated much of New Orleans in 2005) were treated, and the banking scandals of the early years of the 21st century are examples of this. When there is a strong media that does not look the other way when they see destructive action on the part of organizations, the public is alerted to the situation and steps are usually taken to respond and fix the situation. Government agencies are in place to regulate business and impose rules and regulations that benefit the public. Those in powerful positions often complain about the presence of government regulations as they say that it gets in the way of business growth. It also gets in the way of bad business practices that harm the public. When oversight agencies are understaffed and underfunded, they are hampered in their ability to protect the public. Internally, organizations have boards of trustees, one of whose roles is to protect their employees and the public. In some instances, the boards of trustees are themselves part of the destructive leadership team and see their role of exploiting employees and the public "as good business."[8]

Arrogance

For some, there is a fine line between being self-confident and being arrogant. Self-confidence is the belief that you can do something while arrogance is the belief that you are the only one who can do anything important. The arrogant individual's attitude is that there is only one way to behave and "it's my way." Arrogant individuals believe themselves to be above the law and that rules "are for the little people." They are the individuals who claim lack of funds, lay off employees, and then redecorate their office. They appoint their friends to important positions in the organization; they pay themselves and their friends large salaries while at the same time cutting services and programs for others in the organization. They never apologize for their actions as they believe that they are entitled to all they can get.

Richard Nixon, during his presidency, had a passion for secrecy and power and found the normal constraints of democratic politics limiting. In referring to Watergate, Katherine Graham of the *Washington Post* said, "It was a conspiracy not of greed but of arrogance and fear by men who came to equate their own political well-being with the nation's very survival."[9] Nixon plotted in secret, sent agents to break into the offices of those with whom he disagreed, destroyed information in his files that might have been incriminating, and seemed more concerned about being found out than that he had violated the law and his oath of office. One needs only to read the daily papers to see reports of other officials who disregard their public trust and who find ways to improve their situation and those of their friends at the expense of the public they have sworn to serve. While the majority of public servants and business leaders are honorable individuals who have the best interests of those they lead at the forefront of their actions, the dishonorable few often cast a pall over those who truly lead.

Arrogance often leads to a feeling of overconfidence, a feeling that it will always be possible to exert one's will over others and over the social/political/economic environment in which one lives. The Enron experience is an excellent example of what happens when the arrogant overreach. Enron[10] was a large power company supplying utility companies in the western part of the United States. In 2000–2001, California had an energy supply crisis. When an energy shortage would occur in one area, Enron would jack up the prices and make large profits as it filled their energy needs. Enron also intentionally created shortages by calling for plants to be shut down for maintenance when no maintenance was needed. Californians were experiencing rolling blackouts and high energy costs because of the deliberate manipulation of the resource by Enron who was the supplier. In the summer of 2001, Enron as a corporation began to unravel financially because of relying on bookkeeping that did not accurately reflect the health of the company. Arthur Anderson, a reputable accounting firm, audited accounts and said that all was well even though there was suspicion on the part of investors that all was not well. The chief operating officer resigned suddenly, refusing to admit that anything was wrong with the financial accounting of the firm. Ken Lay, chairman of Enron, continued to insist that the company was sound while its stock kept falling in value and debts kept increasing until the company failed. Just before the company failed, the leadership sold their stocks for enormous profits. The three top leaders of the company were indicted and arrested as were numerous officials at Enron. Ken Lay, the chairman, insisted throughout the scandal that he was unaware of the situation and that he had been lied to by his financial officer and that the whole problem was someone else's fault. Often, the last resort of the arrogant leader when caught misusing the trust and resources of others is to whine and try to blame others.

This is arrogance and unscrupulous practice at its worst. Individuals out to make money cared little about the legality or the integrity of their actions or about the damage done to thousands of honest people working for Enron who lost their jobs, their pensions, and in some cases their reputations. After Enron imploded one could meet individuals in communities where Enron had had facilities who had lost their jobs and retirement benefits, and instead of having the comfortable retirement they had earned and anticipated had to find jobs bagging groceries or delivering newspapers just to make ends meet. Enron is a cautionary tale of the damage that can be done when the arrogant find a way to manipulate the system for their own purposes with no concern for others and when government regulations are too loose to put a stop to such actions.

BELIEVING WHAT OTHERS SAY

Believing what others say about one's leadership has both positive and negative elements. Leaders can become caught up in the trappings that accompany a leadership title. They like the power of the position and the praise that may be honestly earned for a job well done or may be unearned accolades given by individuals who wish to demonstrate their loyalty or receive special favors. Successful leaders who gain a great deal of approval may become complacent and neglect to use the power of the position for maximum benefit of those they have promised to serve. If the leader has a loyal constituency, the devotion of their followers may cause them to believe that they are untouchable and that what they say or do is the right thing regardless of the effect it has on others.

Negative comments or rumors can cause mistrust and harm the leadership ability of an individual. These can come from outside the organization or internally. Individuals outside the organization have the opportunity to observe the impact of the leader's actions and how they affect others.[11] Leaders in positions of public trust, such as elected officials, those who tend to the educational, social, and health needs of the community, and those responsible for public safety need to be particularly sensitive to how their leadership actions are viewed by the public. They need to be as transparent in their decision making as possible and to represent the highest ethical and moral standards. They also need to have a thick skin as there will always be members of the community who disagree with them and wish them harm. Positive comments are always welcome but the savvy public servants always know that they are not universally loved and that there will always be those whose agenda is to spread negative information. Within the organization, the leader's ways of leading will foster either positive or negative comments. Here again, integrity and high ethical standards are essential as are good management skills and transparency.

Some leaders have difficulty in understanding feedback, what to accept as valid and what not to accept. Some leaders want staff members who give them only positive feedback and are unwilling to accept negative comments or suggestions for improvement. Staff members quickly learn when the leader is unwilling to accept negative feedback and can respond in several ways, each of which is detrimental to leadership. They can edit feedback so that it contains only positive statements. They can share the negative feedback with colleagues and others who might find it useful in building a case against the leader, or they can follow a course of action somewhere between the two. The successful leader has a healthy ego and a strong sense of self. Most importantly, the leader needs to know the value of listening, assessing the message, and incorporating helpful parts of the message into the way things are done.

Success or failure as a leader depends on learning to differentiate between criticism that is valuable and that which is not. It also depends on being able to know enough about the organization, the situation, those who are supportive and those who are not, and keeping one's ear to the ground so that surprises do not occur. Others both in and out of the organization will try to second guess the leader, to try to second guess the leader's actions, and perhaps even to impute motives that do not exist. The leader needs to be very clear and unambiguous about decisions made and actions taken so that this type of noninformation has less of an opportunity to spread. A fine line is drawn between being clear and ambiguous and cutting off discussion. The best advice one can give is, "don't believe your own press." Know yourself well enough to have confidence in what you are doing and be able to evaluate both praise and condemnation in terms of its relation to the facts and to the source.

COMPROMISING ONE'S INTEGRITY

Most leaders intend to lead ethical organizations and to be proud of their accomplishments. Unfortunately, there are circumstances in which choices must be made and which may compromise one's integrity. While there is no excuse for this, it is important to understand how such situations occur and how to deal with them. One of the most glaring examples of poor choices being made is that of the Pinto, a small car developed by Ford Motor Company to compete with Volkswagen and other small cars. Not long after the Pinto went into the market, there were several instances in which when the Pinto was rear-ended in a traffic accident, it would leak fuel and burst into flames. It took several such accidents, some fatal, before Ford issued a recall. In studying the situation, it was found that even before production, the potential danger of fuel leakage had been identified "but the assembly line was ready to go and the company's leaders decided to proceed."[12] In doing a cost-benefit analysis, Ford determined that it would be cheaper to pay off lawsuits than to fix the assembly line. The company's greater emphasis was on the bottom line than on the safety of the public. Those who were concerned about the decision to proceed said nothing for fear of being fired. This is but one example of what can happen to ethical behavior when it competes with those more interested in personal gain.

Bazerman and Tenbrunsel[13] analyzed this situation to determine if there were lessons to be learned and they identified four things that went wrong and then generalized this situation to the larger environment of organizational decision making and the role of leadership. The first of these was that the organization had poorly conceived goals. When the organization and its leadership set goals, what are they expecting, what are they empowering their members to do? Are they rewarding the wrong things? If an attorney in a firm is expected to increase billable hours, is the pressure so great that the attorney is less than honest in the hours billed or perhaps the attorney increases charges on the hours billed in order to meet expected goals? The housing crisis in the 2007–2012 years was due in part to the goal of ensuring that every family owns a home. While this was a laudable goal, what happened was that families without the financial resources to own a home were given mortgages and when they were unable to meet the payments, went into foreclosure. Goals are necessary but leaders should consider the level of pressure these goals place on employees and what employees feel they must do to meet them.

Motivated blindness is the second element the authors cite as an issue. People tend to see what they want to see and may decide to turn a blind eye to small lapses. Leaders may bring an individual to the team because that individual has certain skills needed by the team. They may ignore some questionable aspects of that person's behavior and hope for the best. If a staff member has been known to treat women with disdain or worse, is that person's skill set worth a lawsuit? What about the individual who has been known to steal ideas from others and claim them? What about sports team leaders who ignore the use of performance enhancing drugs by their athletes? If the athlete takes steroids and becomes a star, the stands will fill, money will be earned, and everyone will get rich. What about the ethics of winning unfairly? What about the ethics of ignoring the fact that athletes who take performance enhancing drugs are destroying their own bodies? "A decade of research shows that awareness of them [ethical lapses] doesn't necessarily reduce their untoward effect on decision making. Nor will integrity alone prevent them from spurring unethical behavior because honest people can suffer from motivated blindness."[14]

The third element is indirect blindness. This occurs when a third party is tied to the ethical lapse. For example, a company knows that it has a faulty product and sells it to another company which then sells it and gets in trouble. The first party can claim ignorance and the company that bought the product in order to sell it is in difficulty. The final element is the slippery slope; if a little bit of unethical behavior hasn't gotten us into trouble, a bit more will probably be overlooked. There is no such thing as being a little bit honest or mostly ethical. The responsible leader always asks "what ethical implications might arise from this decision?" and does not sign off on those decisions that harm others. If the leader turns a blind eye to a small lapse and then if another lapse occurs, it is more difficult to say "no" the second time as it would also be necessary to admit having allowed the first lapse.

Why do leaders go down unethical and destructive paths? Do they lack a strong sense of moral and ethical values? When selecting a leader, it is important to know from their interactions with others and from their personal behavior if they have the character and integrity one demands in a leader. Things one can look for in selecting a leader include the following:

- Does the individual see leadership as a responsibility or as an entitlement?
- Does the individual require recognition, take undue credit, or blame others for failure?
- Does the individual have a sense of responsibility toward others?

The individuals "whose values stressed contribution to others as opposed to personal gain, exhibited greater integrity in making decisions."[15] Those whose loyalty is to the organization and what it stands for are less apt to ignore ethical lapses than are those who put the individual first. The values and moral development a leader brings to the organization not only have a great impact on the organization but also define the ethical stance of the organization to the public.

Ethical and moral lapses can occur whenever money and power are involved. A very sad example of this was the experience at Penn State University in late 2011 and into 2012 when it was broadcast on the news that a former assistant coach of the football team had been reported to have been seen with a young boy in a shower room on campus. What was in itself an illegal and immoral act rapidly became even worse when it was found that the assistant coach had been molesting boys for many years and that this was known to the football coach and to at least some of the University administration who decided they should take care of the issue internally. What was involved was the reputation of a beloved coach and the integrity of the University administration as well as a multimillion dollar football program. As the situation unfolded, and the University trustees were informed, the president of the University, a vice president, and the coach were removed from their jobs and a thorough investigation begun. How much each of these individuals knew about what was apparently years of molestation, how much they ignored or hoped would go away, will probably never be clear but what was clear was that they were responsible for the ethical and moral reputation of the University and that for whatever reason, they failed to honor that responsibility. Power and money were involved in that the football program is a multimillion dollar activity and not something to tamper with without good reason and apparently those in power did not pay sufficient attention to what was going on in the shower rooms. Perhaps they hoped it was a rumor. The coach's reputation as a leader, as an individual of moral courage who demanded the best from the many young men who played football for him, was also at stake. The charges didn't go away, were held up in court, and the University suffered penalties to its football program that will take decades to overcome. Because of the actions of a few, the integrity of the University suffered.

Organizations are reflections of the traits of those who are at its center; "the leader's ethics, the people he chooses to hire, and the way he conducts business" set the tone of the organization.[16] Leaders who lead with integrity "[do what they say they will do]" are the foundation for ethical leadership, without which, "the organization will turn against itself . . . destroy [ing] communication, cooperation, and creativity—and ultimately the company."[17] Another way of saying this is "don't advertise your principles, live by them." None of us is perfect, yet most of us do our best to be honest, honorable, and respect others. A leader is human and small lapses will occur when a decision must be made quickly or when there has been insufficient information to make a decision. When they are dealt with as small things and serve as learning experiences, it shows the leader's willingness to learn. It also shows that the leader cares about others and what they think.

APOLOGIZING

Kellerman[18] says that leaders are responsible for their own behavior and that of their followers. When the leader apologizes, it is for the leader plus the entire organization. She said that apologies are high stakes political actions. Apologizing is becoming a part of our culture as more and more individuals apologize for more and more things they have done or have been perceived as having done. Look at the careers of most politicians. They apologize for stances taken, stances not taken, and stances they might take in the future.

Why Apologize?

An apology is a tactic used to put errors behind one. "I said I was sorry, so forget it." It is a way to defuse a situation or so the apologizer may hope. One can apologize for the past deeds of an organization, for example, Brown University's founders were in the slave trade. One can apologize for poor judgment as was the case when Harvard president Larry Sommers apologized for his comments about the possible reasons for the success or lack thereof of women in the sciences. His apology didn't take, and he stepped down from his post as president. Apologies are an important part of international relations as missteps can occur when one communicates across cultures or in response to events that are reported in real time without the opportunity to determine what actually happened and the context within which it happened.

When leaders apologize, their reputation is at stake and this is a serious action. Therefore one should not use an apology unless there are extraordinary circumstances. The general principle is that "leaders will publicly apologize if and when they calculate the costs of doing so to be lower than the cost of not doing so."[19] Kellerman cites four purposes of apologies.

- *Individual.* The leader makes a mistake and publicly apologizes.
- *Institutional.* Someone in the organization makes a mistake and the leader publicly apologizes in order to restore organizational reputation.
- *Intergroup.* Someone in the leader's group makes a mistake which inflicts harm on another. The leader apologizes to repair relations with the injured party.
- *Moral.* One has genuine remorse for personal or organizational mistakes and forgiveness is requested.

The first three purposes are strategic and are used for specific purposes. The fourth purpose, moral, is authentic and if real is very powerful.

Kellerman says that the perfect apology consists of five elements:

Acknowledge the problem.

Accept responsibility.

Express regret.

Assure that it won't be repeated.

The apology is well timed.

An instinctive reaction by some is to deny that there is a problem or that the problem is that someone or someone's organization is at fault. Research has shown that leaders often overestimate the cost of an apology and underestimate its benefits. In a crisis situation, any apology is better than denying or ignoring a situation. Crisis situations that are not faced immediately and action taken, even if it is bruising to the ego, tend to get worse and rarely if ever are mended on their own.[20]

An excellent example of how an organization dealt with a crisis in leadership were the steps taken by the Smithsonian Institution in March and April, 2007, after concerns were raised in the media about "compensation, expenses, and governance at the Smithsonian."[21] Within days, it was announced that the secretary of the Smithsonian had resigned and an acting secretary appointed. A letter went out immediately to those in any way connected to the Smithsonian announcing a change in leadership. The letter also announced that the Smithsonian's board of regents had created an independent review committee that was charged to "review reports on compensation, expenses and donations and the regent's response and actions and to report in about sixty days."[22] In addition to actions taken and to be taken, numerous new programs that were underway were listed to show that the Smithsonian continued to serve. Continuing with its openness, a website was listed which provided detailed information on steps taken and steps to be taken. Finally, contributing members of the association were invited to contact the contributing membership office "by phone, e-mail, or mail," to share thoughts and concerns. Such immediate action, transparency to members, and an indication of steps to be taken are what the responsible institution does in such a situation. After an extensive search, The Smithsonian appointed a new secretary and announced the selection to contributing members and to the public. In this same announcement the board of regents noted that new ways of dealing with compensation and expenses had been put into place so that there would be greater accountability in the future.

After the Apology

If an apology doesn't help the situation and the leader's career, what are the next steps? Sonnenfeld and Ward[23] conducted a study of 450 CEO successions (1988–1992) at large publicly traded companies. The CEOs studied lost their jobs because of natural disasters, illness, misconduct, honest errors, or unjust conspiracy on the part of others. Of the CEOs studied, 35 percent returned to active executive duty within two years, 22 percent took advisory roles often in smaller companies or found other employment, and 43 percent retired. Those who did not return to work tended to blame themselves, and those around them also blamed them, even though they may not have been responsible for the action. Over a period of 22 years, the authors interviewed numerous fired CEOs and other derailed professionals and this information plus consulting assignments indicated that leaders can come back if they take conscious steps to do so.

1) Decide how to fight back. Do you confront the situation that resulted in being fired? Do you sue or fight back in some other way? Do you come to closure over the dismissal? The key determinant of which step to take is the potential damage to one's reputation and one's reputation is a key personal resource. If you were unfairly fired, and you can prove it, one course of action is taken. If you made mistakes that led to dismissal, another course of action is appropriate.

2) Recruit others into the fight who can provide resources, advice, and can help you gain perspective. They also have connections that will help you find other opportunities. If a firing was unfair, the business or the not-for-profit community of which you are a part knows the situation and will usually be supportive. If you are known as a person with integrity, you will have support.

3) Recover your heroic status. You must publicly show that you survived the situation. You do this by getting your story out to others. If you can't tell your story, this often means that you can't get another position. Often, a severance package will require that an individual not disclose the reasons for the termination and if the individual does disclose the reasons, the severance bonus will be forfeited. Those who fire someone often just want that person to go away and not bother or embarrass them and this may make it difficult for the individuals fired to tell their story.

4) Prove you still have the ability to do the job.

5) Rediscover your mission.

Some individuals lose their jobs because they are incompetent, are a poor fit for the job, exhibit lack of ethical judgment, or have displeased those to whom they report. This latter reason may have nothing to do with the leader's ethics and abilities. The leader may be standing in the way of other ambitious individuals whose power is increasing or the leader may have a vision that no longer fits that of the larger organization. Leaders who have left an organization because of reasons not related to incompetence or lack of ethical judgment often have a chance to move forward in another, more positive environment.

MOVING BEYOND FAILURE

Failure is a natural part of our lives and leaders need to accept that they will fail at times. Everyone and not just leaders need to learn how to build a culture that celebrates intelligent failure. When one succeeds, the tendency is not to question the success. Was I a success because we were so smart, was it luck, or could we have been even more successful? The attitude of "if it ain't broke, don't fix it" can lead to mediocre success. Otherwise, if we did some questioning, the result could be truly outstanding. Questioning what we do can also identify potential failures while they can be fixed or another course of action taken. We should treat success and failure alike in that we should investigate the reasons for both and learn from them.

Dattner and Hogan[24] said that different individuals see the same situation differently. They list personality types "likely to have dysfunctional reactions to failure." They then group these types into three broad categories: those who blame others, those who blame themselves, and those who deny the blame for failure. They also group the types in the following way: skeptical individuals who are very smart about people but oversensitive to criticism; bold individuals who are often in error but never in doubt; and diligent individuals who are hardworking, detail-oriented, and with a tendency to need to control. Each of these groups handles failure differently.

The authors list a number of reasons why leadership can fail:

- The leader chooses to go against stated practices or procedures.
- The leader inadvertently goes against stated practices or procedures.
- The practices or procedures no longer fit the situation and need to be changed.
- The leader lacks the experience/knowledge to deal with the task at hand.
- The task becomes more complex due to external influences.
- The goal or task becomes less certain for external or internal reasons.

The authors then go on to suggest that the individual leaders identify their reactions to failure and then try new strategies around the following: listen and communicate, reflect on the situation and the people involved, and think before acting.

Failure usually has more than one cause and rarely is it the responsibility of a single individual. Edmondson suggests that the leader build a psychologically safe environment in which members of the organization can learn and in which the focus is on "what happened," not on "who did it?"[25] Within this environment, reasons for past failure can be discussed and clues to potential future failure can be identified. Should the vision or the mission of the organization, or both, be revised in response to changing external and internal factors? Does the team need to rebuild to include individuals with different skills? Does the team need to be reeducated in order to include new skills, abilities, approaches? Edmondson suggests the following:

1) We need to understand what kinds of failure may occur.
2) Don't shoot the messenger. Reward those who see problems early and report on them.
3) Be open about what you don't know.
4) Ask for ideas and create opportunities from difficult situations.
5) Know what kinds of failure are blameworthy, those that arise from trying new things, and those that arise from a changing environment.

SUMMARY

Leadership failures can occur because of changes in the external environment or changes in the vision of the organization. They can occur because of a mismatch between the skills of the leader and the requirements of the situation, or they can occur because the leader lacks the interpersonal skills necessary to build teams and achieve goals. Leaders who lack integrity or who do not recognize the lack of integrity in others damage not only themselves but also the organizations they represent. Those who look up to leaders in the workplace and in public life expect and deserve leaders whose integrity is without question and who serve the public to the best of their ability rather than seeing leadership as a route to personal wealth and recognition.

NOTES

1. Andrew Ward, *The Leadership Life Cycle: Matching Leaders to Evolving Organizations* (New York: Palgrave Macmillan, 2003), 5.

2. James M. Kouzes and Barry Z. Posner, "To Lead, Create a Shared Vision," *Harvard Business Review* 87, no. 1 (January 2009): 20–21.

3. Ibid., 21.

4. Jeffrey Kluger, "Why Bosses Tend to Be Blowhards," *Time*, March 2, 2009, 48.

5. Adam Bryant, "Corner Office: Mario Batali," *New York Times*, August 26, 2012, B-2.

6. Birgit Shyns and Tiffany Hansbrough, eds. *When Leadership Goes Wrong: Destructive Leadership Mistakes and Ethical Failures* (Charlotte, NC: Information Age Publishers Inc., 2010), x.

7. Paul W. Mulvey and Art Padilla, "The Environment of Destructive Leadership," in *When Leadership Goes Wrong*, eds. Birgit Shyns and Tiffany Hansbrough, 52.

8. Ibid., 60.

9. Katherine Graham, *Personal History* (New York: Vintage, 1998), 504.

10. "Enron Scandal," *Wikipedia*, http:en.wikipedia.org/wiki/Enron_scandal, accessed September 20, 2012.

11. Nanerl O. Keohane, *Thinking about Leadership* (Princeton, NJ: Princeton University Press, 2010), 6.

12. Max H. Bazerman and Ann E. Tenbrunsel, "Ethical Breakdowns," *Harvard Business Review* 89, no. 4 (April 2011): 59.

13. Ibid., 58–65.

14. Ibid., 62.

15. Diane J. Chandler and Dail Fields, "Ignoring the Signposts: A Process and Perspective of Unethical and Destructive Behavior," in *When Leadership Goes Wrong; Destructive Leadership Mistakes and Ethical Failures*, eds. Birgit Shyns and Tiffany Hansbrough, 109.

16. Robert H. Rosen, "Integrity," in *Leading People. Transforming Business from the Inside Out* (New York: Viking, 1966), 314.

17. Ibid., 284.

18. Barbara Kellerman, "When Should a Leader Apologize and When Not," *Harvard Business Review* 84, no. 4 (April 2006), 73–81.

19. Ibid.

20. Ibid., 81.

21. Laura Brouse-Long, "Letter to Smithsonian Contributing Members and Friends," The Smithsonian, Washington, D.C., April 13, 2007.

22. Ibid.

23. Jeffrey A. Sonnenfeld and Andrew J. Ward, "Firing Back: How Great Leaders Rebound after Career Disasters," *Harvard Business Review* 85, no. 1 (January 2007): 77–84.

24. Ben Dattner and Robert Hogan, "Can You Handle Failure," *Harvard Business Review* 89, no. 4 (April 2011): 117–21.

25. Amy Edmondson, "Strategies for Learning from Failure," *Harvard Business Review* 89, no. 4 (April 2011), 49–55.

11

Mentoring

Leadership in context requires knowledge of a profession, an organization, and a team as well as individuals and how each can contribute to the common good. Formal knowledge about these elements is found in statements of policy and procedure, mission statements, organization charts, position descriptions and similar types of recorded information that describe and define the leader's role and responsibilities. In addition to these formal statements, a great deal of informal information is available: (1) tacit information that describes such things as organizational culture, (2) behavioral norms in specific professions, organizations, and teams, and (3) how individuals are expected to interact. A great deal of learning needs to be done in order to understand what it means to be a leader and to be a team member in a specific environment. While the formal organization is relatively easy to identify, tacit information is passed on informally and is often difficult to pin down. One of the most successful ways in which tacit information is transmitted is through the process of mentoring.

Until relatively recently, mentoring had not been seen as a topic of study separate from teaching, managing, or leading. The Random House Dictionary's[1] brief definition, that a mentor is "an experienced and trusted advisor," does not begin to define mentoring. In seeking out relevant research and in discussing the topic with colleagues, there seems to be consensus that mentoring is difficult to describe, but "I know it when I see it." It is generally agreed that mentoring is a mutually beneficial activity in which individuals learn from one another. An experienced individual who understands the dynamic of an organization, its culture, and the ways in which one can work within the organization to succeed and prosper and who is willing to share this with a new member of the organization is mentoring the individual. It is also agreed that the successful mentor is one who listens, asks questions, provides constructive criticism, and guides an individual along a path that helps that individual succeed.

In an earlier era, it was common for young men to be apprenticed to someone in the trades or professions and learn the skills of the trade as well as the tacit information necessary to build a reputation, a business, and succeed.

Lawyers learned their skills in the offices of other lawyers. Business people learned their skills by working their way up through the ranks of the company and learning about the organization from the bottom up. In our current society, education has been largely separated from apprenticeship, and individuals gain their formal expertise and skills in their schooling and then join an organization after they have received their academic degrees or certificates. They have shown that they have the formal information but unless they have served as interns or worked in other organizational settings, they have little or no understanding of the tacit information necessary to become part of a team and certainly not to become the leader of a team.

We have general agreement that we always need new leaders, leaders who can take our institutions forward. Where are they? Where will they come from? What is the responsibility of our leaders today to prepare for the next generation of leaders? Some say that there is a crisis in commitment and individuals are often criticized for not working to their full potential. Members of the organization often feel bogged down by ever increasing job demands and lack of recognition of the fact that they are trying to succeed. Rosen[2] says that the role of leaders is to be "keepers of the big picture" and that today's leaders have a responsibility to develop tomorrow's leaders. They do this by creating an environment in which individuals can take charge of their work life, receive guidance when appropriate, and learn to succeed, that is, mentoring.

Leadership development is a conscious process that takes time. It is done by putting people in situations and on projects that matter and thus stretching their view of what they can do when they are expected to perform. Leaders lead by example and share their experience and expertise with others. They must have a teachable view of what leadership is, how it contributes to the health of the organization, and how it is used to create change. Numerous authors stress that leaders must look toward the future, develop a shared and compelling vision of the future, and welcome what the future may hold. If leaders are not future-oriented, how can they mentor tomorrow's leaders? Leaders who are in the comfort zone of believing that "all is well and we can coast for a while" are out of touch with reality and are not competent to be mentors of tomorrow's leaders, nor are they themselves good leaders for today.

ORGANIZATIONAL CULTURE

Each organization has a distinct culture and that culture provides "an invisible guidebook for employees." It serves as a compass for making decisions when the policy manual doesn't work. This culture can be a mentoring culture in which employees are encouraged to look at things from new perspectives, try new things, and transform mistakes into learning experiences. Bennis[3] said that the organization itself can be a better mentor than an individual as turnover in many organizations limits the continuity in mentorship which an individual may find useful. He also said that the organization's leaders as mentors in areas including organizational behavior, tone, pace, and values can provide either a positive or negative mentoring experience. Suppose a culture existing within the organization is biased against women, people of color, those with disabilities and does not welcome creativity and open communication. Unless the leader aggressively works to change the culture, neither the leader nor the culture is a desirable role model.

A good mentoring culture welcomes and encourages new individuals. Its purpose is to grow new talent and to find tomorrow's leaders. It recognizes good work and the desire to succeed. It is not as supportive of the individual who lacks the incentive to move ahead nor is it tolerant of behavior that violates the ethics and values of the organization. It encourages shared values and mutual respect. In this way, the new employee gains knowledge of the organization and a commitment to the organization is fostered while at the same time fostering desired values and a strong work ethic.

Within this environment, leaders trust that more experienced staff members will mentor others and thus themselves gain self-confidence while reinforcing cultural values in others. This is what happens when the coach of a basketball team relies on upper-class players to work with new members of the team to teach them the expectations of the coach when they play the game. The coach continues to observe the mentoring process as someone who is just beginning to be a mentor may try to overmanage the interaction and thus not provide the new team member the opportunity to grow and learn, or conversely may be too "hands off" and not know when to step in and provide direction. As the coach works with the team members to foster a culture in which there is mutual support and mutual responsibility, the coach is building a team with the greatest chance of being a winning team.

In some organizations, a formal mentoring program is in place. For example, new employees may be assigned to a leader in their work area who is responsible for "guiding professional growth." The mentor and the assigned employee would be expected to meet regularly and discuss current job performance and future aspirations. Regular meetings and required discussions would allow for a clear understanding of the professional possibilities and required achievements expected. In other organizations, a team of mentors may be identified as "go to" people when staff members have a question or concern. These individuals can be anywhere in the organization and have been identified by their managers or peers as having the information and skills to mentor. These formal approaches provide the opportunity for every new employee to have guidance within the organization and to learn about its culture and expectations. This also allows leaders in the organization to monitor individual progress of new employees and to determine which ones have leadership potential. It also provides the mentor with the experience of working with another individual to achieve organizational goals. Every organization is looking to recruit new talent and to retain the talent it has. The mentoring organization is by definition a learning organization in which everyone involved is continuously learning how to do a better job and how to help others succeed in order for the organization to fulfill its mission and goals.

In the global workplace, mentoring is an essential activity that provides bridges between and among cultures. Given our culturally rich workforce, it is important that ways of mentoring interface appropriately with the needs and expectations of the current workforce. Zachary said that "the definition of mentoring varies among cultures. How the word mentor is culturally understood can alter the very essence of a mentoring relationship . . . or it could connote a negative association because of a perception that it is a position of weakness to seek a mentor."[4] Different cultures mentor in different ways and the success of mentoring is heavily dependent on context. "Like culture, it [context] is social, not individual and is defined as structure, framework, environment, situation, circumstance, and ambiance. Changing the context can have powerful effects on changing the beliefs and behaviors of those who are functioning within it."[5]

The mentoring culture, when it is fully supported, provides a safety zone in which individuals can learn and prosper and if difficulties arise, a mentor is there to help work with the situation. It is difficult for some employees to turn to their boss or to peers for assistance as they think it shows weakness and an inability to solve one's own problems. Others have been in difficult situations, have asked someone for assistance, and having been poorly treated have no desire to repeat the experience. The mentoring culture requires trust, trust by managers that employees are doing their best and trust by their employees that asking for help will result in some level of support that will be a teaching moment rather than an unpleasant experience.[6]

The workplace culture of organizations in the past tended to be more stable than it is today and it was not unusual for someone to stay in the same organization for many years. It tended to be relatively structured and its leadership was usually white male and culturally similar with everyone's role and status well understood. DeLong, Gabbaro, and Lees[7] say that the workplace culture has changed from that of a loyal cooperative culture where people stayed for many years to one in which individuals stay as long as they see opportunity and when something better beckons, they move on. Staff members are less apt to invest in mentoring as there is less loyalty to the organization and to one another. This is costly to the organization both in terms of the lessening of the strength of the organizational culture and the cost of training new staff members. DeLong et al. also stress that everyone in the organization can benefit from mentoring or being a mentor. They further stress that mentoring is essential in an increasingly global world in which cultural issues play a role in each work environment. Not only must one understand the job assignment, but one must also be aware of how to interact with coworkers who may represent different cultures and with those they serve who may also represent different cultures.

WHAT DOES A MENTOR DO

Mentoring is a very personal kind of leadership. It is an informal relationship usually between two people whose purpose is to share knowledge in order to enhance performance. It is not a reward-related activity. Rather, it is a way of connecting compatible people and promoting talent.[8] While in some cases a mentor may be assigned to an individual, more often an individual wishing to learn about how to succeed in a profession or in an organization will identify an individual with whom there appears to be a level of compatibility and ask that person for advice. The mentor pays attention to the individual wishing to be mentored and listens, asks questions, shows interest, and provides suggestions about what to do or try in the workplace. The mentor is also interested in the individual's personal goals, perceived strengths, and interests. The mentor does not cross the fine line between mentoring to enhance performance and professional growth and getting too personal.

The high performing organization includes individuals with a diversity of views and experiences who can share their different views in order to solve problems. A leader as mentor appreciates the diversity of the organization and encourages others to look at issues from new perspectives, champions the free flow of ideas, and supports experimentation. Errors that occur are turned into learning experiences in order to move forward.[9] In preparing tomorrow's leaders, the mentor provides learning opportunities that stretch the individuals' self-perceptions of what they can do and thus build self-confidence. In this way, the organization can identify tomorrow's leaders and at the same time enrich the organization. One way by which to attract talented individuals to an organization is to promise that they will have the opportunity to be mentored by senior leaders who will teach them and give their advice about professional aspects of the job as well as how to work with others and become strong contributing members of the team.

Not everyone is a good mentor. To be a mentor, it takes someone who is honest about personal strengths and failings and who expects similar honesty from the person to be mentored, someone who respects others and demands respect. A person who has a personal agenda of wanting to train someone to be "just like me" or someone who wants to benefit from the hard work of others is a poor candidate to be a mentor, and will probably not offer any guidance of real value. Mentors do not control, do not micromanage, and do not use individuals being mentored for personal gain, for example, taking credit for that person's ideas or research. The successful mentor instills confidence in others by being willing to help them maximize their potential by providing opportunities for new learning experiences, by teaching new skills, and by offering positive encouragement and constructive criticism. The mentor provides candid advice about behaviors or approaches that have not worked and what can be done to make improvements. The mentor is willing to share ideas, to listen, to guide, and to assist in navigating difficult situations when appropriate. The mentor also knows when to back off and let the individual work through a situation without intervening with advice. The mentor who has a "help everyone personality" and is always giving advice is more of a yenta than a mentor.

Not everyone is leadership material, but everyone in the organization benefits from being able to ask others for advice. Most individuals in the organization are solid, steady workers who aren't seeking the top positions but who stay in the organization for a fairly long time, who hold its institutional memory, who have a longer term perspective of the organization, and who appreciate stability.[10] They are often overlooked by fast-track individuals who may look down on them and may underestimate their competence. The wise leader knows that these are often the individuals in the organization who have the greatest amount of tacit information about how the organization works and how to get things done. Solid steady workers are valuable mentors when it comes to this type of knowledge and expertise and they too deserve to be mentored so that they can maximize their opportunities and their ability to do their job.

Trust and trustworthiness is the most important characteristic of a mentor and the strength of the mentoring relationship depends on this. If there is a lack of mutual respect, if the mentor has a rigid way of looking at issues and what is expected of an individual or a situation, the relationship will not work. Each mentoring relationship is different depending on the individuals involved and the situation. The relationship may be brief or may last for many years depending on how compatible those involved feel and how valuable each individual sees the relationship as.

WHAT THE MENTORED PERSON WANTS

Every person wishes to maximize their potential and an important way of doing this is to find someone who is knowledgeable about a field of endeavor, who has experience in a particular area, and who has both the interest in and the ability to teach others and help them grow professionally. The ideal mentor is someone who is genuine and who is truly interested in helping others reach their potential. The ideal mentor is not judgmental but is willing to listen and to provide guidance. A high level of mutual rapport and respect allows for honesty.

Potential mentors are everywhere. When a person joins the organization, part of their orientation is to figure out who knows what and who is willing to share that information. Sometimes a supervisor will suggest or assign an individual to act as a mentor and sometimes this works. In other cases, there is not a good fit between personalities and the individual may need to find someone else to ask for assistance. Some new employees will find an individual in the organization who appears to have the requisite mentoring skills and ask them outright if they will be their mentor. Rarely does that individual say no. Often they are honored to think that they have demonstrated the skills and abilities to help someone else. Sometimes an individual will ask someone for help in one aspect of the work day and another person for help in another aspect. In some cases a mentoring relationship will be short-lived and in other cases will last for an extended period. Mentoring relationships tend to last as long as they are mutually beneficial. The amount of time it takes to be a mentor depends entirely upon the dynamic between the individuals involved. For some, mentoring consists of being readily available to respond to questions and concerns and for others it involves discussions from time to time that deal with one's potential and how to develop opportunities. Individual needs and interests change and their need for mentoring or a particular type of mentor changes. What does not change is an understanding of the mutual benefit of the relationship and the flexibility of how it plays out.

Mentors can open doors as well as give advice. They know who to ask if an individual wants some specific information, wants to learn about a new program, or asks to participate in activities of interest. Someone new to an organization doesn't know these things and it may take a long time to figure them out alone. The mentor can serve as a sponsor, introduce the new individual to the right people, and be available to provide guidance if necessary. The mentor may suggest additional sources of information, other programs to investigate, or other people to meet who can provide further opportunities. Opening doors provides the mentored person an opportunity to learn new things, to meet new people, and thus to expand their horizons.

The number of choice assignments in which one can grow and learn is limited. To provide additional opportunities, the leader could place a more experienced individual in the choice position and then assign a new staff member who would shadow the position. Another way to provide experience within the organization is to give the new staff member a research assignment or pose a problem that needs to be solved. This gives individuals a chance to show what they can do. The mentor should look for real, not contrived opportunities that truly contribute to the organization or to the individual's experience to learn and grow.

Individuals looking to gain understanding of what it means to be a leader will often seek out someone they respect, who is willing to teach in a very personal way, and who will be available over an extended period to guide them toward leadership. Bennis said that "some people are particularly adept at recruiting the mentors they need . . . this ability is more complex and more important than mere networking. It is nothing less than the ability to spot the handful of people who can make all the difference in your life and getting them on your side."[11] Bennis goes on to discuss the need "for mentors and friends and groups of allied souls." These can be teachers, parents, older siblings, senior associates, or others they have met who "demanded more from them than they knew they had to give." One can also learn about leadership from reading the classics, biographies of others who lived through hard times. Friends and friendships act as a very strong kind of mentoring. Mentoring can go beyond professional activities to include teaching of values, ways to deal with adversity, and many lessons we can use throughout our personal and professional lives.

The individual being mentored needs to have enough sense of who they are to avoid trying to fit into someone else's image of them. That never works, nor does allowing oneself to be pushed into daily activities that are not personally of interest or enriching. Saying no to a mentor's suggestion, so long as it is done carefully and with options, helps the mentor better understand what the interests and needs of the individual being mentored are. Regardless of who your mentor may be, you are still responsible for your career and it is your choices that will guide it.

Lyndon B. Johnson[12] chose his own mentors using a very specific strategy. Robert Caro, one of the major biographers of Johnson, said that LBJ made himself a "professional son," picking out of the organization of which he was a part or wished to join an older man who held great power but who had no son and was lonely. "With older men of authority in general, Johnson would do literally what the cliche says: sit at the feet of an older man to absorb his knowledge." He started using this technique while in college and continued to use it throughout his career. LBJ picked his mentors carefully. When elected to the U.S. Senate, he learned who really held power, Sen. Richard Russell of Georgia, and made sure he became close to him by serving on the committee Russell chaired, learning his work habits and working similar hours so he could naturally see him in the hallways, learning his likes and dislikes, and adopting similar ones in order to develop a relationship. He used similar methods to get close to Sam Rayburn who was speaker of the House of Representatives. According to Johnson " . . . all men were tools and to use them he had to know their weaknesses . . . ." While this is a very cynical approach to choosing a mentor, it seemed to work for LBJ in his political career.

While seeking the right mentor is an important component of learning how to lead, selecting the wrong mentor can lead to disaster. If one becomes associated with a mentor and the mentor becomes embroiled in illegal activities or other scandals, some of the scandal may rub off on everyone associated with the mentor. Richard Nixon was a mentor to a number of his staff members and as the Watergate scandal played out, their careers were tarnished by his actions. The mentor needs to be cautious as well when agreeing to work with someone who is thought to be brilliant or who believes they are brilliant or at least that "they know everything." Brilliance and leadership often do not reside in the same individual. The genius may well be a disaster when it comes to social interaction or meeting a schedule. The task of the mentor is to appreciate their abilities while at the same time making them aware that they have limitations.[13] Mentors also need to be wary of individuals whose main objective in asking to be mentored is so that they can boast of their connection to an important person and thus make themselves appear more important.

Role Models

Role models are individuals one can look up to and wish to emulate. A role model can be a mentor or can be someone we respect for their values, their integrity, and the way in which they lead. Barbara McClintock, the Nobel Prize–winning scientist whose work in genetics was ridiculed for years by her male colleagues and who had difficulty in obtaining research funds but who kept working on her theory of "jumping genes" in corn, persevered and in doing so, changed the face of her science. She generously gave of her time to new scientists and was a role model to women because she would not quit, because she persevered in what was seen as a man's world, and she won.[14] We may find role models in every facet of our lives and our profession. They are the ones who dared, who persevered, and who did it with class and integrity.

Other Ways to Mentor

In addition to the traditional one-on-one mentoring, several variations exist including mutual mentoring, self-mentoring and virtual mentoring. One can also include coaching and sponsoring in this list although these are often more formal arrangements that go beyond mentoring.

Mutual mentoring occurs when individuals, often those working together, learn that the other has skills they need and vice versa. An example of this was the pairing of an expert in business processes and a software development expert. Each was hired for their expertise to work together to improve the operation of an automated software system and each was expert in only half of the job. Each taught the other and together they learned what they needed to do to be successful. One taught the other the software skills necessary to improve the system while the other showed the importance of the business processes that the new system was intended to support. Mutual mentoring easily expands into peer mentoring when members of a team or those working on a project help one another and learn together.

If an individual has a position that is high up in the organization or is working at a distant location, there may be no opportunity to find a mentor. Despite this, it is essential to get feedback on how well they are communicating the vision and priorities of the organization, how efficiently the time and effort of the organization is being used, and the extent to which they are making progress toward stated goals.[15] Kaplan suggests that such an individual should develop feedback systems that involve those working in the organization to be sure that one is on the right track and is using the organization's resources wisely. A combination of honest self-evaluation and feedback from others in the organization can be considered a form of self-mentoring.

Virtual mentoring[16] is useful when the mentor and the mentored are at a distance or work in different organizations. E-mail and other online connections allow individuals to develop and maintain a close relationship. This is also a useful technique for peer mentoring as it can bring together individuals from many places with similar needs and interests. Although e-mentoring expands the opportunities for mentoring, those included in the process should be selected carefully to assure that the mentoring process focuses on specific needs and interests and does not become overly social. Those who have participated in e-mentoring appreciate the built-in reflection time that accompanies receiving a message and thinking about it before responding. Others say that while reflection time is helpful in some situations, what if there is an immediate need to discuss an issue and waiting for a response is unacceptable? For some individuals, communicating via e-mail is more comfortable than face-to-face interactions partly because it is time and distance neutral. For others, the absence of visual cues makes this a less desirable format. As is true of any form of mentoring, one size does not fit all individuals or situations. However, we can expect to see more and more virtual mentoring as we continue to find our way in a networked global world.

Women and Mentoring

Since the 1990s more and more women have entered the workplace and have earned the requisite degrees and experience to aspire to higher levels of management and leadership. For several reasons, they often have difficulty finding individuals who will mentor them and who have the requisite experience and ability to do so. In many workplaces women continue to be valued less than men, or women who agree to be mentors may be thought of by their peers as having agreed to mentor individuals with fewer abilities and opportunities to be tomorrow's leaders. CATALYST, a nonprofit research and advocacy organization that studies women at work, reported that in 2005, women held 16.4 percent of corporate officer positions, up 0.7 percent from

2002. At this rate it will take 40 years to reach parity. The researchers found that a lack of access to informal networks, lack of role models, and sex-based stereotyping are the problems. Mentoring is a solution to at least two of these. Networks for women and minorities are not as strong as those for men and the ways to network are less clear. Those in power tend to keep others out of their "clubs" and it is in those networks and informal clubs that decisions on who wins and who moves up the ladder are often made. Because of the small number of women who are leaders in their organizations, there are relatively few role models and women who do not have mentors have to learn on the job how to do the job. One CATALYST researcher said that it is assumed that women "are good citizens . . . helpful to colleagues and clients." It is expected that they will do this and therefore they are not rewarded for doing so, but they are penalized for not doing so. Men however are not expected to be supportive of others, and when they are, they are rewarded. This is but one example of how mentoring can help those not part of the informal networks and those who don't understand some of the arcane ways in which decisions are made, to break the code.[17]

A long-standing discussion continues about why women in science are typically poorly represented in tenure ranks. The 1999 report at MIT on science faculty and the more recent national report by the Women in Science Panel chaired by Donna Shalala[18] say that there is a need in science "to tap a deeper talent pool . . . to maintain a competitive edge" internationally. This demands that one cannot rely solely on white males as a source of all ideas to maintain that edge. The problem for women is not inability or the lack of women in the pipeline. It is not that "women are uncompetitive or less productive, that they take off too much time for their families . . . extensive previous research showed 'a pattern of unconscious but pervasive bias [that is] arbitrary and subjective' . . . evaluation processes and a work environment in which 'anyone lacking the work and family support' traditionally provided by a 'wife' is at a serious disadvantage." Shalala expressed surprise at the strength of the evidence of bias in the 21st century and said that it is essential to level the playing field, for example, send out prepublication journal articles for review minus the names so that the gender of the author is unknown. It is also necessary to provide equal access to resources so that everyone gets an even chance. Without networking, access to resources, mentoring by those who have made it up the next steps on the ladder, and a fierce determination to succeed is difficult.

This raises the issue of why is it so often true that women, individuals of color, and others poorly represented in leadership positions are often unwilling to mentor others and thus help them succeed? Is it because mentoring can be time consuming, because they see mentoring women and minorities as a poor use of their time, or because they think that to mentor "others like them rather than white males" may jeopardize their personal situation? A study reported in 2012 by researchers at Yale University[19] concluded that "the professors [in science] were less likely to offer the women mentoring and a job. And even if they were willing to offer a job, the salary was lower. The bias was pervasive, the scientists said, and probably reflected subconscious cultural influences rather than overt or deliberate discrimination. Female professors were just as biased against women students as their male colleagues, and biology professors just as biased as physics professors—even though more than half of biology majors are women, whereas men far outnumber women in physics."[20] The researchers concluded that the path to leadership by women in the sciences has changed little in the past decade despite attention given to this issue, both positive and negative, by such academic luminaries as Lawrence Summers, president of Harvard University, who questioned the abilities of women in science and resigned his presidency over the uproar that resulted.

Women, over the past decades, have developed ways of showing leadership and finding mentors that differ from the paths men most likely take. "For a woman in any business, it's easier to focus outward where you can define and deliver the services required to succeed, than to navigate the internal affiliations and power structure within a male dominant firm . . . women cultivate external relationships because of uneasy in-house relationships, poor mentorship, neglect by colleagues, and a vulnerable position in the labor market."[21] Most women who have achieved leadership positions have had mentors but they were more likely to be treated as probationary employees than as potential leaders. Because of this they missed out on the most valuable opportunities available to new members of the organization and were rarely introduced to the internal and external network of relationships that existed. Some men were reluctant to mentor women "because of the risk that he would be wasting his time, as the women might leave the organization." In fact ". . . men who do mentor women can't offer much in the way of psychosocial support—how to deal with sexism, how to balance a career and family."[22]

What women have done in many areas is to develop external relationships with others, often women, who can provide the mentoring support and external networks. This provides them opportunities outside an organization to gain recognition. An informal study by this author several years ago showed that women who were active in professional societies and community groups and who published their research and other articles externally were more highly regarded by the organization for which they worked. Apparently, women within the organization need external validation before their male coworkers appreciate their abilities. Women also look for positions that are transparent in terms of expectations so that their abilities can be validated by effective measures, and they are not subjected to biased reviews. When they do change positions, their productivity continues unlike men whose productivity tends to drop when they accept a new position. Because of their external relationships, women have a better understanding of other organizations and their work environment, and transitioning from one organization to another is smoother. When women consider changing employers, they are much more deliberate than men "probably because experience has taught them the importance of environment and culture in both their performance and job satisfaction . . . and look at the culture of a department in terms of how women fit in along with its values, atmosphere, and tone."[23] Only then do they consider salary.

We often hear of "the old boy's club" which is defined as follows: "It is not necessarily purposeful or malicious, but . . . it entails establishing business relationships on high-priced golf courses, at exclusive country clubs, in the executive sky-boxes at sporting events . . . arenas from which women and minorities are traditionally excluded." It is also in these places that the "truly serious" business transactions or conversations occur.[24] It is also in these environments that senior members of the organization select those they will sponsor as tomorrow's leaders. Since women tend to be excluded from these venues, they need to make their own opportunities. CATALYST researchers have found that "women who highlighted their achievements advanced further, were more satisfied with their careers, and had greater compensation growth than women who failed to blow their own horns."[25] While there are those who consider self-promotion unladylike, it is the most efficient means for women to move ahead and since the more traditional venues are closed to women, it is the only way. As more and more women assume positions of leadership and excel in their roles, it may be easier for them to find sponsors and mentors who are in senior roles within the organization rather than needing to go outside it.

Networking

Someone new to a profession or an organization wants to meet other individuals with whom they have interests in common and with whom they can share ideas. Part of the mentoring process is to introduce individuals with similar interests to one another so that they can learn from one another. This also provides the opportunity to interact with individuals outside the organization who can look at issues from a position not biased by loyalty to an organization or group of individuals. As has been noted above, networking consists both of external networking and internal networking and an important role of the mentor is to introduce new hires to each network.

External networks may be both formal and informal with the formal networks often being represented by professional societies whose members have professional interests in common and who provide a meeting place for people of like interests. Professional societies often invite new professionals to participate in their various mentoring activities, which can lead to participation in committee assignments, meeting leaders in the field, and otherwise getting introduced to the field of their interest. Other external networks can be developed based on one's personal interests and on relationships developed during one's graduate professional program or similar relationships. Linked-In, the online social networking resource, grows daily and is a useful means of finding and connecting with individuals who share similar interests and concerns.

SUMMARY

Mentoring is the process by which leaders pass on to the next generation the lessons they have learned. Where once these lessons were passed on through apprenticeships, it is more common today for individuals to receive required formal education to fill a position, be hired, and then learn from those in the organization how to do their job and work as part of a team. Mentoring is the way in which the organization's culture and its expectations are passed on. It is also the way in which tomorrow's leaders are identified and groomed for their future roles. Mentors can be anywhere—in an organization, in a professional society, in the community. They may be selected to assist a new staff member, or staff members can select as a mentor an individual they respect and with whom they feel comfortable in discussing issues related to their career. Mentoring can be a very personal activity in that it involves the sharing of knowledge and skills that pertain to the professional needs and interests of a particular individual. A personal mentor is like a personal trainer for your career.

NOTES

1. *The American Heritage Dictionary of the English Language*, 4th ed. (Boston: Houghton Mifflin, 2000), 1098.

2. Robert H. Rosen, *Leading People: Transforming Business from the Inside Out* (New York: Viking, 1996).

3. Warren Bennis, *On Becoming a Leader* (New York: Basic Books, 2003), 180.

4. Lois Zachary, "Tips and Practical Advice for Mentors and Mentees and Anyone Involved in the Mentoring Process or Beginning the Mentoring Experience," *Lois Zachary's Mentoring Expert Blog*, retrieved April 10, 2011 from http://mentoring expert.wordpress.com/

5. Frances K. Kochan and Joseph T. Pascarellil, eds. *Perspectives on Mentoring: Transforming Contexts, Communities, and Cultures* (Greenwich, CT: Information Age Publishing, 2003), xi.

6. Linda Hill, "Becoming the Boss," *Harvard Business Review* 85, no. 1 (January 2007): 55.

7. Thomas DeLong Jr., John J. Gabarro, and Robert J. Lees, "Why Mentoring Matters in a Hyper Competitive World," *Harvard Business Review* 86, no. 1 (January 2008), 115–21.

8. Paul Oestreicher, *Camelot, INC. Leadership and Management Insights from King Arthur and the Round Table* (Santa Barbara, CA: Praeger, 2011), 11.

9. Rosen, *Leading People: Transforming Business from the Inside Out*, 37.

10. Bennis, *On Becoming a Leader*, xiii.

11. Ibid., 83–86.

12. "Lessons in Power: Lyndon Johnson Revealed. A Conversation with Historian Robert A. Caro," *Harvard Business Review* 84, no. 4 (April 2006): 51.

13. Rob Goffe and Gareth Jones, "Leading Clever People," *Harvard Business Review* 85, no. 3 (March 2007): 72–79.

14. Evelyn Fox Keller, *A Feeling for the Organism: The Life and Work of Barbara McClintock* (New York: W. H. Freeman, 1983).

15. Robert S. Kaplan, "What to Ask the Person in the Mirror," *Harvard Business Review* 85, no. 1 (January 2007): 86–95.

16. David Clutterbuck and Zufi Hussain, eds. *Virtual Coach Virtual Mentor* (Charlotte, NC: Information Age Publishing, Inc., 2010), 3–18.

17. Ibid., 7.

18. As reported in the *New York Times*, November 19, 2006. p. A20.

19. Nancy M. Carter and Christine Silva, *Mentoring: Necessary but Insufficient for Advancement*, www.catalyst.org.publications

20. *Beyond Bias and Barriers: Fulfilling the Potential of Women in Academic Science and Engineering*, www.nationalacademy.org

21. *Proceedings of the National Academy of Science* http://www.nytimes.com/2012/09/25/sciencebias-persists-against-women-of-science-a-study-says.html.

22. Ibid.

23. Boris Groysberg, "How Star Women Build Portable Skills," *Harvard Business Review* 86, no. 2 (February 2008), 76.

24. Ilene Lang, "Co-Opting the Old Boy's Club: Making it Work for Women," *Harvard Business Review* 89, no. 11 (November 2011), 44.

25. Ibid.

12

Following the Leader

Many leadership opportunities arise when the current leader, for one reason or other, leaves a position. This may occur when the current leader is promoted from within to another leadership position in the same organization or is recruited to become a leader in a new organization. The organization may be experiencing a change in vision because it is moving in a new direction and wants a different kind of leader. Financial or organizational changes may result in restructuring that eliminates the leader's position. Differences in how to carry out the organization's vision or even in what that vision should be may motivate a leader to move to another organization or to start a new organization. The leader may not be performing at the level desired by the organization and is asked to leave. The leader may step down for health or family reasons that make it impossible to meet the requirements of the role of leader. Every leader reaches retirement age at some point and will step down from the position to pursue other interests. In each situation, the individual who is selected to replace the leader has to face issues and make plans for the future of the organization.

When the motivation for a change in leadership comes from the individual currently in a leadership position, it is usually the result of an informed decision to do so. A new position may provide new opportunities to learn new things; provide more resources to support activities; a chance to change responsibilities, to work within or even change a new organizational structure; and perhaps to live in a new location and at a higher salary. New positions carry a sense of the opportunity for growth, of challenge, of excitement. When individuals arrive on the scene to assume new leadership positions, they expect to be on a very steep learning curve and to learn quickly how to lead within the new environment. If the previous leader was a good leader who understood how to develop and grow a good organization, the transition can be relatively smooth because the staff will have a positive, wait-and-see attitude toward the new leader. The new leader will step into a smoothly running organization and the transition will be relatively easy.

If the previous leader was unwilling or unable to manage the responsibilities of leadership because of illness, lack of interest, or difficulties with leadership further up in the organization, the new leader may find that there are numerous issues to be resolved. When interviewing for a leadership position, difficulties may be touched on but rarely discussed at length and the individual selected for the position typically will not fully understand the situation until actually on board. The absence of leadership in a situation quickly becomes evident. The staff may lack interest in what they are doing or they may be anxious to tell the new leader everything that is wrong, what needs to be fixed, and that it needs to be fixed now; or they may have tuned out and say little or nothing about the gaps in leadership. In a service organization, those using the service may express disappointment that the quality of service has declined and will exert pressure to ensure improvement in service. Individuals who resign from their leadership position because of health or family issues tend to retain the sympathy of those who worked for them and although leadership may not have been at the desired level, there are few negative feelings toward the former leader. If the former leader was arrogant, did not treat staff with respect, did not represent staff well, and did not serve as a positive influence, the new leader may find that there is a need to reassure staff members and to rebuild their trust in the leadership of the organization. When new leaders join an organization, they need to move deliberately but quickly to assess the situation, seek information from peers and those higher in the organization, and talk with staff in order to prioritize issues, develop a plan, and act.

LEADERSHIP CHANGES

Organizational Change or Change in Vision

The vision of an organization may change for any number of reasons: external circumstance, changes in needed workforce skills, or changes in leaders who are looking for a new direction. For example, the move to more and more online education by universities will change the nature of on-campus services. In addition to being a "go to" place for the individual who is on campus, the university library also becomes an electronic "go to" place for students located in many places. This change in delivery of courses and the need to deliver information to students in new ways requires a change in the library's vision of the appropriate range of services and how they will be provided. Will the university library's leaders be part of the leadership team to effect a new vision or will university leaders look for someone outside the organization who has had experience implementing a similar new vision? In addition to changes motivated by technological changes, the vision may change because it may need to adapt to financial changes, to changes in the demography of those the institution serves, or for a number of other reasons. The leaders need to be change agents who determine the new vision. If not, new leaders who have a different vision will emerge.

Mergers, downsizing, or changes in direction due to any number of events result in leadership changes in the organization that emerges. Former leaders of one organization may find themselves assisting the leader of a merged organization. Leadership for these individuals has changed into followership and they may be expected to follow a vision not necessarily in agreement with their own or the one that influenced their leadership. For individuals accustomed to being the leader, this can be very difficult and may result in that individual looking for another position, particularly if the new leader has a style that is in conflict with that of the now follower.

In major reorganizations in business in which a company redesigned its vision, members of the existing workforce no longer had the skills to implement the vision. IBM is an example of a company that shifted its vision from manufacturing to consulting. Their leaders identified a new vision and rebuilt the workforce to match the new vision. Unlike many organizations whose vision and needs change, IBM attended to the needs of those who no longer fit the new vision. For example, a number of IBM employees were given a year's salary and benefits if they agreed to retire early.

When an organization is downsized, positions will be lost and leaders may find themselves leading fewer people, leading an organization that no longer fits the vision under which it was established, or they may find themselves without a job. In situations in which leadership is lost through no fault of the leader, there is a moral responsibility on the part of the new leaders to work with them to help them transition to new opportunities. In some situations, leadership accepts this responsibility while in others they show little if any concern for those whose positions have been lost through no fault of their own.

Leadership Changes Due to an Inability to Lead

We have only to read the news or watch television to see examples of leadership that has gone wrong, and it fails for a number of reasons. The leader who is dishonest, inept, arrogant, or falters in other ways often loses the position of leadership. The leader may come in conflict with leadership further up in the organization whose directives negate the leader's ability to lead. The person who follows in the leadership role has the task of rebuilding the vision, restoring the health of the organization, and helping it move on. If the leader who was dismissed had a strong following in the organization, the new leader has a particularly difficult rebuilding process. No one likes to be associated with a loser and when staff members have worked for someone who lost power in a public way, their self-image and the attitude of others toward them will be affected. If they are not part of the problem, the new leader needs to take their feelings into consideration and involve them in the rebuilding of the organization. If they continue to support the former leader and are unwilling to move forward, they need to be removed from the organization.

Some individuals are not successful leaders. They may lack the vision, the organizational skills, or the interpersonal skills to achieve the goals of the organization. Perhaps they would do better in another situation. If this is the case, they need to be removed and replaced by a new leader who has the confidence of the board of directors or other group or individual who is responsible for the entire organization. Those individuals who develop health problems and can no longer lead an organization need understanding and a graceful way to leave their position so that they can step down without negative consequences. Any situation in which leaders are removed because they cannot do the job will have repercussions in the organization they were responsible for leading. The individual coming in as the new leader here again needs to take into consideration the personal concerns of the staff while working to rebuild the organization.

Retirement

When the economy is slow, the expectation is that more and more individuals will tend to remain in the workforce longer than anticipated because of uncertainty about economic conditions. If this happens, it creates a bottleneck in the normal flow of one's work life from first job through retirement. As the economy improves and a larger than usual number of retirements are expected to occur, there will be major leadership changes. It has been noted by many, if not most, not-for-profit organizations that there will be a serious deficit of experienced individuals to lead these organizations. This is in part because senior leaders have stayed in their positions longer than they otherwise might have and the opportunities for middle-level managers to gain experience have been limited. As the baby boomer generation moves on to retirement and as a new generation arrives to assume leadership positions, there will most probably be changes in vision, in leadership skills, and in attitudes toward leadership.

How does a leader prepare for retirement, for letting go? Most of one's life, the emphasis is on "what will I do when I grow up?" Educational preparation, positions held, passions pursued all focus on what the individual will do for a life's work. Often little thought is given to what to do after one has accomplished what one wants to do, when one wants to do something else, or when the law or circumstances say that it is time to let go. Many of us look forward to the time when we won't have to get up and go to work each day or when we have more time to pursue other interests. Still the awareness we must face the reality that when we step down from a leadership position, there can be a big hole in our life as we have lived it.

In the military, individuals serve for a specified time. Officers know that each rank above the one they hold admits a smaller number of officers than there are candidates. They are constantly aware of the fact that if they don't make it to the next rank, they will need to retire from the military and build the next chapter of their life. Politicians are elected for stated terms. Some can run for reelection for as long as they and their constituents wish (U.S. Congress) while others are limited to one or two terms (many mayors and governors). They know that they will retire from political office after a stated period. Limits on one's leadership position make it necessary to plan ahead to the next career or life steps so that when the change comes, and it is known when that change will come, there is a path ahead.

For many professionals, retirement is more likely to be determined by the work we do, how much we enjoy it, our financial position, the condition of our health, or the strength of our desire to do something different. Those in leadership positions can easily become accustomed to the perks of the position.

One gets to pursue a vision, to lead others to pursue that vision, and, with the help of others, to accomplish good things. Leadership has power, and it is often hard to let go of that power, to turn it off, and to turn away from one's life's work. Holding a leadership position also opens doors to many interesting experiences including travel, meeting interesting people, invitations to special events, opportunities to give speeches, invitations to serve on boards and commissions and to be treated as someone who is somehow special. These are all part of the leadership position and stay with the position after the person holding that position leaves. For leaders whose work has been their total life meaning their work life, their social life, the one place where they have friends, retirement can be devastating for when they retire they have little to replace it. One often hears of individuals who become depressed after retirement or individuals who drive others to distraction by trying to micromanage the home front. One of the important contributions women have made to the world of work is that they have brought the concept of balance to the table. Partly because they tend to be the primary caregivers in the family, they have learned to work smarter and to balance the personal and the professional. While this is an important element when one is in the workforce, it is particularly important when one retires and the routines and responsibilities of one's career no longer fill large amounts of the day.

What do the individuals nearing retirement age do to assure that the process works well for all? What they do is to look at their career and decide what else they want to do while in a leadership position, and identify priority items. How long will it take to accomplish them? Can they be done in this current position? If not, what can be accomplished in this position? What can I do after I retire to further my professional goals? Then set retirement goals and a mental timeline. This does not mean gearing down. On the contrary, it usually means that there is a timeline for accomplishing desired goals and where possible preparing connections from current activities to post-retirement activities. If you are an academic and wish to write a book, start preparing the project you will pursue. Find a potential publisher, contact individuals you wish to interview. Identify research resources you will need to access. This is all a legitimate part of a leader's activities and signals to others that you are looking long term at the issues of importance to you and how you can continue to contribute. If you have built relationships with community organizations, you may find many ways in which your leadership activities can be of value to them.

Retiring leaders need to go out at the top of their game. They should not stay on in the position until they hear comments such as "she's getting a bit slow, don't you think?" or "he was really good a few years back but doesn't seem to have that edge anymore." Leaders when they step down from leadership positions do not stop leading unless they want to. Leadership just takes other guises: consulting, writing, teaching, being a mentor, or accepting the leadership of a specific project in the community. One can also lead by showing that life after retirement is not a grey, grim existence but is full of possibilities. Retirees become their own leaders who are accountable to themselves for the power of their vision and their accomplishments.

When the leader retires, there is a responsibility to leave the leadership role in good condition. The organization should be healthy with high-quality staff accustomed to working together, and they should be looking positively to new leadership and different ideas. The retiring leader should tell the incoming leader that "should you have questions about anything, I'm available. Just call me. In the meantime, I'm gone." Few things are worse than a retired leader hanging around to be helpful.

Reluctant Retirement

In an organization, some individuals with leadership positions are less than successful and, although it is evident that they should retire or move to another position, they don't really want to leave. They may make the motions that will lead to selecting a replacement but they will do whatever they can to slow the process of giving up control. The process of giving up control by the leader and assuming control by the designated follower is full of emotional stress for both the individuals involved and those around them. In the business arena, less so in not-for-profit organizations, the CEO may designate or accept from a board of directors a successor from inside or outside the organization several months prior to actual retirement, so that they can work together to assure a smooth transition. While this may sound like a good idea, having two individuals working in the same area on the same tasks invites difficulties. It is expected that there will be a gradual power shift from the senior person to the successor. A person who has become accustomed to being the leader does not necessarily step aside gracefully. If the leader is ready to step down and wants to groom a successor, the power struggle may be relatively small, but if the leader is resistant to leaving the position, each time a bit of power is ceded, there is stress. Often, when an individual has been hired to lead an organization, the board of trustees or other employer may ask the new leader to overlap with the individual who is leaving or the individual who is leaving may suggest sticking around for a while to help with the transition. This is never a good idea as staff cannot work for two leaders in the same place at the same time. They cannot pursue the old vision and the old leader and a new vision and a new leader at the same time. If there are staff loyalties to the person leaving, anything other than a clean break is painful to all. The new leader should come in, gracefully assume leadership, discuss any new directions, and start working on a plan of what to do next, and ask staff for patience and support.

Developing New Leaders within the Organization

The old social model of "come here, work hard, advance in the company, get regular raises, and after an appropriate number of years of at least adequate service, receive retirement benefits" no longer applies. The new social model is one of "find an employer who can help you with your long-term goals and who will pay you what the market says you deserve" and then you move on when a better personal opportunity arises. Company loyalty lasts only as long as you work there. When one looks at turnover rates in both profit and not-for-profit organizations, it is evident that fewer and fewer individuals are making one institution their home forever but are moving to other institutions in response to personal opportunity for growth. This is part of the larger trend, particularly of professionals, to resist authoritarian environments, expect more from employers, give more of their creativity and ideas to employers, and then move on when another challenge beckons. This new model has major implications for the way in which leaders develop. The gradual process of identifying tomorrow's leaders, guiding them gradually so that they understand the organization and how it functions, gradually giving them new responsibilities, and then when it is time for one leader to step aside, another leader is ready to take over is no longer the norm.

WHAT FOLLOWERS MAY FIND

Each leadership position is different depending on the organization, the organizational culture and the vision of the organization. The position is strongly influenced by the individual who came before. If the previous leader understood how to develop and maintain a creative, forward-looking vision and a workforce to match, the transition can be relatively smooth because the staff will have a positive image of leadership and will be looking forward to new ideas. If the former leader was unwilling or unable to perform at the required level, it may take the new leader time to gain the confidence of those to be led and to bring the organization up to the required level of performance.

Following a Successful Leader

Staff members who have followed a successful leader tend to expect successful leadership from the new leader. A positive situation allows the new leader time to study the situation, get to know members of the staff, and identify changes that can be made to enhance the organization and its vision. In this situation new leaders can add value to a good situation by using their own style and approach. New ways of looking at things and doing things can refresh an organization. It isn't necessary to feel obligated to make changes in order to "make the job mine." Changes that are not well thought out and are implemented just for the sake of change rarely work as it becomes evident quickly to everyone that the change was ego motivated rather than leadership motivated. The new leader who steps into a good situation may take it for granted and rather than build on it, sit back and relax. This is never a good idea as the organization that is not growing and changing will not function efficiently unless it receives continuous motivation to grow and change. Encouraging and expecting forward movement is the primary role of the leader.

The Unprepared Leader

When the new leader steps into a leadership position without sufficient preparation and lacks information about expectations that will make the transition easier, the learning curve necessary to assume control is steep.

When President Franklin D. Roosevelt died in 1945 near the end of World War II, Harry Truman became president without having been included in discussions and decisions about plans for ending the war. He had not met foreign leaders with whom he would now have to negotiate and was thus at a major disadvantage. He had been selected as vice president largely for political reasons, and Roosevelt rarely if ever included him in discussions of foreign policy. He had leadership thrust upon him, and he rose to the occasion. A similar situation occurred in 1963 when John F. Kennedy was assassinated and Lyndon Johnson, also a political choice as vice president, assumed the presidency. The Vietnam War was not going well and it was dividing the country. Kennedy disliked Johnson and did not include him in many of the policy and decision making sessions necessary to understand the issues. Johnson, like Truman, had to learn a lot very quickly as a restless nation depended on him. These events bring to mind the "what if I were hit by a truck" philosophy which is that one should be prepared for the unexpected and make plans accordingly so that there will be a smooth continuation of activities. Today's vice presidents tend to be members of the president's councils and participate in the decision-making process. Our world is too complex and dangerous to permit unprepared leadership.

Following an Unsuccessful Leader

The absence of leadership in an organization is quickly evident to the new leader and often to the larger community. In addition to a general aura of uncertainty and perhaps a reluctance to have a positive attitude toward the new leader, there are usually tasks that need immediate attention that the former leader for one reason or other did not attend to. A personnel situation must be addressed, such as the faculty member who had been denied tenure but was not informed of this because the previous leader lacked the courage or was too disorganized to inform the individual. A pending budget cut requires reduction in programs and requires immediate attention. A planning document or report is way overdue and that must be completed immediately. Staff may have the feeling that all is collapsing around them, and they are not sure that the new leader is their best hope. During the period of faulty leadership, someone in the informal organization may have gathered power and may use subversive means to undermine the authority and potential success of the new leader. Many agendas, both internal and external to the organization, both hidden and overt, may also be at play and the new leader must take charge immediately.

When new leaders enter such a situation, they need to move deliberately but quickly to assess the situation, seek information from peers and those higher in the organization, and talk with staff in order to prioritize issues, develop a plan, and act. A colleague who was director of a major not-for-profit organization said that when she was working her way up in positions of increasing responsibility, she would look for a leadership failure and apply for the position as she could do so much more in a short time to demonstrate her own leadership skills and make dramatic, visible changes. Her thinking was that there was less challenge if one moved into a position in which there had been a history of good leadership as in that situation, all one could do was to continue the good work but with one's own style.

Challenges for the New Leader

Many of the challenges result from a poor workplace culture in which the former leader lacked vision and the ability to follow through, communication is uneven, tasks are not completed and the former leader seemed not to be aware of the problems or not to care and let things slide. Problem employees may need either to be retrained, reassigned, or removed, and the former leader did not deal with the situation. The role of the incoming leader is to look at a dysfunctional situation and provide a perspective on what needs to be done and then to act.

Some organizations seem to run on tacit information. Nothing is written down. No documentation, no project requirements, status reports, or other documentation is available to guide how the organization functions. The new leader needs to figure out how the organization currently functions, or not, by observation, by interviewing staff members not all of whom necessarily want to work in a situation where there are written rules, and then needs either to develop processes and procedures to guide current operations or to set new processes and procedures to guide a newly structured organization. At the opposite end of the spectrum, the former leader may have micromanaged the organization to the extent that everything had to be approved centrally and staff members had no independence of action and in this case, a new way of working needs to be instituted that will create an environment of respect and individual responsibility.

Sometimes the leader is promoted to a position elsewhere in the organization and has no authority over activities in the earlier position but cannot seem to let go of that position and regularly "makes suggestions" to the new leader about how to lead. Such activity leads to stress and confusion. Incomplete transfers of power never work and should not be allowed. The new leader must insist on clear lines of authority and a clear transfer of power. When an individual takes responsibility for an organization, the prior leader must step aside.

When one steps into a situation in which leadership has been absent and one inherits a staff that is not motivated, that may be unqualified to do the job, or that is just plain difficult, it is necessary to determine what one can do to improve the situation. This is an opportunity for the new leader to put a personal stamp on the position and to set a direction that benefits from the positive elements found in the organization plus the new leader's ideas. This will include understanding the culture of the workplace and how it influences staff motivation. If the unit being led has had a history of not being productive or of having poor interpersonal relations, one may need to look to higher levels of management to learn why this situation has been allowed to fester. The culture of the entire organization may not be conducive to fostering a positive workplace. As one wise mentor said, "there are some situations that are too messed up to fix," and if the new leader finds such a situation, the best thing to do may be to look for another situation.

STEPPING ASIDE

One of the ways in which great leaders are evaluated by those who follow is the manner in which they step aside. Some do so with grace, others are forced aside, and still others use the process as an opportunity to make statements some of which would have best been left unsaid. Others might resemble Michael Collins, the Irish revolutionary, who was assassinated before he had the chance to fulfill his promises to the people of Ireland. Another example is Dorothy Day who began her public life as an idealistic anarchist and spent her working life serving those who were in need. She and a friend began a movement, the Catholic Worker, for which she became well known. As she aged, she became physically frail and gradually stepped aside so others could follow her.[1]

Katherine Graham, publisher of the *Washington Post*, assumed her leadership role after the death of her husband and led the newspaper for a number of years. Her son, Donald, worked with her and gradually assumed the leadership role as she moved from direct leadership to becoming a consultant and advisor. She "was always concerned less inertia or the lack of desire to give up, lead me to stay too long on the job. . . . [she] had seen companies hurt or even ruined by an owner/CEO not stepping down at the right time."[2] Knowing when it was time to go, she made the transition gracefully.

Shirley Chisholm of New York served seven terms in the U.S. Congress and was a vocal advocate for African Americans and the disadvantaged. She was a coalition builder and leader who never forgot who elected her and why they sent her to Congress. As the political climate became increasingly conservative and as her political alliances were disappearing, she decided to retire so that she could continue her work teaching political science and women's studies courses at Mt. Holyoke College and remaining politically active outside of elected office. She gave up one political power base and then developed another power base by becoming the first president of a new group, the National Political Congress of Black Women, and continued her work for the rest of her life.[3]

Sir Edmund Hillary,[4] the noted explorer and leader of the first team to reach the top of Mount Everest, in 1958 took part in the first expedition led by Dr. Vivian "Bunny" Fuchs to cross Antarctica by way of the South Pole. He was responsible for leading a New Zealand team in the reconnaissance of the western part of the main expedition to establish food and fuel depots so that the main British crossing party would remain fully supplied after reaching the Pole. Having done this, he joined the crossing party led by Fuchs. He was no longer a leader or decision maker and was consulted only when difficulties arose. Fuchs refused to recognize Hillary's leadership experience and treated him as hired help unless his expertise was needed. Because it was difficult to impossible for Hillary to leave the expedition and because he felt a responsibility for the safety of the men in the expedition, he continued to serve. Fuchs's ungracious actions were an excellent example of the insecure leader who is unwilling to recognize the contributions of the former leader.

Golda Meir[5] resigned as president of Israel and was resentful that her colleagues, full partners in the struggle to form the Israeli government, did not stand up for her when she received criticism. They were members of a strong movement to have a coalition of political parties, including her own, and she did not support this as a viable action. Because of conflict within her party, she opted to resign and let others follow a course with which she did not agree.

Mary Breckenridge,[6] founder of the Frontier Nursing Service at the beginning of the 20th century, realized her vision of providing free medical care to the children of Appalachia. She was accustomed to being in charge and continued to manage the Service even after it became evident that others should take over. She refused to step aside and her activities were gradually taken away and given to a chosen successor. While she reluctantly agreed to relinquish day-to-day activities to her successor, she still refused to resign. Inflexible to the end, she resigned symbolically at the age of 80.

Greg Smith of Goldman Sachs[7] left his organization in a different way. He wrote an article for the *New York Times* titled "Why I am Leaving Goldman Sachs." His opening statement was as follows: "TODAY is my last day at Goldman Sachs. After almost 12 years at the firm—first as a summer intern while at Stanford, then in New York for ten years, and now in London—I believe that I have worked here long enough to understand the trajectory of its culture, its people and its identity. And I can honestly say that the environment now is as toxic and destructive as I have ever seen it."[8] He went on to say that this is because of changes in the way the firm thought about leadership, from leadership being about ideas, setting an example, and doing the right thing to being about making money. His very public resignation was designed to be a wakeup call to the board of directors that unless the client and not money again became the focal point, it would not survive. He demonstrated the courage of his conviction in the way he resigned and may have done it in this way to gain the attention of both Goldman Sachs and the public. Whether or not he was successful, he did what he thought was the right thing to do. Those who followed him would, in some way, need to respond. Leaving a position in anger rarely improves a situation and Greg Smith who was a respected member of the financial community had to have felt very strongly about the situation if he was willing to put his future career on the line.

Because their activities are so public, the ways in which presidents of the United States deal with stepping aside in many ways represent their final public actions. Truman,[9] although he was angry at Eisenhower because of things said in the campaign and still hurting from having lost the election, guaranteed that there "would be an orderly transfer of the business of the executive branch." He put personal feelings aside to do his duty and invited Eisenhower to the White House. Eisenhower went but "was taciturn to the point of surliness."

Sutton[10] reported that "people's memories of experiences are shaped by peak moments, whether good or bad, and by how those experiences ended when individuals leave office, whether forced out or by choice, their last chance at affecting how they will be judged by history is "to create a favorable impression with your exit." If your last actions include "bragging about accomplishments, grabbing goodies for yourself, and settling personal scores," you will be remembered as a selfish narcissist while if you thank those who helped you and wish them well, you will be remembered more positively. Sutton also noted that how the retiring CEO treats the successor says a great deal about the quality of leadership. Those in the organization "will devote particular attention to how you interact with your successor . . . they will note whether [the retiring CEO] shows deference and respect for the new boss or treat [s] him or her as the same old underling—by interrupting, for example or lecturing, or insisting on having the last word."[11] A graceful exit is the way for the outgoing leader to leave with reputation and legacy intact.

SUMMARY

New leaders join an organization for many reasons—to lead the organization in a new direction, to provide new ideas, or to repair a situation in which there had been faulty leadership—and in each instance the new leader builds on or rebuilds the legacy of the leader they follow. If the previous leader left an organization that was forward-looking and well managed, the transition is relatively easy. If the previous leader left an organization that was dysfunctional or not functioning at the desired level, the new leader's role is to assess the situation by listening, observing, asking questions, developing a plan of action, and moving forward.

Leaders step aside for many reasons: new opportunities, changed vision of the current organization, lack of success in a leadership position, personal interests and concerns, or retirement. When the time comes for the leader to step aside, a graceful and gracious exit is the most appropriate means of saying goodbye.

NOTES

1. Robb Coles, *A Radical Devotion* (Boston: Addison-Wesley, Longmans, 1987).

2. Katherine Graham, *Personal History* (New York: Vintage, 1998), 611.

3. Shirley Chisholm, *Unbought and Unbossed* (Boston: Houghton Mifflin Harcourt, 1970).

4. Vivian Fuchs and Edmund Hillary, *The Crossing of Antarctica: The Commonwealth Transarctica Expedition, 1955* to 1958 (London: Cassell and Co., 1959).

5. Deborah Hitzeroth, *Golda Meir* (Stamford, CT: Sengate Press, 1994).

6. Marie Bartlett Maher, *America's First Nurses-Midwife Service and School* (Jefferson, NC: McFarland & Co., 2008)

7. Greg Smith, "Why I Am Leaving Goldman Sachs," *New York Times*, March 14, 2012.

8. Ibid.

9. David McCullough, *Truman* (New York: Simon and Schuster, 1992).

10. Robert Sutton, "On Stepping Down Gracefully," *Harvard Business Review* 89, no. 6 (June 2011), 40.

11. Ibid.

Leadership in the Digital Age

As we look toward the future, we need to identify the contexts within which we live and which will to an extent determine the kinds of leadership necessary to move forward. In their study of Geeks and Geezers, Bennis and Thomas said that the era in which we have lived influences how we see the world and how we see our role in that world. "Older leaders [were] trained to think of the world in Newtonian mechanical terms; younger ones tend to look at it in terms of constantly changing living organisms and biological systems."[1] While Geezers value experience and seniority, Geeks value fresh insights. Regardless of age, each leader studied had experienced a severe test of patience, belief, or other test and this "crucible experience" teaches that crisis provides an opportunity to learn and that one is not defined by crisis but by how one deals with it. For Geeks, 9/11 was a national crucible that defined many individuals and affected how they built or rebuilt their belief systems and lives. For Geezers, it was the Korean War or the Vietnam War.[2] In any instance, each of us has had specific experiences that define us as individuals and influence how we contribute to the society in which we live.

We can also define the era in which we live by the technology we have developed—television, computers, advanced telecommunications. In the not so distant past, we lived in an era in which communication was slow, inter-action with other individuals, groups, and countries was more leisurely, and now we live in real time where there is little space between actions and state-ments and those actions and statements becoming known worldwide. As our ability to interact with one another on a worldwide stage has increased our knowledge of one another, it has also magnified the opportunity for misin-formation to enter into the dialogue. Speeded up communication leads us toward more rapid decision making and the possibility that we will make decisions we would not have made had there been time for more reflection. Speeded up communication also increases our ability to take advantage of opportunities that might have passed us by in a slower world. Whether we are Geeks or Geezers, despite having grown up in different eras and despite having different worldviews, we are alike in that we are curious about the world around us, are always learning new things and trying new things, and doing so with enthusiasm and a positive attitude toward the future. We are living in a world in the midst of major social, economic, and political change and it is comforting to know that the combined expertise and worldviews of both Geeks and Geezers is available to us as we move ahead in a world of risk that is reinventing itself as we speak.

An additional element in how we look toward the future is the need for balance; a balance between work life and personal life, a balance between looking forward and looking backward, and a balance between art and science. In the years after World War II, the stereotypical leader was the man in the gray flannel suit, someone who sacrificed everything for his work life. He hardly knew his family, had few friends outside his work life, and died young usually from a heart attack brought on by lack of healthy habits and too much stress. Mintzberg's *Study of Managerial Work*[3] showed that men of that era focused on the workplace to the detriment of the rest of their life. As women entered the workplace, the single-minded focus on the workplace tended to change and as we move toward a global economy with its variety of cultural approaches to work, the balance between work and personal life continues to evolve.[4]

The information age has brought with it major change in the ways we acquire information and use information. Our decision making has speeded up and we have faster access to the information available to make choices. Information is also more freely available than when it was seen as power that needed to be guarded rather than a resource to be shared. There continue to be individuals who long for the "good old days" when everyone knew their place, a minimum amount of information was doled out to them, and they did what they were told without argument. Life moved at a relaxed pace and tomorrow, for those in power, wouldn't be too much different from today. That era is history and today we live at a much more rapid pace in a much more participatory world. For some it is exhilarating while for others it is terrifying, a response that has less to do with age than it does with one's comfort level with the rate of change and changing roles.

On a more esoteric level, there is the balance between the sciences and the humanities; the need to understand and appreciate not only how things work and what new devices we can invent but also the beauty of our universe and the need to appreciate one another. Steve Jobs said that his success was due in part to his appreciation of creativity and technology, of the melding of the arts and engineering. From Ben Franklin, another creative giant who delighted at scientific discovery, writing, publishing, being a diplomat, and generally stirring things up, to the present, there are always a few individuals who truly understand that to have an interesting life, we must learn of the need to include artistic, scientific and organizational elements when setting direction and making decisions. Like Ben Franklin, they are the ones who ask why and then look for answers in both likely and unlikely places.

In concrete terms, this means that we need science and art to solve the problems we must face particularly when combining economic well-being with environmental sustainability. How do we deal with the need to move from current energy resources to sustainable energy resources that do not destroy the environment? What are the economic, social and political implications of reducing a reliance on coal and oil? How do we go about educating and reeducating a workforce that will fill the jobs required in the information age? How will we feed a world population that continues to grow? How do we move to the future without destroying the positive aspects of the present? New realities require new ideas and new ways of looking at what we do and what we need to do. The leader in a digital world fosters an environment that encourages others to look at these issues from different perspectives, to try new approaches, to learn from these activities, and to continuously reshape what we do in light of what we have learned. The leader surveys this big picture within which we all live and work, asks how it affects the environment, and with those they lead, plots a direction that recognizes global as well as local expectations and directions.

To be successful, organizations of all types must be future-oriented and have leaders willing to consider a range of different futures. While the manager's comfort zone is determined by what is known and familiar, the leader tends to see the comfort zone as a complacency zone that can quickly insulate the organization and put it out of touch with reality.

In an increasingly global society, as we interact with a diversity of value systems and learn to respect the customs of other cultures, how does this impact the ways in which we define leadership? How can we lead in a global society unless we are aware of the fact that in different cultures, different approaches to leadership exist? How can we lead unless we have empathy for the issues others confront and the solutions they propose to make the world a better place? These are difficult issues that need discussion and are some of the contexts within which today's leaders function and from which tomorrow's leaders will emerge.

THE KINDS OF LEADERS WE NEED FOR TOMORROW

The first step in identifying tomorrow's leaders and being a leader tomorrow is to have a sense of history. History is the story of human experience and while history shows that the demands of leadership change depending on time, place, and culture, its basic elements do not change.[5] David McCullough, historian and biographer of several 20th-century leaders, and a Geezer according to Bennis's definition, stressed that the ability to spot talent and good ideas and let them develop is essential to leadership. His criteria for successful leadership included knowing how to analyze problems and to implement solutions, and having the courage, resilience, and strength of character to see the positives in others. He also stressed that observing how individuals handle failure is important as we all fail and the individual who has never dealt with failure will not be prepared when it happens. McCullough praised President Harry S. Truman as a successful leader because Truman understood people, had common sense, and wanted smarter people around him who could contribute their best advice. He knew who he was, knew how to deal with failure, and wasn't intimidated by other individuals or by difficult circumstances. Truman is an excellent example of a plainspoken man from Missouri who became president of the United States at a critical time in our history and who made difficult decisions which were usually the right ones. He is an excellent example of the statement "character counts above all."

The Ideal Leader

Tomorrow's ideal leader is the same as today's ideal leader in that the ability to work with others to achieve a common goal is the hallmark of success. Personal characteristics do not change but the problems we will face change and may require new ways of gathering information, new ways of organizing resources, and new ways of using technology. In a multicultural environment with its many versions of human interaction, each individual, each leader must have an ethical compass or as Jill Ker Conway said, know their True North. Such leaders have not only the education and experience that helps them understand the ethical complexities of organizations. They have also learned that different cultures have different views of what is appropriate practice. For example, passing out favors in order to receive special attention in negotiations is acceptable practice in some cultures while in others it could result in a fine or worse.

Some leaders put self before the organization they represent. They enjoy the power that leadership entails and use this power to make decisions that improve their own financial standing. We find them in financial circles where they use inside information to make decisions that increase their personal fortunes. Some leaders enjoy the power of reorganizing companies and making them more efficient moneymakers. If in doing so, they fire a few or a few hundred people and they say that it is all in the name of efficiency and wealth for stockholders. Such individuals who seek either wealth or the exercise of power that puts others under their control lack the essential self-knowledge that comes with having a moral compass.

The experience of modern China provides an example of what happens when ethical leadership meets class warfare. Traditionally, Chinese interactions were based on Confucianism in which the importance of harmony and trust in interpersonal relationships was expected. Maoism broke down traditional relationships and demanded loyalty to the Communist Party and emphasized class struggle rather than harmony. As China modernized and the Communist Chinese government developed relationships with foreign businesses that brought their own ethical thinking to the table with the expectation that business be conducted through contractual duties and legality, one has an interaction of not just past history and present conditions but also a potential clash of cultural expectations. Czeto[6] suggests that the only way forward from such an interaction of cultures is to agree on what ethical behavior is and to base decisions on trust which takes us full circle to a core value of Confucianism. While the definition of ethical behavior will vary somewhat depending on the culture, trust and the integrity of leadership is a universal understanding.

Tomorrow's leader has a vision, a believable plan to make that vision a reality, and the ability to communicate both vision and plan to those who will collaborate in making the vision a reality. Perhaps more than in the past, successful leaders will go outside their comfort zone of ideas, technological opportunities, and individuals of like mind to seek new solutions.

Flexibility while keeping the vision front and center allows for changes and adaptations that enhance forward movement. This includes a willingness to take informed risks. Collaboration within the team, within the organization, and with those the organization serves has been made much easier with the advent of social networking as interested stakeholders can be included in discussions that keep the vision relevant. It is the leader's role to collaborate with stakeholders, recognize their contributions and at the same time not become overwhelmed with too much information, too many details, and too many suggestions. The leader's role continues to be to make the decisions that steer the team in the direction of the vision.

Tomorrow's leaders also communicate by example. They believe in what they are doing, that it in one way or another makes life better. They are passionate about their work and are willing to do what it takes to move forward in a manner that is consistent with their ethical standards. Pat Summitt, women's basketball coach at the University of Tennessee from the early 1970s until 2011, wanted women to have the opportunity to play the game and to learn the many life lessons that sports teaches as well as to participate in an enjoyable activity. She built her team and the game from its early days when she was coach, chauffeur, and mender of uniforms to what has become a nationally recognized and very popular college sport. Not only did she become the winningest basketball coach, male or female, in history with over a thousand wins, many of her assistant coaches went on to coach women's basketball in other universities and carried with them the passion for education and for the sport that she had instilled in them. Her expectations of her team were high and students met them. Every team member left the University of Tennessee with a degree in hand and graduated having learned from a powerful role model about hard work, honesty, sportsmanship, and the importance of caring for one another.

Tomorrow's leaders need to be aware of the fact that events such as natural disasters, technological innovations, and political upheavals in all their many dimensions will create disruption in how our society functions and how the organizations they lead respond. While natural disasters are unstoppable single events, other disruptions tend not to be single events but rather a series of events over time. Disruptive innovations "stem from technological or business model advantages that can scale as disruptive businesses move upmarket in search of more demanding customers." Resisting this type of disruption is not an option and leaders find ways to accommodate the disruption in positive ways.[7] It may be a new idea or new technology that allows us to do something faster, more efficiently, and cheaper. It may be a new way of doing things that requires new training and new jobs. Sometimes we have the time to observe a disruptive innovation as it grows, such as the changes in higher education in which the online model of course delivery is becoming ever stronger in response to the demand for a more highly educated workforce to fill the many positions opening up in our increasingly high-tech society.

Social networking has become a part of many organizations and the leaders who have incorporated it into their organizations and who have tamed or tried to tame it are examples of leaders who have welcomed disruptive technologies. Successful leaders treat disruptive innovations such as these as a challenge and find ways to make them part of their vision and plan for the future.

We are still in the process of moving from a command-and-control society to one in which collaboration prevails. Leaders who lead because they have the power of the position are gradually losing out to those who know that they have to prove daily that they are qualified to lead, that their team knows that "they get it." Given the power of social networking and the opportunity for everyone to be involved in a team environment, it is much more difficult for a leader to be anything but transparent. Feeding the team inaccurate information is much more difficult than when information was difficult to access. Claiming credit for something done by others is usually found out. The leader who takes credit for success that is really a team success is less likely to get away with this than in the past. No one has all the information available and not all information is of equal value, but the leader who works with the team to achieve the best outcome, keeps team members informed, discusses issues with team members, expects their best ideas and efforts, and gives credit where due will have the best chance to succeed as a leader. Leaders, particularly those in high-profile positions, are under constant scrutiny by the media; their actions are critiqued regularly; and they are held accountable for their actions. Leaders who have made unethical decisions, who have not been forthcoming when questioned about their actions, or who have faltered in other ways may well find themselves the subject of social media discussion. In an information-rich world, leaders need to be able to support their actions when asked. Some criticism may be unfounded and the result of personal or political maneuvering on the part of those with contrary views. The leader needs to deal with unfair criticism and to continue to lead despite unfounded negative statements. Some leaders who have faltered are able to rebuild their reputations and gain a second chance while others disappear from public view.

In tomorrow's leaders, we are looking for those who have an open mind, who respect the members of their team and who work collectively to build team confidence and bring out the team's best performance. The leader uses soft skills rather than those exhibited in a command-and-control environment. The leader has a true north, has a vision for the future, and uses all available organizational and technological skills to move ahead. Tomorrow's leader reaches across roles, functions, and organizations in order to achieve goals. Ghani's statement that "[the leader] understands her organizations as living systems within an interconnected world[8] . . . and aids it in collectively creating systems designed to enhance the human condition and co-construct cultures of inclusion"[9] neatly encapsulates the role of tomorrow's leader.

Where Will We Find Tomorrow's Leaders?

In addition to the traditional sources of leadership, such as our universities, our laboratories, the business world, where will we find leaders? Rather than looking locally and within our own organizations and professions, we need to look globally to include individuals from developing countries. For many years the United States has been the destination for students wishing to obtain the best possible education and while many stayed in the United States to help us build our scientific and technical economy, many others returned home to share in the building of the economies of their home country. Economies in China, India, Latin America and elsewhere are now producing their own

leaders for a technological world and are rapidly building their own economies. International companies are growing and leaders of these companies
representing different cultures may find themselves working anywhere in the
world. Within many developing countries, women are gaining in influence and
leadership opportunities. Social networking brings potential leaders together
and provides opportunities for identifying leaders wherever they may be. We
also need to "seek out the demographic invisibles," those who may or may not
have access to social networking or fast-track training or those whose leadership style is more low key, for example the quiet leader who without a lot of
talking about what needs to be done just goes to work and gets the job done.[10]
We have just begun to appreciate that many cultures and societies with many
leadership styles are on the move and that from this new leaders and new
ways of leading will doubtless emerge.

In the United States, we have "The New Greatest Generation," young men
and women who have served or are serving in the military which plays an important role in preparing leaders for tomorrow by providing education, training,
and opportunities to lead others in many types of situations. "The returning
veterans are bringing skills that seem to be on the wane in American society,
qualities we really need now; crisp decision making, rigor, optimism, entrepreneurial creativity, a larger sense of purpose, and patriotism."[11] While the
traditional view of the military is "command and control," today's all-volunteer
military is more highly educated and more highly motivated than during some
periods in the past and provides a better platform for building leaders for tomorrow who understand the importance of mutual responsibility.

Research has indicated that we are revising our definitions of leadership
to include those who don't fit the conventional model of the leader. The un-
assuming individual who learns about the organization and moves it ahead
steadily and does so without a lot of self-advertisement, the quiet leader,[12] is
gaining respect. The leader who creates the opportunity for collective action
and who leads by facilitating the activities of others rather than by dictating
what is to be done is also gaining respect. It has been said that the younger
generation of leaders has a greater ability to empathize and its members are
willing to concede fallibility. They see opportunities rather than barriers and
are less interested in "where the lines are drawn" than in "where the lines connect." We have no lack of leadership; we just need to know how to recognize it
and to be part of it.

LEADERSHIP GOING FORWARD

More than a decade ago, Rosen[13] commented that there is a crisis in commitment, that people are not working to their full potential but are preferring
to use the basic job description as their guide. Individuals often feel bogged
down by management structures, by the glass ceiling, or new requirements
imposed from above or from the outside. He said that people want leaders who
create an environment that is conducive to their doing their best work. They
expect leaders to be "keepers of the big picture." Covey[14] suggested that this
lack of creative moving forward is because our management practices derive

from research and practice carried out in the industrial age which often does not mesh well with the needs of the information age. Today's workforce is different from that in the past in that it is better educated, and today's jobs are different in that they require a higher level of education. The hierarchical structure of an industrial-age organization does not fit well with these new jobs and the better educated, more independent workforce. Further, the workforce is more varied demographically (e.g., gender, ethnicity, age, cultural background), which further differentiates it from the traditional workforce. Today's workforce expects to be involved in discussions about the work being done and to contribute to decisions that are made. While more than limited participation is not possible for many regimented jobs or service jobs, there is still opportunity to participate in decisions about working conditions and to make suggestions about ways to improve processes. Social networking has made a broader understanding of the work we do and why we do it widely available.

Bill George's introduction to the "Special Report on America's Best Leaders"[15] included the following statement:

> The time is ripe to redefine leadership for the 21st century. The military-manufacturing model of leadership that worked so well fifty years ago doesn't get the best out of people today. People are too well informed to adhere to a set of rules or to simply follow a leader over a distant hill. They want to be inspired by a greater purpose . . . [The 21st-century leaders] not only inspire those around them, they bring people together around a shared purpose and a common set of values and motivate them to create value for everyone involved . . . they are more concerned about serving others than they are about their own success or recognition.

The concept of management and leadership has expanded since women, individuals of color, and individuals from other cultures have become managers and leaders. When once management and leadership positions were dominated by white males who tended to follow an authoritarian, hierarchical model, many women have introduced an inclusive, mutually supportive mode. Others who have joined the ranks of leadership have brought their own cultural strengths to the mix so that now management and leadership benefit from a wide range of models and combination of models that can be used depending on the situation and the leader's personal strengths and style. No longer is there one way to lead. There are many ways to lead and the workplace is stronger because of it. We are gradually moving beyond the "us or them" view of the workforce and are coming to understand the strength of a variety of different perspectives as we work to solve today and tomorrow's problems.

SUMMARY

Leadership is about going somewhere and about having a vision to guide that journey. Leadership is the journey, and you never reach the vision as the vision is always just out of reach. As you close in on your goals, you renew the vision and set new goals, always keeping the vision ahead of you. You continuously examine the vision and adjust it as needed. Pfeiffer[16] notes that leaders of the future need the ability to teach others and to maintain a climate of continuous learning so that those being led have the tools to move forward. Pfeiffer also said that tomorrow's leader has the ability to ask good questions that cause others to think about issues and to explore new ideas and new directions. Ghani,[17] in discussing the leader as integrator, said that tomorrow's leader is one who has multiple perspectives and who is "consciously connecting [them] and applying a variety of skills to establish new directions, options, and solutions for the organization . . . [tomorrow's leader] has a strong commitment for continuous learning for themselves, their employees, their organization, and organizational partners."

NOTES

1. Warren Bennis and Robert J. Thomas, *Geeks and Geezers: How Era, Values, and Defining Moments Shape Leaders* (Boston: Harvard Business School Publishing, 2002), 12.

2. Ibid., 14–18.

3. Henry Mintzberg, *The Nature of Managerial Work* (New York: Harper and Row, 1973).

4. Sally Helgesen, *The Female Advantage: Women's Ways of Leadership* (New York: Doubleday Currency, 1990).

5. Brownyn Fryer, "Timeless Leadership: A Conversation with David McCullough," *Harvard Business Review* 86, no. 3 (March 2008), 45–49.

6. Ricky Szebo, "Chinese Folk Wisdom: Leading with Traditional Values," in *Ethical Leadership: Global Challenges and Perspectives*, eds. Carla Millar and Eve Poole (New York: Palgrave Macmillan, 2004), 148–64.

7. Maxwell Wessel and Clayton M. Christensen, "Surviving Disruption," *Harvard Business Review* 90, no. 12 (December 2012): 59.

8. Usman A. Ghani, "The Leader Integrator, An Emerging Role," in *The Leader of the Future 2*, eds. Frances Sesselbein and Marshall Goldsmith (San Francisco: Jossey Bass, 2006), 244.

9. Ibid., 299.

10. Paul Hemp, "Where Will We Find Tomorrow's Leaders? A Conversation with Linda Hill," *Harvard Business Review* 86, no. 1 (January 2008): 123–29.

11. Joe Klein, "The New Greatest Generation," *TIME* 178, no. 8 (August 29, 2011): 26–34.

12. Susan Cain, *Quiet: The Power of Introverts in a World That Can't Stop Talking* (New York: Crown Publishers, 2012).

13. Robert Rosen, *Leading People: Transforming Business from the Inside Out* (New York: Viking, 1996).

14. Stephen R. Covey, "Leading in the Knowledge Worker Age," in *The Leader of the Future 2*, eds. Hesselbein and Goldsmith, 218.

15. Bill George, "Special Report on America's Best Leaders," *U.S. News and World Report*, October 30, 2006, 52.

16. Jeffrey Pfeiffer, "Are the Best Leaders Like Professors: Teaching, Asking Questions and Evidence Based Management," in *The Leader of the Future 2*, eds. Hesselbein and Goldsmith, 227–39.

17. Usman A. Ghani, "The Leader Integrator: An Emerging Role," in *The Leader of the Future 2*, eds. Hesselbein and Goldsmith, 241–45.

Appendix
Biographies Consulted

Babcock, B. *Woman Lawyer: The Trials of Clara Foltz.* Stanford, CA: Stanford University Press, 2011.

Bernstein, Carl. *All the President's Men.* New York: Simon & Schuster, 1994.

Beyer, Kurt W. *Grace Hopper and the Invention of the Information Age.* Boston: MIT Press, 2009.

Bloomberg, Michael. *Bloomberg by Bloomberg.* Hoboken, NJ: John Wiley & Sons, 2001.

Brinkley, David. *David Brinkley: A Memoir.* New York: Ballantine, 1995.

Brinkley, Douglas. *Gerald R. Ford.* Waterville, ME: Thorndike Press, 2007.

Bundles, Aielia. *Madame C.J. Walker.* New York: Facts on File, 1992.

Carnegie, Andrew. *The Autobiography of Andrew Carnegie and the Gospel of Wealth.* Memphis, TN: General Books LLC, 2010 (reprint).

Carter, Jimmy. *Jimmy Carter: From Plains to Post-Presidency.* New York: Scribner, 1997.

Cash, Johnny. *Cash, The Autobiography.* New York: Harper Collins, 2003.

Chernow, Ron. *Alexander Hamilton.* New York: Penguin, 2004.

Chernow, Ron. *Washington: A Life.* New York: Penguin Books, 2010.

Chisholm, Shirley. *Unbought and Unbossed.* Boston: Houghton Mifflin Harcourt, 1970.

Coles, Robb. *A Radical Devotion.* Addison-Wesley, Longmans, Inc., 1987.

Colver, Anne. *War Nurse.* New York: Facts on File, 1992.

Conway, Jill Ker. *True North.* New York: Knopf, 1994.

Dalton, Kathleen. *Theodore Roosevelt: A Strenuous Life.* New York: Knopf, 2002.

Folsung, Albrecht. *Albert Einstein, a Biography.* New York: Viking, 1997.

Franklin, Benjamin. *The Complete Autobiography of Benjamin Franklin.* Washington, D.C.: Regenery Pub. Inc., 2007.

Fuchs, Vivian, and Edmund Hillary. *The Crossing of Antarctica: The Commonwealth Transantarctica Expedition, 1955–1958.* London: Cassell and Co., 1959.

Gerber, Robin. *Leadership the Eleanor Roosevelt Way.* New York: Prentice Hall, 2002.

Goodwin, Doris Kearns. *Lyndon Johnson and the American Dream.* New York: Penguin Group, USA, 1977.

Goodwin, Doris Kearns. *Team of Rivals.* New York: Simon & Schuster, 2005.

Graham, Katherine. *Personal History.* New York: Vintage, 1998

Greenstein, Fred I. *The Presidential Difference: Leadership Style from FDR to Barack Obama,* 3rd ed. Princeton, NJ: Princeton University Press, 2009.

Griswold del Castillo, Richard. *Cesar Chavez: A Triumph of Spirit.* Norman, OK: University of Oklahoma Press, 1995.

Hitzeroth, Deborah. *Golda Meir.* Stamford, CT: Sengate Press, 1994.

Isaacon, Walter. *Steve Jobs.* New York: Simon & Schuster, 2011.

Jackson, Troy. *Becoming King: Martin Luther King, Jr. And the Making of a National Leader.* Lexington, KY: University of Kentucky Press, 2008.

Jardine, Anne. *The First Henry Ford: A Study in Personality and Business.* Boston: MIT Press, 1970.

Keller, Evelyn Fox. *A Feeling for the Organism. The Life and Work of Barbara McClintock.* New York: W. H. Freeman and Co., 1983.

Keohane, Nanerl. *Thinking about Leadership.* Princeton, NJ: Princeton University Press, 2010.

Kopp, Wendy. *One Day All My Children: The Unlikely Triumph of Teach for America.* New York: Public Affairs, 2003.

Logue, Mark. *The King's Speech: How One Man Saved the British Monarchy.* London: Quercus, 2010.

Maher, Marie Bartlett. *America's First Nurse-Midwife Service and School.* Jefferson, NC: McFarland & Co., 2008.

Maraniss, David. *First in His Class: A Biography of Bill Clinton.* New York: Simon & Schuster, 2008.

Maraniss, David. *When Pride Still Mattered: A Life of Vince Lombardi.* New York: Simon & Schuster, 1999.

Mayank, Chhaya. *The Dalai Lama: Man, Monk, and Mystic.* Tullamarine, Victoria, Australia: Bolinda Pub. Ltd., 2009.

McCullough, David. *John Adams.* New York: Simon and Schuster, 2011.

McCullough, David. *Truman.* New York: Simon & Schuster, 1992.

Meacham, Jon. *American Lion: Andrew Jackson in the White House.* New York: Random House, 2008.

Mortenson, Greg. *Stones to Schools: Promoting Peace with Books not Bombs in Afghanistan and Pakistan.* New York: Penguin Group USA, 2009.

Mortenson, Greg. *Three Cups of Tea: One Man's Mission to Promote Peace.* Stamford, CT: Cengage Gale, 2007.

O'Connor, Sandra Day. *Reflections of a Supreme Court Judge.* New York: Random House, 2008.

O'Connor, Ulick. *Michael Collins and the Troubles: The Struggle for Irish Freedom.* New York: Knopf, 1996.

Orr, Tamrak. *The Life and Times of Susan B. Anthony.* Hokessin, DE: Mitchell Lane Pub. Inc., 2006.

Rogers, Mary Beth. *Barbara Jordan: American Hero.* New York: Bantam Books, 1998.

Schiff, Stacy. *Cleopatra, A Life.* New York: Little, Brown & Co., 2010.

Seifer, M. *Wizard: The Life and Times of Nikola Tesla, Biography of a Genius.* Secaucus, NJ: Carol Pub., 1996.

Sirleaf, Ellen Johnson. *This Child Will Be Great: A Memoir of a Remarkable Life by Africa's First Woman President.* New York: Harper, 2009.

Thomas, June Resh. *The Life of Queen Elizabeth I.* Boston: Houghton Mifflin, 1998.

Tough, Paul. *Whatever It Takes: Geoffrey Canada's Quest to Change Harlem.* Boston: Houghton Mifflin, 2008.

Whiting, Jim. *The Life and Times of Abigail Adams.* Hokessin, DE: Mitchell Lane Pub. Inc., 2009.

Williams, Charles. *Adenauer: The Father of New Germany.* Hoboken, NJ: John Wiley & Sons, 2001.

Wood, Ian. *Churchill.* New York: Palgrave Macmillan, 2007.

Woodward, Bob. *Five Presidents and the Legacy of Watergate.* New York: Simon & Schuster, 1999.

Index

About the Author

ANN E. PRENTICE, DLS, is professor emerita of Library/Information Science and former dean at the University of Maryland, College Park, MD. Her published works include Libraries Unlimited's *Public Libraries in the 21st Century* (2010) and *Managing in the Information Age* (2005), as well as more than a dozen titles dealing with management and related topics.